Pitt Series in Russian and East European Studies

Jonathan Harris, Editor

THE ARCHAEOLOGY OF ANXIETY

The Russian Silver Age and Its Legacy

Galina Rylkova

UNIVERSITY OF PITTSBURGH PRESS

Published by the University of Pittsburgh Press, Pittsburgh, PA 15260
Copyright © 2007, University of Pittsburgh Press
All rights reserved
Manufactured in the United States of America
Printed on acid-free paper
10 9 8 7 6 5 4 3 2 1

Library of Congress Cataloging-in-Publication Data
Rylkova, Galina.
　The archaeology of anxiety : the Russian Silver Age and its legacy / Galina Rylkova.
　　　p.　　cm. — (Pitt series in Russian and East European studies)
　Includes bibliographical references and index.
　ISBN-13: 978-0-8229-4316-7 (cloth : alk. paper)
　ISBN-10: 0-8229-4316-6 (cloth : alk. paper)
　ISBN-13: 978-0-8229-5981-6 (pbk. : alk. paper)
　ISBN-10: 0-8229-5981-X (pbk. : alk. paper)
　　1. Russian literature—20th century—History and criticism. 2. Russian literature—20th century—Political aspects. 3. Russian literature—20th century—Social aspects. 4. Russia—Civilization—1801-1917. 5. Soviet Union—Civilization. 6. Akhmatova, Anna Andreevna, 1889-1966—Criticism and interpretation.　　I. Title.
　PG3021.R895 2007
　891.709'003—dc22　　　　　　　　　　　　　　2007039148

CONTENTS

Acknowledgments vii

1. Introduction: Anxiety and the Russian Silver Age   1
2. Literature and Revolution: The Case of Aleksandr Blok   23
3. The Russian Silver Age: Its Makers and Undertakers   45
4. No "Room of Her Own": Anna Akhmatova's Tenure in Soviet Culture   66
5. The Winged Eavesdropper: Kuzmin and Nabokov   108
6. The Silver Age in Translation: Boris Pasternak's *Doctor Zhivago*   127
7. Braving the Thaw: Anna Akhmatova in the 1950s and the 1960s   154
8. The Apocalypse Revisited: Viktor Erofeev's *Russian Beauty*   179
9. Coda: The Silver Age Up Close   200

Appendix: Original Russian Texts   211

Notes   217

Index   261

ACKNOWLEDGMENTS

I chose the "Silver Age" as the subject of my research in the summer of 1996. At the time, most people I hoped to write about and talk to were gone or out of my reach. After graduating from Moscow State University, I worked for the Academy of Sciences and followed the burgeoning "Silver Age" studies in the late 1980s only from a distance. I left Russia as an experienced technical translator and not as a student of literature. My North American list of lost opportunities includes Nina Berberova, whom I missed at a graduate students' conference in Philadelphia in 1993 (she was sick); and also Joseph Brodsky, whom I failed to see at a writers' festival in Toronto in 1994 (I had to stay at home with my daughter).

I am extremely grateful to many people who not only enriched my knowledge about the "Silver Age" but also made my academic life meaningful and the writing experience less lonely and infinitely more rewarding. I am particularly grateful to Christopher Barnes, Irene Masing-Delic, Irina Paperno, and Irene Kacandes for their mentorship, for being a source of inspiration, and for challenging me to write a better book. Tony Naldrett made me a more versatile human being by teaching me what it takes to be an academic.

I am indebted to Yuliia Evgen'evna Galanina, Galina Timofeevna

Savel'eva, and other researchers at the Blok Museum in St. Petersburg for their help and hospitality in the years 2000–2005. Marina Vital'evna Bokarius shared her insights into the St. Petersburg literary scene and made me stay a few days in her apartment surrounded by various literary relics and Maximilian Voloshin's inimitable watercolors. I am grateful to Evgenii Borisovich Belodubrovskii for his kindness and for showing me parts of Petersburg I would never have seen otherwise. Evgenii Borisovich also introduced me to Irina Nikolaevna Punina and Anna Genrikhovna Kaminskaia, who were sympathetic enough to answer my convoluted questions about Punin and Akhmatova in 2000 and 2001. I would like to thank Tatiana Mikhailovna Dviniatina for showing me the Pavel Luknitskii archive at Pushkinskii Dom in 2005 and for making a photocopy of a chapter of Vera Luknitsikaia's book for me at a time when it was impossible to get hold of the book anywhere. Seeing Luknitskii's archive in its actual physical state—which, among many other things, contains numerous scraps of paper, envelopes with Akhmatova's hair, photographs of her, and other relics of the bygone era—was truly one of the most memorable experiences of my academic career.

I want to thank Olga Glagoleva, Robert Mulcahy, Michael David-Fox, Bill Wolf, Angela Brintlinger, Anna Krylova, Sara Dickinson, Timothy Sergey, Ruth Rischin, Michael Gorham, E. C. (Land) Barksdale, Keith Bullivant, Annemarie Sykes, Frederic Corney, Ivan Esaulov, Ralph Lindheim, Radislav Lapushin, Margarita Odesskaia, and Anna Dormady for years of support, advice, and interest in my research. I am also grateful to my students—Patricia Flaherty, Meredith Meadows, Lisa Booth, Adam Grunzke, Adam Oberlin, and James Slater—for their wit, patience, and willingness to study the Russian modernists.

Aleksandr Burak, James (Frank) Goodwin, and Irina Men'shova have read and heard about more versions of various chapters than they should have been asked to. To them, my daughter, my aunt, and my Canadian-born cat Thomas I owe my deepest thanks for not giving up on me and for keeping me sane and going.

At the University of Pittsburgh Press, this book has received unfailing support. I am particularly grateful to Peter Kracht for his faith in my final product, expert advice, and encouragement. I am also indebted to the anonymous reviewers for their intellectual generosity, insightful suggestions, and thorough criticism of my manuscript. Deborah Meade and Jane Flanders deserve credit for their expert handling of the book at the production stage.

Earlier versions of chapters 2, 5, and 8 were previously published and are reprinted here with permission: chapter 2: "Literature and Revolution: The Case of Aleksandr Blok," *Kritika: Explorations in Russian and Eurasian History* 3 (Fall 2002): 611–30; chapter 5: "Okrylyonnyy Soglyadatay—The Winged Eavesdropper: Nabokov and Kuzmin," in *Discourse and Ideology in Nabokov's Prose*, ed. David H. J. Larmour (New York: Routledge, 2002), 43–58; chapter 8: "The Apocalypse Revisited: Viktor Erofeev's *Russian Beauty*," in *Gender and Sexuality in Russian Civilization*, ed. Peter Barta (New York: Routledge, 2001), 325–43. I am grateful to the editors of these publications for their interest in my work.

Parts of my research were generously supported by a postdoctoral fellowship from the Social Sciences and Humanities Research Council of Canada (SSHRC, 1998–2000) and by the Humanities Enhancement Foundation of the University of Florida (summer 2001, 2004).

I am grateful to the Department of Germanic and Slavic Studies of the University of Florida for defraying the cost of having my book indexed.

Unless otherwise indicated, all translations are my own, as are any mistakes and/or deficient interpretations.

1 Introduction

ANXIETY AND THE RUSSIAN SILVER AGE

> Part of the meaning of Stonehenge is that we do not remember what it means.
> —Gary Taylor, *Cultural Selection*

> In the course of a conversation [with her son, Lev Gumilev] about the Russian poetry of the nineteenth and twentieth centuries, Anna Akhmatova mentioned the Golden Age of Pushkin, and they had roughly (as preserved by prison camp memory) the following exchange: "That's fine, but the twentieth century may just as well be called the 'Silver Age' . . ." "A remarkable characterization! Sell it to me!" Anna Andreevna exclaimed. "Only for a quarter-liter bottle of vodka!" Lev Nikolaevich was quick to respond and was rewarded immediately with the required sum of money, whereupon the vodka that appeared on the table was consumed in a convivial atmosphere, and Anna Andreevna earned the right to a period description that subsequently became a common label. Without attempting to join a historico-literary discussion of the origin of the term, I'm just relating faithfully Lev Nikolaevich's story, whether it is true or not. However, he sincerely believed himself to be the creator of this formula.
> —L. A. Voznesenskii, "Mozhno ia budu otvechat' stikhami?"

The postperestroika restaurant the Silver Age (Serebrianyi vek) is an important landmark on the Moscow scene. It is one of the few enterprises that can boast a ten-year survival history through the most turbulent times that have gripped Russia in recent decades. It occupies the glamorously refurbished building of what used to be the Moscow Turkish Bathhouses. Located only a few blocks from the infamous Lubianka, it combines the late imperial grandeur of its decor with the dullness (and emptiness) of a big Soviet restaurant of the Brezhnev era. In the summer of 2005, I made my third visit to the Silver Age. The doorkeeper greeted us with the disconcerting question: "Whom would you like to see? *(Vy k komu?)*" He looked anxious. When I explained that all we wanted was to have lunch there, his face showed puzzlement, but he opened the door. The service was impeccable, as usual, and the food was good. However, the buffet where they kept the wine and liquor was locked after last night's banquet, and we had to wait for the owner (who was in no hurry to get there on a rainy afternoon) to unlock it. The restaurant's main mission, as we were told, was to host various receptions and weddings. People rarely came there in small groups for lunch or dinner. Back in 1999, in response to my question about the appropriateness of such a name for their restaurant, one of the waiters replied, "I guess we called it the Silver Age because we hoped that it would make the Silver Age come back."

Why would a Russian nouveau riche, who opened this restaurant in 1993, care about the Silver Age? Why would anybody want the Silver Age to come back? Although the restaurant has changed hands several times, the name has remained intact. Apart from eating alone at an expensive restaurant, until recently one could get a taste of the Silver Age by gambling in two Moscow floating casinos named after the most prominent representatives of the Silver Age, Aleksandr Blok (1880–1921) and Valerii Briusov (1873–1924). The promotion flier for the Aleksandr Blok Casino said that their "aquarium fish never stopped the act of reproduction, hinting to the customers how nice it would be to spend the night in the arms of a loving beauty in the Blok Hotel on board." Both casinos went out of business in 2005. At other casinos, one can still celebrate one's good fortune or cool down one's disappointment with a glass of sparkling wine called "The Silver Age." Would everyone who drinks the so-called Russian champagne know what the Silver Age was all about? Most likely not. It would seem, however, that the name is expected to stir some forgotten memories of something vaguely beautiful and familiar; otherwise, why would anyone promote a businesses in such a manner?

In her essay "Pushkin's Children" (1992), the writer Tatiana Tolstaya describes the Silver Age as "that legendary time" and as "the *Titanic* floating in the night and gloom on its way to destruction":

> During the years before the revolution, the arts flourished in an extraordinary manner. . . . Now when we look back with a feeling of sorrow and loss at that legendary time, which seems separated from us by a transparent but impassible barrier, when we hear the dim, underwater voices of those people—their debates and quarrels, their amorous admissions, their unrealized and realized prophecies—we have a vision of the *Titanic* floating in the night and gloom on its way to destruction, a vision of a huge ship brightly illuminated, full of music, wine, and elegant people, a bit afraid of the long ocean voyage, of course, but hoping that the journey will end well. After all, the ship is so large, strong and reliable![1]

Will this majestic boat be forever floating in the darkness? Will we or should we ever start looking at its passengers in broad daylight? Will this adulation of the Silver Age survive into another century or two? Or will it eventually perish like the *Titanic*, despite (or, most likely, because of) being so "strong and reliable"?

For years, the Silver Age has been one of the most intensely studied topics in Russian literary studies, and for years scholars have been struggling with its precise definition. The term is often employed to denote loosely a period in Russian cultural evolution that ended with the advent of the Bolsheviks in 1917. What is generally known as the era of modernism in Western cultures (1890–1939) was frequently divided into the blossoming Silver Age (the flourishing of the arts in the years immediately preceding the revolution) and the decaying age of socialist realism (the sterile formations of the arts in the late 1920s and beyond). Many literary scholars, both within and outside Russia, still see Russia's Silver Age as a charmed lost era or as a historical period in cultural evolution on a par with romanticism and the Enlightenment.

They have argued about its temporal boundaries, about its primary participants, about the chronology of its "seminal" moments, indeed, about the applicability of its very name.

What's in a Name?

Omry Ronen is duly credited with starting a debate on the appropriateness of the term *Silver Age.* "My purpose in this inquiry," he states in the opening chapter of his celebrated *The Fallacy of the Silver Age* (1997), "[is] to trace the history of the term 'Silver Age' as applied to the first two (or three or four) decades of the twentieth century and to scrutinize its appropriateness for this particular stretch of time in Russian literary history."[2] What, in part, inspired Ronen's inquiry was the "manifestly uncritical attitude toward the metallurgical metaphors" that he detected in the works of his colleagues.[3] The specific book he had in mind was *Cultural Mythologies of Russian Modernism: From the Golden Age to the Silver Age* (1992), edited by Boris Gasparov, Robert Hughes, and Irina Paperno.

The unity of the articles comprising *The Cultural Mythologies*, as Gasparov explains in his introduction, is anchored by the "self-conception" that Russian modernists shared. For all their diversity, they "all shared an essential interpretation of their age."[4] This was the modernists' keen awareness of their cultural past, which meant their creative appropriation of Pushkin, both his life and his work. Gasparov, however, hastens to do away with the discussion of the trickiest part—what was the time frame of Russian modernism? "With the historicizing vision of hindsight," Gasparov writes, "as the early twentieth century receded into the past, Russians were able to view the culture of the era as a single, unified phenomenon which may be designated—at least provisionally—as 'the age of Russian Modernism.'"[5] To explicate the book's subtitle, *From the Golden Age to the Silver Age*, and to avoid tautology, he uses modernism and Silver Age as synonyms. Gasparov goes on to trace the genealogy of the term Silver Age, attributing some of its first usages to Anna Akhmatova, Sergei Makovskii, and Nikolai Berdiaev, to conclude that the "phrase's indefinite origin as well as the multiplicity of later references may indicate that the expression was simply 'in the air,' a commonplace in early twentieth-century oral usage, and thus implicit in the period's figurative language, although not directly incorporated into contemporary texts."[6] In his study, Ronen sets out to complete Gasparov's unfinished list of the Silver Age's attributions.

Despite his remarkable erudition, Ronen fails to answer one of the questions that he himself outlines in his introduction, namely, how appropriate is the term Silver Age regarding Russian culture of the beginning of the twentieth century?[7] Nor is his list of usages as exhaustive as he implies. Petr Pertsov's review of *The Anthology of New Poetry* (*Antologia novoi poezii*, 1914), published in *Novoe vremia* on the brink of WWI, offers yet another use of this term: "There is absolutely no doubt, that 'from a certain distance,' a future historian of Russian literature will describe the last twenty years as the second revival of Russian poetry, some sort of its 'silver age,' following the 'gold age' of the 1830s and the 1840s and a barren interval between 1860 and 1880 dominated by civic concerns."[8] Unlike the futurist Gleb Marev and the literary critic R. V. Ivanov-Razumnik, who highlighted derogatory connotations of the term, Pertsov used Silver Age to denote a period of cultural vitality, a definition very similar to the generally accepted meaning of this term, which Ronen attempts to deconstruct. A salient feature of Pertsov's definition was that full appreciation of contemporary poetry required time. It is also significant that Pertsov drew his conclusions on the eve of a major upheaval in world history. As I shall demonstrate, both "the historicizing vision of hindsight" and the interconnectedness of the Silver Age with major political and social upheavals are the cornerstones of this cultural construct.[9]

On more than one occasion, Ronen highlights inconsistencies in how the term the Silver Age is applied—hence the alleged "fallacy" in the book's title. However, inconsistency does not necessarily mean fallacy or inappropriate usage. What is missing in Ronen's inquiry is a conceptual framework. He does not relate these differences in the use of the term Silver Age to particular cultural and political situations in Russia (and Russia Abroad) throughout the twentieth century. His task is to invalidate and discredit the term. Ronen goes so far as to suggest alternatives that might "help exorcize [the Silver Age's] pallid, deceptive and meddlesome ghost."[10] One such candidate is the Platinum Age, a term coined by Oleg Menshikov and wholeheartedly approved by Roman Jakobson.[11] Ronen appears unaware of how much his own prescriptions and perceptions of prerevolutionary Russian culture stem from the same unfounded adoration for the Silver Age that initially inspired him to question the validity of this term. Like the Golden Age, only more so, the Silver Age is a multilayered sociocultural phenomenon. However earnest Ronen may be in his call for correction, it is virtually impossible to conduct any large-scale revision of the Silver Age's cultural resources and to evaluate its merits definitively.[12]

Gasparov's and Ronen's approaches to the Silver Age nicely illustrate Paul Ricoeur's argument that hermeneutics is driven by "double motivation." According to Ricoeur, there are two ways of obtaining the "truth"—one by restoring a meaning (as exemplified by Gasparov's and his collaborators' careful reading of the Silver Age through the prism of Pushkin) and the other by demystification and "reduction of an illusion" (as exemplified by Ronen's exposure of the "fallacy" of the Silver Age).[13] Here I attempt to preserve some balance between these polar motivations but approach the Silver Age in a radically different way. Instead of a thorough reevaluation of the prerevolutionary literature or a search for a unifying idea, I posit a different question: how did the idea of the Silver Age come to occupy such a prominent place in the Russian collective consciousness? Several provocative studies of the Silver Age have expanded our understanding of its cultural sources (and resources) and describe how its legacy evolved in subsequent epochs.[14] Yet this imperative question has still not been answered. Here I focus not on the history of cultural evolution, but on the collective experience of this evolution, traced through the larger portion of the twentieth century. I submit that the Silver Age is a cultural construct of retrospective origin brought to life as a means of overcoming the existential anxieties unleashed by the Bolshevik Revolution, the civil war, and the Stalinist terror. At the same time, it was also one of the main sources of anxieties that dominated the Russian cultural and political scene through the greater part of the twentieth century. I chart these anxieties through case studies of Anna Akhmatova, Boris Pasternak, Vladimir Nabokov, and Viktor Erofeev. Because the two phenomena I examine are obviously connected but not identical, I address them separately.

In Search of the Silver Age

In the eyes of many beholders, the Silver Age ended in 1917.[15] Its immediate rediscovery was instigated by the death of Aleksandr Blok in 1921. However, unlike Howard Carter's celebrated discovery of Tutankhamen's tomb that instantly put ancient Egypt back on the map in 1922, the rediscovery of the Silver Age stretched over most of the twentieth century. It is not surprising, therefore, that the cultural excavating machines, while removing historical sediments from one side of the dig, often dumped them on the other. Thus when the future *shestidesiatniki* (people whose coming of age coincided with the 1960s) were sorting through the treasures of a perfectly preserved Silver Age, which in their eyes had somehow cheated and survived the Bolshevik Revolution, they were unaware that the perceived totality of that "period" owed its conceptualization and existence mostly to that same revolution. The Bolshevik Revolution not only claimed people's lives but also enhanced the ever-present sense of uncertainty and existential anxiety. In "Anxiety and the Formation of Early Modern Culture," William Bouwsma hypothesizes that any culture is the product of "man's ability to impose a meaning on his experience that can give to life a measure of reliability and thus reduce, even if it cannot altogether abolish, life's ultimate and terrifying uncertainties."[16] Bouwsma sees culture as "the collective strategies by which societies organize and make sense of their experience. Culture in this sense is a mechanism for the management of existential anxiety."[17] I argue that the Silver Age was created as a result of the collective appropriation of the historical experience that befell the Russian people in the first third of the twentieth century.

Despite the widespread assumption that the Bolshevik Revolution consigned the Silver Age heritage to oblivion, the voluminous material written about this "period" suggests otherwise. The Silver Age has inspired a profusion of memoirs, letters, various other testimonies, and works of fiction, not to mention numerous scholarly articles. Many of these works were produced in the 1920s and 1930s—that is, during the first twenty years after the end of the era. Thus, having read Andrei Bely's memoirs about Blok in 1923, Bely's friend and long-time correspondent Ivanov-Razumnik described them as "a unique (in the whole of Russian literary tradition) monument to a cultural epoch, erected by its own contemporary."[18] To be in a position to create such a monument, Ivanov-Razumnik further stipulates, one has to feel completely cut off from one's own past, which Bely would have experienced while residing in Berlin in the early 1920s.[19] It would appear, therefore, that the perceived rift between pre- and postrevolutionary cultures was in fact beneficial in creating an entire cultural apparatus, or even an institution, that became seriously engaged in reproducing the Silver Age's legacy for a contemporary audience, thus securing its vitality for later periods. It was this institution, for example, that was responsible for generating new mnemonic spaces where memory about the Silver Age would be stored and conserved for the greater part of the twentieth century. Such mnemonic spaces include the myth about the continuation of the Silver Age in Russian emigre circles; museums, cemeteries, private photograph albums, and even private literary graveyards, such as Vladislav Khodasevich's collection *Necropolis* (1926–1939); the *Tartu Blokovskie sborniki* (1964–); and the Silver Age restaurant mentioned earlier.

The reason we now remember almost every name and every detail connected with the Silver Age is because of the all-preservationist approach toward the Silver Age adopted in literary studies in the 1950s and prevalent ever since. Angela Brintlinger describes her writers-cum-historians-cum–literary critics of the 1920s and the 1930s, Tynianov, Bulgakov, and Khodasevich, as "sifting through patches of historical data—characters, events, places—and choosing which patches to piece together into a story."[20] With contemporary critics, this ability to sift and differentiate seems to have largely atrophied. Russian cultural archeologists do not want to lose anything remotely related to their revered past. They fill in their boxes with bones, jewelry, pottery, and other precious artifacts, together with tons and tons of soil that had enveloped those relics of the bygone era. When Akhmatova claimed in 1964 that "almost nobody has been forgotten; almost everyone has been remembered," by "everyone" she meant a group of outstanding representatives of the prerevolutionary culture, such as Andrei Bely, Boris Pasternak, and Viacheslav Ivanov, Igor Stravinskii, and Vsevolod Meyerhold.[21] By the beginning of the twenty-first century, this group of the "remembered" has expanded to include much lesser-known cultural figures succeeded by members of their families and distant relatives. Not surprisingly, works of literature that deal directly with literary history and tradition, such as Dmitrii Galkovskii's *The Endless Dead End* (*Beskonechnyi tupik*, 1988, 1998), average 700–1,000 pages in length.

The boom of interest in the Silver Age in Russia coincided with the late 1980s when many Russians were made aware of their political and cultural history. One of the achievements of Gorbachev's perestroika was to make the new revelations about the political and cultural past a priority on the pages of scholarly and popular journals and newspapers. By the early 1990s, following numerous publications that emphasized the hardships endured by its many representatives in the Soviet period, the Silver Age truly became a popular symbol of democratic development and of moral and artistic freedom. As Kathleen Smith observes, "Politics always has a symbolic dimension. Politicians in general have a particular interest in shaping versions of past events because shared memories of nationally significant events provide grist for the formation of collective identities."[22] Because the "truth" about Russia's cultural history tended to be presented along with the "truth" about Russia's political history, these phenomena became permanently entangled in the eyes of beholders. The Silver Age was like a territory once annexed by a foreign power and then reunited with the mainland. In this situation, the euphoria of reconciliation with the past eventually gave way to torturing queries and concerns.

Renewed interest in the Silver Age and its position within Russian cultural history stemmed to a large extent from various popular attempts to reevaluate the past, particularly the experience of the October Revolution, which has been blamed by many for all the atrocities of the Russian twentieth century. In such reconstructions, evaluation of the period immediately preceding the revolution plays a major role. The famous study by Boris Groys, *The Total Art of Stalinism* (1988, 1992), in which he convincingly demonstrates kinship and continuity between the Russian avant-garde movement and socialist realism, made readers ponder the existence of similar links between the Silver Age and the Stalinist culture of the 1930s.[23] In 1997 the journalist Boris Paramonov took credit for extending a special service to Russian speakers in 1989 while working for Radio Liberty by exposing the traps that people infatuated with the ideas entertained by popular figures of the Silver Age might have fallen into:

> I guess I had rather unconventional ideas at the time.... I have worked for Radio Liberty since 1986, and when, in the course of "perestroika," Russia began to resurrect new cultural personalities and subjects in its search for alternative ideas to communism, I had the following comment to make. During the "period of stagnation," the philosophical and religious works by cultural figures of the Silver Age were beneficial reading by way of an antidote to the dominant ideological clichés. But having arrived in the West and having put all those writings in the context of normal, so to speak, civilized life, one begins to realize that all of them are mere intellectual fantasies.... I just want to say that, when everybody began to talk about going to the representatives of the Silver Age for the truth, I set as my aim to show that this ground had already been covered and the results were disastrous. All of those people were undoubtedly very interesting, vivid, and talented, but they were evil geniuses, as the saying goes, and that applies to Berdiaev,

Florenskii, and, of course, to Viacheslav Ivanov—a totally ominous character. . . . My main idea was the following: Bolshevism in Russia wasn't something absolutely alien to the general cultural developments at the turn of the twentieth century. It was [part of the same] flood. An orientation toward a total transformation of being was characteristic of both religious philosophers and Bolsheviks. The project of a new heaven and a new earth. They never reached the heaven but fouled up the earth. . . . I discussed this for several years, based on concrete analyses of books, events, and intellectual conflicts. I never came across any definite expression of such ideas in the press. Today I believe they have been absorbed by public consciousness and are generally not unexpected.[24]

Even if one disagrees with Paramonov's pronouncements, his assessments are typical of the 1990s and are shared by some free-spirited Russian intellectuals. In a recent episode of the Russian literary broadcast *The School for Scandal* (*Shkola zlosloviia*, May 2005), the writer Sergei Gandlevskii suggested that one of the main reasons for the popularity of the Silver Age in his youth was "because it was forbidden." It also allowed him and his friends "to be different from the gray Soviet people." When prompted to talk about Anna Akhmatova, Gandlevskii did not conceal his animosity toward one of the Silver Age's renowned cultural icons. He dismissed Akhmatova both as a poet and a human being because of Akhmatova's "need for [some sort of] a narrow-minded audience—a dependence that doesn't do you a lot of credit," and also because of "her ability to strike an attractive classicist pose in any kind of situation." As Paramonov's and Gandlevskii's comments suggest, in the past decade the near-surface cross-cultural and cross-temporal studies of the Silver Age, so typical of the 1960s, because of the abundance of new information about this period, coupled with rising nationalism, have given way to meticulous "excavation" of the lives of its representatives. Probing the past by digesting and analyzing previously concealed official documents, personal diaries, memoirs, official and private letters, professional and amateur photographs—and on the basis of these new discoveries rejecting that past or reconciling oneself with it—all this has been on the agenda of many Russian newspapers and "thick" journals for the last twenty years. I maintain that because of its political dimension, the myth of the Silver Age reveals many conflicting attitudes. To paraphrase Foucault, the Silver Age is "a place of rest, certainty, reconciliation, a place of tranquillized sleep."[25] It is also a source of anxiety and insatiate ambitions and an active battleground. To borrow from Stephanie Sandler's elegant summation about Pushkin's enduring popularity in Russia, "one would think that other, more urgent needs might take priority, and of course in many forums they have, but Russians still argue" about the Silver Age.[26] It wouldn't be an exaggeration to say that although in the eyes of the rest of the world twentieth-century Russia came to be primarily associated with the Bolshevik Revolution and its aftermath, it was the myth of the Silver Age through which Russian collective consciousness in fact revealed its identity and, in Bouwsma's words, "managed its existential anxieties."[27] Even the prevailing discourse on the Stalinist terror that has gained popularity over the last twenty years has not eclipsed the ongoing debate about the Silver Age and its legacy. And this is only to be expected: while the Stalinist terror has been perceived in general as an abominable past experience that one should either try to forget or never stop speaking about, the Silver Age so far continues to resist clear-cut definitions.

The Silver Age and the "Anxiety of Influence"

In his study of what he calls cultural selection, Gary Taylor observes, "Culture is the gift of the survivor. It is always bereaved, always retrospective, always at war with the present."[28] For Taylor an emblematic example of the very mechanisms by "which culture is made" was the story of Nadezhda Mandelstam (1899–1980). For many years after Osip Mandelstam's death in 1938, Nadezhda Mandelstam was the sole custodian and interpreter of her husband's poetic legacy and of his life in general. In Taylor's brief analysis, Nadezhda Mandelstam succeeded in preserving the memory of her dead husband for posterity despite all odds and repressions. Would she have been more successful had she had to promote her husband's legacy under more favorable conditions? The answer is probably no. Most likely, her name and the name of her husband would have been known to a limited group of people with a developed taste for great poetry. What added tremendously to the popularity of Osip Mandelstam's work and Nadezhda Mandelstam's memoirs was the fact that they were both seen as victims of Stalinist terror.[29] As revealed by the controversy surrounding the publication of Emma Gerstein's subversive and provocative *Memoirs* (*Memuary*, 1998), without the protection of being seen as a martyr and an unjustly persecuted person, Nadezhda Mandelstam could have been subjected to severe criticism and accused of perjury and amoral behavior.[30] In 2001 Elena Chukovskaia published posthumously her mother's *The Poet's House* (*Dom poeta*), a lengthy critique of Nadezhda Mandelstam's second book of memoirs, *Hope Abandoned* (*Vtoraia kniga*, 1978).[31] Written largely in the late 1970s, *The Poet's House* was not meant for publication. Rather, it served Chukovskaia as an outlet to vent her indignation about Nadezhda Mandelstam's unscrupulous approach to portraying her illustrious contemporaries, such as Anna Akhmatova, Boris Pasternak, and Nikolai Khardzhiev, to name but a few. Both Gerstein (1903–2002) and Chukovskaia (1907–1996) were upset that Nadezhda Mandelstam usurped the right to speak for the dead, refused to recognize any other influence on her husband's creativity apart from her own, and dishonestly appropriated other people's ideas. In a 1999 interview, Gerstein went even further by trying to expose Nadezhda Mandelstam as a double-dealer and accused her (and not the Soviet authorities, as one would expect) of impeding the first Soviet publication of Osip Mandelstam's poetry.[32] She did this, according to Gerstein, for purely selfish reasons—to promote her own memoirs (they achieved much wider recognition, while Osip Mandelstam's poetry was banned in the Soviet Union) and to establish her unquestionable authority outside the Soviet Union on all issues related to her husband's legacy.

Both Chukovskaia and Gerstein were cultural historians and memoirists by vocation. Why then did they wait for over twenty years to challenge Nadezhda Mandelstam's stories? The answer is obvious for anybody familiar with the cultural and political situation in Russia in the 1970s. What took Gerstein so long to come out with her memoirs and what made Chukovskaia suppress the publication of *The Poet's House* indefinitely was a self-imposed moral obligation to keep silent while so-called unofficial literature was under a cloud. Such heightened feelings of obligation toward one's culture, along with anxiety both about its loss and omnipresence that many Russian intellectuals shared in the twentieth century, are at odds with Harold Bloom's famous pronouncements about literary sons and daughters always wanting to oust their so-called forefathers and foremothers. For example, Bloom sees the relationship between Christopher Marlowe and Shakespeare as a poetic rivalry that did not end with Marlowe's untimely death.[33] According to Bloom's theory, Chukovskaia and Gerstein would have seized an opportunity to topple Nadezhda Mandelstam and, given their talents and access to information, would have gained fame by erasing her version of the past forever. However, Bloom's otherwise illuminating theory has its limitations when applied to the cultural situation in twentieth-century Russia.

Whether we ponder it explicitly or not, our relationship with the past is mediated through a set of anxieties regarding its influence on our present and future lives. With writers (and artists in general), such anxieties are inextricable from the creative process, since no writer creates in a vacuum and no writer can be oblivious to the works of his or her predecessors. Vladimir Nabokov, who was notoriously secretive about his actual sources of inspiration and particularly loathed being compared to Dostoevskii, by the end of his life composed and disseminated through his *Strong Opinions* (1972) a list of writers that he himself was willing to be compared to. Bloom describes the attitude of an artist toward the achievements of his predecessors as an explosive mixture of admiration, jealousy, and "the anxiety of influence."[34] The artist evokes earlier works not in order to repeat them or to establish some special bond with them, but in order to "swerve" from them and produce something essentially new out of this contact. Russian literature was no exception. The classical case study is Yurii Tynianov's illuminating exposure of Dostoevskii's appropriation of Gogol's legacy in *The Village Stepanchikovo and Its Residents* (*Selo Stepanchikovo i ego obitateli*, 1859).[35] By intentionally reducing Gogol to the victimized and victimizing self-professed writer Foma Opiskin, whose literary and other influence did not exceed the circle of certain senile old ladies, Dostoevskii successfully purged himself from the burdening influence of his distinguished predecessor who was inadvertently present in Dostoevskii's early fiction. As Bloom reminds us, "Poets are neither ideal nor common readers.... They tend not to think, as they read: 'This is dead, this is living, in the poetry of X.' ... For them, to be judicious is to be weak, and to compare, exactly and fairly, is to be not elect.... Poetic history ... [is] indistinguishable from poetic influence, since strong poets make that history by misreading one another, so as to clear imaginative space for themselves."[36]

A collection of memoirs by such "ordinary talents" as Leont'ev-Shcheglov, Moshin, Iasinskii, and Ezhov offers further support for Bloom's theory, revealing how little some contemporaries cared about Chekhov and the preservation of his memory after his premature death in 1904.[37] These memoirs, although not written to be published as a group, capture a kind of primordial state in which geniuses did not know that they were geniuses and weaker talents were unaware of their inferiority. This was the merry time when the literati drank and ate together, exchanged anecdotes, sold land to each other, played cards, visited monasteries, went hunting, traveled by train—that is, did anything but write and read. Most of the memoirists were fortunate to know the majority of Russian writers of the last third of the nineteenth century; however, they frequently referred to "our great writer" and "our esteemed author" primarily to ridicule the thought that this or that figure might indeed be considered great. The title of this collection, *Among the Great* (*Sredi velikikh*), underscores this sense of being oblivious to greatness, a kind of being-lost-in-the-virgin-woods situation.

Likewise, when the acmeists vehemently attacked the symbolists in the 1910s for their addiction to mysticism, detachment from mundane experience, and failure to live in the three-dimensional world, and themselves cultivated an obsession with the "real," material world, they did so not out of piety toward their declining predecessors, but to expose the novelty of their own ideas and to emphasize their superiority over their former teachers.[38] Such a rebellious mood left no time to consider what was fair and ethical. Thus, in the early twenties, Osip Mandelstam—at that time himself preparing to switch from poetry to prose—was particularly vicious toward Andrei Bely, whom he compared to "a *grande dame*, sparkling in the blinding brilliance of universal charlatanism," and whose novels he likened to "exhibition pavilions soon to be dismantled."[39]

By the 1930s, however, Mandelstam had changed his negative view of Bely.[40] This happened not because by the end of his life Bely started to behave differently or adopted a different way of writing, but because in the 1930s Bely and everything he stood for—a prerevolutionary culture that received the name of the Russian Silver Age—had acquired in the eyes of Mandelstam and many other intellectuals a distinct aura of martyrdom and respect. In his otherwise laudatory review of Bloom's *Anxiety of Influence*, Paul de Man saw one of the major weaknesses of Bloom's theory to be its initial assumption that the past had such a strong appeal in the eyes of his poets-beholders. According to de Man, this was "a mere assertion without evidence to make it convincing."[41] However, Russian literature of the twentieth century provides ample support for Bloom's assertion, for Russian writers were not merely attracted to their past, they were obsessively attached to it. It is precisely this obsession with the immediate cultural heritage, rather than any attempts to overcome it, that distinguishes the twentieth-century Russian writers from their English counterparts cited by Bloom.

Although representatives of prerevolutionary culture were often criticized for their irresponsible, highly individualistic, and hedonistic behavior, some of their memoirists, like Nadezhda Mandelstam, even held them accountable for the atrocities of the subsequent periods. Open battle with tradition was virtually impossible, since many of its representatives had met with tragic deaths or persecution by the authorities. In such a situation it was more important to preserve what was left than to attack or rebel against it.[42] In the effort to preserve the effaced and forgotten, political revolt against the present substituted for artistic revolt against the past. Writers were looking to European or "classical" Russian literature for inspiration while addressing their numerous poems to their older contemporaries and peers. In the 1930s, any "sophisticated" mockery of the early twentieth-century culture and its representatives—such as one can find in the memoirs of Andrei Bely or Georgii Ivanov, for example—was regarded by most of their contemporaries as indecent behavior. This unhealthy prohibition against wrestling with tradition, a restraint that many artists seem to have imposed on themselves, resulted in the conscientious smuggling of numerous quotations and references to forgotten or forbidden names, events, and literary sources into their own works, as can be seen in Akhmatova's *Poem Without a Hero* (*Poema bez geroia*, 1940–1965). Pasternak's slow buildup toward the big novel *Doctor Zhivago* (1945–1955), for which a succession of shorter works published in the late 1930s had laid the foundation, should be considered in the same vein. It was only in the mid-1940s, when the Silver Age started to make its way back into Russian culture, that Pasternak found it possible to commence his revision—or in Pasternak's words, his "translation"—of its legacy into the modern language of his time.

If before the 1917 revolution Russian writers had typically been preoccupied with undermining and destabilizing cultural traditions, after the revolution, they began to see themselves and were seen as the sole bearers of cultural memory.[43] Anna Akhmatova's *Poem Without a Hero* about the rupture between the Silver Age and "the real—not the calendar—twentieth century" is particularly notable in this respect. Even in Akhmatova's lifetime, the *Poem* was generally considered to be a carefully encoded message about the past that required a similarly careful deciphering on the part of the reader, as is amply demonstrated by many of Akhmatova's scholars and admirers. The key idea of Mandelstam's ethics and aesthetics—"to remember," an idea that first appeared in his essays of the early 1920s—was shared to a greater or lesser extent by many of his contemporaries both inside and outside the Soviet Union.[44] For writers like Vladimir Nabokov, who started to write seriously only after emigrating to Europe, the legacy of the Silver Age was an umbilical cord that tied them to Russian literary tradition.

When something is not remembered, it disappears. In *Doctor Zhivago*, a novel largely devoted to questions of memory, and particularly cultural memory, Pasternak depicts the following situation: The same day little Yura forgets to recall his father in his prayers, his father commits suicide a few miles away from the estate where Yura has been invited to stay with his uncle. Not surprisingly, the works of Harold Bloom were unknown to Russian readers until very recently. And those who read him in the 1970s and 1980s, like the poet Joseph Brodsky, were clearly troubled by his parricidal theories. In his "A Note to a Commentary," Brodsky recorded his own anxiety at being subjected to Bloom's scrutiny:

> A true poet doesn't flee influences and continuity but often cherishes and emphasizes them in every possible way. There is no greater physical, even physiological, pleasure than to repeat silently or out loud somebody's lines. A fear of influence or (a fear of) dependence is a disease—the disease of a savage but not of culture, the whole of which is continuity, the whole of which is an echo. Let somebody pass this on to Harold Bloom.[45]

Clearly, Brodsky was not afraid of being influenced by his forefathers and foremothers. As Susan Sontag recalled after the poet's death, "One should write to please not one's contemporaries, but one's predecessors, Brodsky often declared. Surely he did please them—his compatriots agree that he was his era's unique successor to Mandelstam, Tsvetaeva, and Akhmatova. Raising the 'plain of regard' (as he called it) was relentlessly identified with the effortlessness and ambitions and appropriate fidelities of poets."[46] Brodsky's affirmation of his loyalty to the past notwithstanding, by the late 1960s, the strong sense of moral obligation toward the legacy of the Silver Age started to subside and gave way to a healthier curiosity, mixed with amiable irony and sarcasm. This trend is evident in the works of the so-called *shestidesiatniki*, particularly in the novels of Andrei Bitov and, to a lesser extent, Vasilii Aksenov. The new cavalier approach to the Silver Age reached its apogee in the writings of their younger colleagues such as Sasha Sokolov, Viktor Erofeev, and Viktor Pelevin. The 1960s were the time when the Silver Age started flowing back into the mainstream of the Russian culture, while the 1980s and the 1990s saw its complete reintegration.

Accordingly, the anxiety of influence, as a theory, is both an instrument and an object of my research. In this, I follow Bloom, who claims that any "strong" work of art is always "the achieved anxiety." Bloom emphasizes that this statement is true regardless of whether the anxiety was actually "internalized by the later writer" or not.[47] In the case of the writers whose reactions to the past form the substance of my book, there is no need for such a clarification, since there is much evidence that they were all very much aware (sometimes painfully so) of their long-term engagement with the past. More so, these writers' attempts at conceptualizing their relationship with their predecessors accord rather well with Bloom's hypotheses.[48] What gave a boost to her studies of Pushkin in the 1920s was Akhmatova's research on the writers that might have influenced Pushkin and her ex-husband, the poet Nikolai Gumilev. Some of her formulations about Pushkin "unscrupulously" borrowing from other writers everything he liked (which, according to Akhmatova, was the sign of a true genius) long preceded Bloom's statements on strong poets "appropriating for themselves."[49] By the 1960s, Akhmatova had revised her earlier versions of her relationship with Gumilev; from then on she interpreted it primarily in light of her anxiety about his constricting influence on her work and her struggle to develop her own voice.

Gumilev was one of the first victims of the Bolshevik terror. Akhmatova, as she revealed to her confidantes, had been tortured ever since Gumilev's execution in 1921 by the guilt of not having loved him enough. This feeling of moral responsibility for the dead and/or forgotten and forbidden (some of whom were intimately related to her) made her a perfect keeper of the prerevolutionary cultural tradition. It was probably because of that guilt that she later opened up her *Poem* to every other discourse. Years later, in *Russian Beauty* (1982, 1990), Viktor Erofeev parodied the Russian institution of widowhood (of which Akhmatova was a moral beacon and its most famous representative) through his character Irina Tarakanova, who made her body accessible to anyone who wanted to satisfy his or her sexual and textual needs. With Irina Tarakanova, the level of textual and emotional chaos reaches an apogee and she commits suicide. In real life Akhmatova suffered no less. The work on the *Poem* was finished only with Akhmatova's own death. The last years of her life were marked by four heart attacks and bouts of anxiety about the reception of the *Poem*, which she had hoped would surpass any other work in quality.

Obviously, with regard to the Silver Age and its influence on later writers, Bloom's model has to be expanded to accommodate both the piety and suspicion that its image has encouraged in its various beholders. Bloom's Freudian model of literary influence is based on a family of two—that is, a poet always wanting to rid himself of the influence of his poetic father (or fathers) in order to prove himself. But what if a particular "father" is portrayed by neighbors or relatives as a criminal, or, conversely, as an unjustly persecuted person? What if a father is actually a mother? What if there was no father at all?

For any happening to turn into an event proper, it has first to be contextualized and textualized. As is well known, not only the meaning of the Bolshevik Revolution, but even its time span have provoked numerous debates.[50] Its perceived time frame depends on how one chooses to conceptualize its goals and outcome. As Sheila Fitzpatrick explains:

> Since revolutions are complex social and political upheavals, historians who write about them are bound to differ on the most basic questions—causes, revolutionary aims, impact on the society, political outcome, and even the timespan of the revolution itself. In the case of the Russian Revolution, the starting-point presents no problem:

almost everyone takes it to be the "February Revolution" of 1917, which led to the abdication of Emperor Nicholas II and the formation of the Provisional Government. But when did the Russian Revolution end? Was it all over by October 1917, when the Bolsheviks took power? Or did the end of the Revolution come with the Bolsheviks' victory in the Civil War in 1920? Was Stalin's "revolution from above" part of the Russian Revolution? Or should we take the view that the revolution continued throughout the lifetime of the Soviet state?[51]

Likewise, there is no such thing as the "true" history of literary evolution, since its recorded trajectory is a joint effort of a certain group of beholders. Do we shape cultural phenomena to fit the trajectory of political events? Or do we need these political events to make sense of the otherwise inexplicable trajectory of cultural evolution? These are the questions that I attempt to answer in chapters 2 and 3.

Although the riches of the prerevolutionary culture were not confined to literature and literary criticism alone, I concentrate on writers and literary critics, their lives and work, primarily because, as I have mentioned before, Russian writers of this era (unlike their American or Western European counterparts) felt themselves to be charged with the preservation of continuity and therefore were forced to negotiate an intricate balance between cultural conservation and the need to develop their own creative identity. While chapters 2 and 3 concern the ways in which anxieties caused by political and cultural upheavals were managed at the collective level, in the five chapters that follow I focus on the various strategies used by Akhmatova, Nabokov, Pasternak, and Viktor Erofeev in assimilating the legacy of the Silver Age into their writings. My aim is twofold: to determine the contributions of these figures to the myth-making process and at the same time to assess the effect of popular conceptions or misconceptions about the Silver Age on their writings and personal life.

Bloom is often accused of ignoring women writers in his interpretative schemes. Some critics believe that his theory of literary influence was meant to apply only to the sons wrestling with their fathers, while daughters were excluded. Although I am not convinced that these accusations are valid, my analysis of Akhmatova's ingenious strategy of unloading her jealousy and anxiety not on her illustrious fathers and brothers but on their wives and companions addresses a gap in Bloom's theory.

Today the Silver Age has come to occupy a well-defined place in the landscape of Russian culture. What happens to cultural constructs such as the Russian Silver Age when they lose one of their important constituent elements—their delectable "outsideness," "foreignness," and novelty? I address these issues in my conclusion.

2 Literature and Revolution

THE CASE OF ALEKSANDR BLOK

> One could be exhausted and die like a dog, without a ripple. We keep talking about history, but history is a petty and illusory wave, which has as little authenticity as the current recognition of Blok by everyone.
> —*The Diary of Nikolai Punin*, January 28, 1922

In 1980, the Soviet people celebrated the centennial of Aleksandr Blok. The jubilee turned into a large forum at which literary scholars and writers were invited to make their comments on the influence of Blok on Russian culture in general and on their personal development in particular. In response to the questionnaire put together by *Voprosy literatury*, the poet and literary critic Stanislav Kuniaev compared Blok to a sapper whose job had been to build bridges between different epochs:

> After the majority of the old, prerevolutionary intelligentsia had betrayed Russia and the majority of the new intelligentsia was doing its utmost to dissociate themselves from the traditions of the Russian classical arts, it suddenly transpired that it was impossible for them to

do so because Blok, as the workman and engineer *[kak chernorabochii, kak saper]*—not "the tragic tenor"—of the epoch, had already built bridges between the two historical periods.

In the 1920s and 1930s, when the vulgarizers were distorting our great history and vandals were destroying the invaluable monuments of culture and architecture, attempts were made to supplement this destruction by annihilating Pushkin, Nekrasov, Dostoevskii, and Tiutchev. However, Blok had already constructed barricades that blocked this road to destruction.[1]

Although nobody expressed this point of view quite as forcefully as Kuniaev, he was not alone in his celebration of Blok as the perfect cultural intermediary.[2] The bridge imagery featured prominently both in scholarly works and private estimations and recollections. Many respondents spoke of Blok as the "golden bridge" or the "everlasting rainbow arching over Russia's past, present, and future."[3] However, responses to the second question of how an individual would estimate Blok's influence on his or her writing career proved to be difficult to formulate. Most poets answered vaguely that it was Blok's heroic life rather than his poetic technique that they were really striving to emulate, or insisted that the specifics of Blokian poetry were resistant to imitation. Likewise, Mstislav Koz'min (the editor-in-chief of *Voprosy literatury*), in his article "Russia's Great Poet" ("Velikii poet Rossii") appreciatively concluded that "with the passing of time the importance of Blok in the development of Soviet poetry has become more and more pronounced," but he refrained from buttressing his statement with any concrete examples.[4]

It is no easy task to establish Blok's status within the Soviet aesthetic hierarchy. Blok assumed the status of a loner and yet, at the same time, an almighty mediator who in the eyes of many beholders (such as Kuniaev) single-handedly changed the course of literary evolution as well as the outcome of political developments, almost at a whim. A second question is how to account for the (at times) astounding interest in Blok on the part of numerous critics and authorities. This seemingly inexplicable level of interest used to puzzle even such insightful interpreters as the famous art historian and critic Nikolai Nikolaevich Punin (1888–1953). Punin's private notes betray his lifelong preoccupation with the making of cultural icons and, more specifically, the definition of artistic genius. In 1923 he recorded in his diary: "No, I do not agree with the existing appraisal of Blok.... The understanding of the revolution in 'The Twelve,' for instance, is so untrue and superficial. It is also an incomprehensible distortion of his contemporaries. I am not saying that he was not a great man, but his role was not the one they are trying to foist on him now—he is the end, the past, and the despair."[5] Like Punin's, my fascination with Blok lies not so much with his actual oeuvre, but with the subsequent collective re-experience of his life and work. By retracing Blok's elevation to a cultural icon and institution, we can obtain insights, if not into the "actual" trajectory of cultural evolution, at least into the mechanics of its subsequent conceptualization. To the extent that a new round in cultural evolution involves the emergence of new trends and approaches, it brings with it a collective invention and collective experience of this evolution.

There seems to have been more periods or epochs in Russian cultural evolution than in other known "evolutions." What is known as modernism (1890–1939) corresponds in Russia to the Silver Age and the age of socialist realism.[6] So far, there has been no compatible taxonomy of Russian twentieth-century cultural trends, groups, and periods. Instead, there is a crop of impressive studies devoted to revealing various misconceptions about these trends, groups, and periods.[7] Furthermore, there seems to be a widespread myth that Russian cultural evolution was discontinuous, although, as many recent studies have revealed, it is hard to conceive of another culture that has enjoyed such continuity in its development.

How do we know that this or that period of cultural evolution has come to an end? Did modernism really end with the outbreak of World War II, as we are now led to believe? Do we always become aware of the end of an era as result of a meaningful political event or the death of a major figure? All histories of cultural evolution have made use of historical events, some bringing them to the foreground, some moving them to the background, but none has been able to ignore them entirely. Even those histories that center on individuals, styles, genres, and literary reception have to take into consideration such events as the birth or death of this or that cultural figure, thus inevitably entering the domain of historical record, of events and their interpretations and re-presentations.[8] Do political events punctuate cultural shifts, or do these shifts turn minor happenings into major historical events? These are not easy questions to answer. One question we might want to answer is how political and cultural phenomena are built into contexts that endow them both with a codependent meaning.

Not long ago, like Kuniaev, I tended to think about Blok, or the Blokian institution, as I call it, as being a cultural intermediary that was brought to life to bridge the gap between pre- and postrevolutionary cultures. Now I believe that the role of this institution was much more to first create and then expand this gap. In early 1917 Blok was already receiving praise from a number of critics either for his commendable "yearning for realism" or even for turning himself into an accomplished realist on a par with the mature Pushkin.[9] Thus in an article entitled "At a New Threshold" ("U novoi grani," 1917) one critic recorded:

> Talking about Blok some time ago, we noted that he had completed the road upon which he had set out long ago and was standing at the threshold of something new. And true enough, his last long poem ["Retribution"] is the best proof of this development. . . . [This poem] is no longer [an example] of decadent art, it is completely comprehensible and, most important, is of general significance. . . . From a romantic poet, dreaming and impulsive, utterly subjective and egocentric, Blok is turning into a poet of a realistic persuasion, who is capable of taking an objective view of what is happening in the world. However, this abrupt transition is not as radical or fatal as it may seem. . . . Blok has not lost those things that he had previously accumulated, nor has he renounced them. He did not reject them upon choosing

the new road. On the contrary—he used his findings to serve his new purposes in other areas. This is what makes us see this turning point in Blok's writing career not as something accidental or contrived, but as a deeply natural phenomenon and a new stage in his evolution, the evolution to be found in all great poets.[10]

However, such an idyllic view of Blok as evolving naturally from one stage to another did not survive Blok's death in 1921. For the most part, it was only rediscovered and reaffirmed by Soviet critics some twenty years later. The pressing need shared by many in the 1920s and 1930s—to conceptualize the political upheaval that came to be known as the Great October Revolution—called for the reinvention of Blok. Not only the Soviet authorities but also critics of various stripes took part in this gigantic enterprise. Regardless of whether these different people supported pro-Bolshevik developments or opposed them, Blok became a cornerstone in each of the edifices arising out of their discussions. As I will show, the myth of the Silver Age (in which Blok played a leading part) came into being largely out of a necessity to account for either the positive or the negative effects of the October Revolution.

Blok and the Soviet Intelligentsia

Blok's breathtaking ascent to the pantheon of Russia's Great Writers happened shortly after his death in 1921. However, his position within that congregation was rather special. For years, Blok was one of very few cultural figures of late imperial Russia who was portrayed consistently with warmth and reverence. While many other less fortunate men of letters were suffering passengers on Russia's "steamboat of modernity," Blok managed to weather well most subsequent revisionist periods in Russian history (as intimated by Kuniaev). Blok remained staunchly at the helm—an unbending "northern skipper," as memoirists often portrayed him.

Until recently, Blok has been one of the most intensely studied of Russian writers—on a par only with Pushkin, and often surpassing the latter in popularity and attention. More than 800 articles, books, and monographs devoted to Blok and his works were published between 1918 and 1928 alone.[11] The next thirty years produced another 1,000 works devoted to various aspects of Blok's legacy.[12] Each newly released publication of Blok's private letters, diaries, and notebooks was welcomed as an important cultural, social, and political event, and each was widely discussed both in the press and at meetings of various commissions and subcommissions devoted to the study of his legacy and preservation of his memory.[13] Not everybody knows that the 1937 issue of *Literaturnoe nasledstvo* was devoted to the Russian symbolists, primarily to the key representatives of the movement—namely, Blok, Valerii Briusov, and Andrei Bely. The 1978 volume of *Literaturnoe nasledstvo* was devoted solely to Blok's correspondence with Liubov' Dmitrievna Mendeleeva, supplemented by extensive commentary. The issuing of another volume of *Literaturnoe nasledstvo* commemorated Blok's centennial in 1980. In fact, the word *volume* is a gross understatement—this particular volume, number 92, consists of five thick books that encompass the efforts of a group of more than eighty specialists.

In 1944 Blok's remains, along with those of his grandfather, mother, and wife, were disinterred and transported from the Smolensk cemetery to a place deemed more appropriate for Russian literati, that is, the special section of the Volkovo cemetery known as "Literatorskie mostki." To this new grave crowds of people came in 1946 to lay flowers to commemorate the twenty-fifth anniversary of Blok's death.[14] Prior to the actual date (August 7), every effort was made to make the festivities worthy of "the conscience of Russian poetry," as Blok was described by one of his custodians.[15] The year 1946 was marked not only by the launch of a new collection of memoirs and updated biographical monographs, but also by the mass production of Blok's portraits. Likewise, sculptors were commissioned to produce "new busts of the poet," and musical publishers issued a special edition of Blok's works arranged for voice and piano by Soviet composers.[16] In Leningrad people lined up to visit a memorial exhibition in Pushkinskii Dom that featured Blok's unfinished cigarette and other snapshots of his final days.[17]

If in 1946 large-scale celebrations of Blok were a novelty, ten years later they had become part of the annual cultural routine and a well-trodden venue for political propaganda. The literary critic Kornei Chukovskii (1882–1969) described one such meeting in his diary entry for December 1955:

> Last week I delivered a speech about Blok. A magnificent celebration in his honor was organized in the Chaikovskii Concert Hall. Fedin in his metallic voice as [if he had been] the Lord on Mount Sinai delivered his introductory speech with weight and significance. Then all hell let loose. Antokol'skii with artificial energy shouted out his hopelessly shallow presentation. He started in a high pitch as if he had been arguing with someone by offering to the audience his rotten banal concept ("Blok is a realist! Blok is fond of revolutions!"). He honked loudly as if he had been in a barrel and sat down. I was sitting next to Tvardovskii who said, "Antokol'skii shouts as if he were shouting from an airplane." Tvardovskii had also prepared a speech about Blok but declined the honor of giving it after seeing Kirsanov dancing convulsively like a shaman and after hearing the bureaucratic babble of Sergei Gorodetskii. Fedin gave me the floor when everybody in the audience was extremely tired, but nevertheless my speech was the only one that was heard and that reached people's hearts (or so I was told by Fedin, Tvardovskii, and Kazakevich). However, even this speech was not sincere enough.[18]

Even so, despite the officialdom and boredom generated by the Blok industry, as illustrated by Chukovskii's testimony, through the years of Soviet power Blok succeeded in remaining an attractive outsider in the eyes of his beholders, particularly in the eyes of the intelligentsia. One such beholder was Boris Pasternak, a friend and neighbor of the Chukovskii clan in Peredelkino. In his frequently quoted cycle "The Wind" ("Veter," 1956), Pasternak declared that Blok, unlike Pushkin, was not deified by inclusion in school curricula, was not in any sense a man-made product, nor was his image thrust upon its beholders by anyone else. It took almost sixty years for such perceptive observers as Lidiia Ginzburg (1902–1990) to recognize the Blok-related hustle and bustle for what it was, that is, the motions of a gigantic cultural institution. Yet even then Ginzburg attributed her disgust at the pompous celebrations of the Blok centennial in 1980 to the utter incompatibility of "officialdom" (such as various representatives of party organizations, school principals, directors of museums, and representatives of the press) with Blok the artist. "A horrifying exposé of the mechanics of the jubilee machine," she recorded in her diary, "particularly because the machine is processing highly unsuitable material, material that is so fresh and raw. Pushkin festivals have become a habit, they have become automatized. But here with Blok everything is in such a primitive state [vse pervozdanno]."[19]

Moreover, despite the official recognition of Blok's contributions and the large amounts of government money devoted to celebrating him, those studying his life and work (who for the most part held positions in governmental, research, and teaching institutions) felt that they were treading on dangerous ground and were risking everything—their careers, jobs, and freedom—in their choice of subject. This viewpoint was not restricted to these individuals. It was widely believed among intellectuals of the time that these people were heroes, risking martyrdom for their chosen topic.

The recently recorded meetings of "the first Blok seminar" bring to mind the catacombs of the first Christians, where the latter fled to practice their faith and seek protection from their persecutors.[20] The chroniclers highlighted both the underground nature and emotionally charged atmosphere that characterized every such meeting of the group. Although the Blok seminar was held within the framework of the Leningrad State University curriculum, the proceedings soon moved into the private home of its organizer, Professor Dmitrii Evgen'evich Maksimov (1904–1987). The seminars started in the autumn of 1945, and the atmosphere of poverty, disarray, and food rationing was not only evocative of the last years of Blok's life, but also conducive to a budding camaraderie. In the intimate home setting—in the words of one of the memoirists—"all casual participants were soon weeded out." The feeling of serving some unidentified but high goal by studying Blok was shared by all students and was accentuated by Maksimov's own ascetic behavior. Maksimov was admired for being a serious and laconic speaker who soberly imparted his insights into the literary scene. In the course of his life he published a number of monographs devoted to the symbolists. Blok was his lifelong passion, and Maksimov spent sixty years of his life studying Blok and his work.

Maksimov and Vladimir Nikolaevich Orlov (1908–1985) were the key figures in the Soviet Blokovedenie up until the 1980s. The library in the Blok Museum (Muzei-kvartira Aleksandra Bloka) in St. Petersburg has in its possession several folders that previously belonged to Maksimov in which he meticulously arranged his various writings devoted to Blok. These range from commemorative newspaper articles and reviews to scholarly monographs. When read in chronological order, these folders attest not only to Maksimov's changing views with regard to the subject of his research, but also to the fact that apparently he had little difficulty in publishing at least some of his work on Blok during the Soviet period. The fact that Maksimov was not particularly a persona non grata is supported by another folder that includes copies of his routine reports on his teaching of so-called foreign students who came to work under his supervision in the 1960s and 1970s. For me, the most extraordinary parts of this particular folder are the work schedules and, particularly, the reading requirements that every student had to fulfill during the early stages of his or her apprenticeship. These consisted of impressive lists of literature that presumed familiarity with various prerevolutionary editions and periodicals. Apparently, these reading lists were also part of official training. Without doubt, Maksimov was a demanding teacher and a meticulous researcher. Nevertheless, this was not how Maksimov came to be remembered by his colleagues and students. He has always been praised for his notable contribution to Blok studies, but much more for the "great courage and high moral principles" he displayed in pursuing his subject.[21]

Courage and adherence to moral principles seem to have characterized many students of Blok. Thus, Pavel Reifman opens his commemorative article on Zara Grigor'evna Mints (1927–1990) by recalling how she sent a copy of her lectures on Blok, which had been given for external students at Tartu University, to her Czech colleagues in December 1969. "It is not difficult to understand," Reifman writes, "that Mints's gesture was related to the 1968 invasion of the Republic of Czechoslovakia by the Warsaw Pact countries."[22] Reifman continues by portraying the reactions of the Soviet intelligentsia to these events and by reminding his 1998 readers that the year 1968 was the watershed that divided Russian intellectuals into two groups: one supportive of the invasion and the other strongly opposed to it. Mints clearly belonged to the latter group. On the surface she did nothing much, just wrote on the second page "to my dear acquaintances" in Czech, followed by her initials, "Z. M." While it was apparently never Mints's own intention to advertise her sympathies in this particular case (she even took the precaution of making her writing as inconspicuous as possible), in Reifman's account her very private gesture acquires the importance of a public display of heroism, linking Soviet Blokovedenie with nonconformist behavior.

Incidentally, the first page of Maksimov's *Blok's Creative Life* (*Tvorcheskii put' Bloka*), as preserved in one of his personal folders, attests to his anxiety about and disappointment with both his own work and the political situation in general. It bears different inscriptions made in Maksimov's own handwriting at different times and in different inks. It is the color of the ink that makes one immediately aware of the time that might have elapsed between each entry (perhaps he did this to provide a clue for future biographers). In the space above the title and above his own name, Maksimov recorded in dark ink the source and date of his publication: "*Litucheba* 1935, no. 6." In the right-hand corner above his name, he wrote diagonally in violet ink (speaking about himself in the third person): "An article, the authorship of which its author does not renounce, but which now would have been written in a completely different way." And below this, in green ink, Maksimov wrote: "And he renounces it! [*I—otrekaetsia!*]." This last inscription, positioned over Maksimov's printed name, is accompanied by the date in parentheses: 1968 (also in green ink). The sixth line from the top of the opening paragraph has been cut out of the page, presumably with a razor or a knife. In the original, this line contains a reference to Nikolai Bukharin's speech at the First Writers' Congress in 1934.[23]

In my personal collection, I have various editions of Blok's writings that, at different times, were given to their former owners as meaningful presents. Some of the inscriptions include: "And we are no longer what we used to be. Alfredo and Traviata," inscribed on *Night Hours (Nochnye chasy)*; "You know what I mean," on the second volume of Blok's diaries; and "In remembrance of our close friendship from faraway Novosibirsk, December 31, 1941," on the first edition of Blok and Bely's correspondence. At a friend's house in St. Petersburg I saw the 1978 volume of *Literaturnoe nasledstvo*, which features Blok's correspondence with his wife, with a lengthy inscription by Il'ia Samoilovich Zil'bershtein (1905–1988), one of the founding fathers of *Literaturnoe nasledstvo* and a member of its editorial board. Zil'bershtein used the opportunity to explain the shortcomings of that particular edition, outlining the torturous process of its publication and expressing frustration with his own impotence as a supposedly able Soviet administrator.

The Death of a Poet

What was so special about Blok that made him attractive in the eyes of the party-minded, in the eyes of open-minded intellectuals and even of dissidents?[24] To understand, one will have to go back to August 7, 1921, the day Blok died. Every death foregrounds the relationship between the old and the new, and many people were quick to recognize Blok's death for a meaningful watershed and to interpret its significance in accordance with their special needs and preferences. "[He died] only three weeks ago," wrote Ivanov-Razumnik, "but it feels as if many years have elapsed since that day: his death has cut our epoch into two completely different parts—'before' and 'after.' . . . Blok's death—is a symbol: he died—and a whole stretch of life died with him."[25] The spectrum of immediate reactions to Blok's death brings to mind final scenes from Chekhov's *Cherry Orchard,* ranging from the "Good-bye old life! Greetings to the new life!" (Maiakovskii, Tynianov, and Eikhenbaum) to "Here comes the owner of the cherry orchard!" (Trotskii and Lunacharskii) to "My life, my youth, my happiness . . . good-bye!" (Bely, Gippius, Kuzmin, Berberova, and many others).

Despite the occurrence of many deaths at this stressful time, Blok's burial and funeral service attracted a large congregation of intellectuals. Mikhail Kuzmin, who was initially dragged to the service by a friend, immediately felt good about going there: "I am glad we came. Everybody was there. Crying. . . . Many were mourning their pasts, the whole stretch of their artistic lives, and maybe also their own imminent deaths."[26] Kuzmin's instant ability to see Blok's death in a broader context was shared by many spectators. "I was listening to him in May of this year in Moscow: in a half-empty room that was silent like a cemetery; he sadly and quietly recited his old lines about the Gypsy's singing, about love and about the Beautiful Lady—this was a dead end. Only death could follow. And it came," wrote Vladimir Maiakovskii appreciatively in his obituary.[27] Similar descriptions can be found in the memoirs of Bely, Zamiatin, Chukovskii, Pavlovich, and Gippius, to name but a few. Many memoirists chose to concentrate on Blok's physical attributes by highlighting his inability to breathe, eat, see, and even hear at the end—during the first years of the Soviet regime. With the notable exception of Zamiatin, who attributed those impediments to Blok's poor physical state and to the hard living conditions that most people endured at the time, the majority of memoirists preferred to interpret them metaphorically as a sign of Blok's inability to function normally in the Bolshevik-controlled environment.[28] By analogy, Bely claimed that he also stopped hearing the music the day Blok died: "No more music—I am deaf. Blok is dead: therefore I will be a cripple forever (I have lost my hearing). This was my immediate reaction to Blok's death (as if I had lost my eyesight all of a sudden)."[29] However, despite the great shock that many, like Bely, experienced when they heard the news, the general consensus was that Blok himself wanted to die.[30] Some believed either that Blok intentionally starved himself to death or simply credited him with a superhuman control over his destiny.[31]

Speaking about Blok gave intellectuals an opportunity to articulate their own personal feelings. These they presented not so much as personal sentiments or anxieties, but either as something that they wished Blok had experienced or that they felt they had experienced collectively along with him. Some people, particularly women, claimed to have had a personal bond with him that was based not on sexuality but on a deep sense of fraternity. One such person, the budding poet Nadezhda Aleksandrovna Pavlovich (1895–1979), according to Bely, "for some reason was under the impression that [Blok] died on the threshold [na rubezhe] of a gigantic [new] period" that he was about to embrace. She felt that "somewhere at a great depth, everything inside him had undergone a considerable transformation, but none of his friends, relatives, or his wife were aware of it." Pavlovich and Bely, who in his turn claimed to have had a unique fraternal bond with Blok, took delight in divining together the exact nature of that threshold, "the new morning" as they called it, and strove to reinterpret Blok's legacy in the light of their premonitions.[32]

Such Blok-inspired soul-searching was apparently rewarding and dignifying to everybody involved. In the same vein, Bely and Ivanov-Razumnik resolved to give up the mourning of Blok in public and instead devote themselves to quiet contemplation and preservation of their dear friend's memory: "Let our memory about him manifest itself in years of hard work . . . [work that will take] probably what is left of our lives."[33] This would include critical interpretation of Blok's work, as well as preparation of his biography and memoirs. It took only three weeks for these future collaborators to realize the futility of their plan to become the sole custodians of Blok's legacy. Thus, whether they liked it or not, Bely and Ivanov-Razumnik had to turn the commemorative meeting of the Free Philosophical Association (Vol'naia Filosofskaia Assotsiatsiia) on August 28, 1921, into a political arena for staking out their positions in the already thriving Blok-related industry. Bely asserted, "No sooner had Blok died, when from the right and from the left—or, more precisely, from the right and from the right, we started to hear all those casual voices who wanted to make a banner out of Blok; . . . to all those political and literary parties that want to make Blok appear as one of their own, we should tell from the very beginning—hands off Blok!"[34]

In his assertion that Blok was grossly abused to suit his interpreters' needs, Bely was not alone. His younger contemporary Vladimir Weidle also felt that many memoirists lacked compassion and were not really sorry for the dead poet. Instead of "posing in silence" and mourning him like "human beings," they rushed to incorporate Blok's death into their theories and interpretations of the cultural scene "as if they had been wound-up machines."[35] In fact, one of the articles that upset Weidle most opened with an apology for such insensitivity. "We live and die in an Iron Age where tears have no place," Boris Eikhenbaum contended.[36] According to Eikhenbaum, Blok's death was symptomatic of that Iron Age, and what was left of the preceding tradition was simply going to wither away. Moreover, Eikhenbaum welcomed Blok's death as a "retribution" and a long-awaited finale to the whole epoch, the decline of which had been punctuated by the deaths of Vera Komissarzhevskaia, Mikhail Vrubel', and Lev Tolstoi in 1910. That was a year of losses for Blok and other intellectuals, as were the late 1910s, "but somewhere within them or prior to them are years of births still unknown to us. Life goes on and with it the Retribution of History," Eikhenbaum wrote in conclusion.[37]

Eikhenbaum was not insensitive by nature, nor was he hungering for anybody's death, but Blok was too good an illustration of the projected fate of his generation to be dismissed entirely. He was a dying proof of theories that were popular at the time: "Now Blok in reality 'is dead.' And we are shaken because his death appears to us not just a simple coincidence, but a preordained tragic denouement, the fifth act of the tragedy that we were all watching. Above all, we are shaken because we are confronted with two coinciding deaths: the death of a poet and the death of a man."[38] Blok, Eikhenbaum insisted, stopped being creative in 1918. "It should not be an insult to his memory to say that his last published books of poetry revealed a decline of his creative will-power, which had been strained to the breaking point by 'The Twelve.'" The poem entitled "The Twelve," as well as those articles in which Blok articulated his attitude toward the revolution, "were Blok's last attempt to reconcile contradictions" inherent in symbolism, the tenets of which Blok could not shake off easily.[39] Like Eikhenbaum, many literary critics chose to overlook Blok's enormous literary output from 1918 to 1921, which included numerous polemical commentaries on political and literary matters, translations, and works of prose, not to mention the copious minutes, appeals, and evaluations that Blok wrote as a member of various pro-Bolshevik commissions and subcommissions. It was natural to discuss Blok's creative impotence in the atmosphere of the late 1910s, when publications were scarce and poets were forced to recite their poetry publicly. It was a time when contacts between writers and their readers became very intense and the public watched writers very closely, commenting on every change in the appearance, physical health, and mental state of any given individual.

In their desire to give meaning to social and political changes, intellectuals were more than eager to project those changes onto the trajectory of literary evolution. Thus in his review for *Pechat' i revoliutsiia* the symbolist Valerii Briusov singled out the years 1917–1922 as a decisive period for the development of modern Russian poetry. These were the years, according to Briusov, when symbolists either died out one after another or completely lost their voices. Their heirs, the acmeists, found themselves outside the mainstream of Russian poetry, while the futurists, albeit extremely active during this period, nevertheless were faced with a dead end, having exhausted their poetic potential. The future, according to Briusov, belonged to poets of proletarian origin. He asserted that nine-tenths of Blok's poetry in 1917–1921 consisted of repetitions, and if one discounted his poem "The Twelve" (which Briusov described as "antirevolutionary in spirit") his contribution to "the history of Russian literature" after the revolution was minimal.[40] Another literary critic went even further and announced the death of the Blokian tradition: "Despite the huge interest in Blok and despite what can be called the 'Blokocentrism' of the majority of modern writers, Blok left no disciples; to master one's poetic skill [by looking up to Blok] would be senseless."[41] Two years later (not surprisingly, the year of Briusov's demise), Blok's death was upgraded by Yurii Tynianov to become the harbinger of the decline of poetry in general. In his industrialist jargon of the time, "The production of prose has been increasing, while the production of poetry has been decreasing," which was why "Blok's death was *only too* natural." And a few pages later, "There are some disappointing traditions—effaced. (Thus, in our eyes, Blok has been also effaced as a tradition.)"[42]

Survival of the Unfittest

The very qualities that made Blok unfit in the eyes of literary critics endeared him to the hearts of the revolutionary historians and theoreticians. In 1924, Trotskii opened the first chapter of his famous treatise *Literature and Revolution* by observing that "the Bolshevist Revolution . . . did not overthrow the Kerenskii government alone [but] overthrew the whole social system that was based on private property." This system "had its own culture and its own official literature, and its collapse could not but be the collapse of pre-revolutionary literature." So big was this gap that the "pre-October [writers and literature] will sound to the future historian of culture just as ponderous" as medieval history sounds "when contrasted with modern history."[43] As commonsensical as it may have seemed, Trotskii's argument was far from bulletproof. Trotskii felt this himself, since he devoted a whole book to support his assertion that the revolution had indeed divided Russian culture irrevocably into its pre- and post-October parts.

In his book, Trotskii slaughtered many writers, such as Bely, who came of age before the Bolshevik Revolution. There was one exception: Aleksandr Blok. "Blok belonged entirely to pre-October literature. . . . But he overcame this, and entered into the sphere of October when he wrote his 'The Twelve.' That is why he will occupy a special place in the history of Russian literature," Trotskii explained.[44] But was it writing "The Twelve" alone that saved Blok from Trotskii's condemnation? As soon as it appeared, "The Twelve" provoked heated discussion in the press as to whether Blok was sympathetic to the revolution or disgusted by its outcome. As a revolutionary-cum–literary critic, Trotskii was very much aware of the unresolved mystery associated with the poem. What seemed to be particularly attractive about Blok was his "timely" death within three years after the revolution. Not unlike his contemporaries, Trotskii also attributed Blok's death directly to political and social developments: "The convulsive and pathetic break with the whole past became, for the poet, a fatal rupture."[45] However, when Trotskii argued that the Bolshevik Revolution divided Russian culture into two distinct entities, he was not only outlining the trajectory of Russia's cultural evolution but also doing something else. What seemed to be at stake was not so much the history of Russian literature but the legitimacy of the October Revolution. As Frederick Corney subtly observes:

> The October Revolution was fought and won most enduringly not by force of arms on the streets of Moscow or in the hallways of the Winter Palace in Petrograd in late 1917, but in newspapers, in halls and on speaking platforms. . . . Well into the 1920s, battle was joined energetically at the symbolic, artistic, political and aesthetic levels simultaneously. . . . The battle was over the broader story that the events of October 1917 would come to convey.[46]

Trotskii accordingly felt that the revolutionary nature of the October events manifested itself most clearly in an all-consuming cultural rejuvenation: "A profound break in history, that is, a rearrangement of classes in the society, shakes up individuality, establishes the perception of the fundamental problems of lyric poetry from a new angle, and so saves art from eternal repetition."[47]

In other words, if what happened in October 1917 was indeed a revolution, then it should have been accompanied by a revolution in literature and in culture. If there is no evidence of a great cultural upheaval, then what happened was not a revolution. Thus in a debate devoted to the future of Russian literature and drama, a playwright, Anatolii Glebov (1899–1964), ridiculed the idea that someone might want to speak in 1924 about "the last ten years of literary evolution." Such an idea was "absurd" in Glebov's eyes, because "evolution commenced in October [1917]." In its effect on Russian culture, the Bolshevik Revolution was like a surgical operation that left "many Russian intellectuals dead, others castrated, and some rejuvenated." Glebov illustrated his speech with concrete examples, pointing to Vladimir Maiakovskii and Osip Brik (who were present in the audience) as living examples of rejuvenation, complete in the case of the former and "less successful" in the case of the latter.[48] As literary debates of the 1920s reveal, when it comes to convincing people about something less concrete and less obvious, such as the death of a cultural age, one needs to be able to point to the actual corpses of many of the icons of the age in question. Blok's death, following his completion of "The Twelve," made him an ideal candidate to serve as such an icon. "To be sure, Blok is not one of ours," wrote Trotskii, "but he reached toward us. And in doing so he broke down."[49] In other words, even if "The Twelve" might have left some readers confused about the exact nature of the events described in this poem, Blok's own death endowed those events with a full legitimacy and turned them into the revolution proper.[50]

In the hands of zealous revolutionaries and their supporters, Blok soon became a case study in degeneracy. Thus the entry on Blok in *Literaturnaia Entsiklopediia* (1930) opens with Dmitrii Blagoi's analysis of Blok's medical history as well as that of his entire family. Blok, according to Blagoi, suffered from severe pathological disorders that he inherited from his parents and relatives. Moreover, "one month prior to his death he started to lose his mind."[51] Such Nordau-inspired studies culminated in Anatolii Lunacharskii's extended introduction to Blok's collected works of 1932.[52] Like Blagoi, Lunacharskii credited Blok with a full range of psychological disorders and celebrated him as "a brilliant specimen of the final decadent stages of the culture of the gentry and gentrified bourgeoisie, who threw the values of the world he had come to detest under the hoofs of the steeds of the revolution galloping toward an unknown future." However, Lunacharskii stipulated, "this revolutionary ardor was not sufficient: it left Blok standing at the threshold of the revolution in a state of bewilderment and incomprehension, excluded from the revolution's genuine march, whose musicality he did not understand."[53]

If in the eyes of the Bolsheviks and their supporters Blok's death was caused by his inability to transform himself into a new artist, then in the eyes of their opponents Blok was seen as one of the first victims of such a transformation. "He was wasting away in front of our very eyes," reported an anonymous correspondent to his compatriots abroad, "and it was becoming more and more difficult to recognize him. I am sending you the picture of the deceased on his deathbed. You can see for yourselves that, positively, not one feature of that charming image that everybody who had a chance to know him remembers so well remained unaltered. [Blok's death] is symptomatic of the regime in which we are all suffocating."[54]

Any upheaval leaves the masses with a profound sense of disorientation, and the Bolshevik Revolution was no exception. In the atmosphere of postrevolutionary turmoil and uncertainty, the death of a famous forty-year-old poet in his own bed was apparently one of the very few things that made sense, or was at least open to sensible interpretation. There was hardly a literate person in Russia who was completely oblivious of Blok's death and failed to express a reaction to it. Every representation of the event was partial, although no memoirist failed to relate it to the Bolshevik Revolution and its consequences. "They say, 'Blok perished, and Yesenin perished in the same way,'" the critic Georgii Adamovich wrote with indignation in 1926. "I'm sorry, gentlemen, but Blok perished in a different way. His existence was harsh, difficult, and, in his last years, semimonastic; he suffocated, he didn't withstand some inner, mysterious, not-audible-to-all hurricanes."[55]

The end of an epoch and the start of a new one normally pass unrecognized at the time and are only seen for what they "were" in hindsight. Not so with the two epochs that came to comprise modernism in Russian culture. The future proponents of the Silver Age and the Soviet age immediately recognized Blok's death as their final destination and as a point of departure, respectively.

While many other vitae have been conveniently readjusted over the course of the twentieth century, students of Blok and his biographers have been relatively consistent in their inconsistency. Blok's critics were never shy about discussing various aspects of his personality, his private life, and his works. Instead of simplifying Blok's image, they celebrated its multiform character. Articles about Blok's ambiguous attitude to such notions as "people," "Motherland," and "love"—not to mention the Bolshevik Revolution—were produced both inside and outside Russia. Even his most zealous admirers repeatedly questioned Blok's integrity. Blok's natural and "acquired" versatility might have been responsible for the extensive attention paid to him in the Soviet Union. Despite the Bolsheviks' initial intention of erasing the memory of the prerevolutionary culture, they nevertheless succeeded in creating a huge repository of information related to Blok and "his" epoch. Apparently it was not the culture itself but the way it was represented (with all its diversity, contradictions, and unanswered questions) that was objectionable to them. (The period from 1890 to 1917 has traditionally been seen as a history of various schools, groups, and movements.) However, with the Bolsheviks' subsequent acceptance that monolithic key figures such as Ivan the Terrible, Peter the Great, Pushkin, Tolstoi, and Stalin could come to dominate the epochs within which they held sway, Blok was promoted to become the monolith of the prerevolutionary age. Once identified as such, the diversity of this age apparently became more acceptable as diversity within the artistry, life, views, and personality of this one man.

When Andrei Siniavskii "strolled with Pushkin" in the 1960s and shared his views about Pushkin's evasiveness and unscrupulousness, he was (and still is) castigated by many for attempting to destroy one of Russia's most revered cultural icons.[56] Siniavskii's book was read by many in the 1970s and 1980s if not as heresy, then at least as a revelation. This would never have happened if he had "strolled" with Blok. Even crude Soviet critics, such as Aleksei Selivanovskii (1900–1937), celebrated Blok's unscrupulousness and ability to reconcile the most irreconcilable. In his 1929 review of Blok's diaries for Na literaturnom postu, Selivanovskii tried to define Blok's legacy as belonging either to a particular social group or to a particular cultural environment. Not surprisingly, he came to the conclusion that it fully belonged to neither.[57] As a cultural construct that came to symbolize a rupture between two adjacent cultural and political epochs, Blok apparently had to remain a no-man's-land belonging to none of the rival parties. In the words of Lev Lozovskii, "With the help of a pair of scissors coupled with a certain perseverance and sleight of hand, every literary critic can succeed in producing either Blok-the-mystic, or Blok-the-romantic, or Blok-the-realist, or Blok-the-revolutionary, et cetera. [Each new persona] appears in response to the needs of a particular argument."[58]

In 1946, in her commemorative article devoted to the twenty-fifth anniversary of Blok's death, the writer Nina Berberova fantasized about Blok surviving into the 1940s. Like many literati, Blok would have emigrated to Europe, according to Berberova, and would have lived in seclusion, a long way from the hustle and bustle of Russian editorial offices. By sheer accident, one might have run into him at the theater, caught sight of him leafing through a book at a Russian bookstore, or happened to hear his name mentioned in casual conversation.[59] Berberova's sentiments aside, in the mid-1940s, her desire to transport Blok over the watershed of the Bolshevik Revolution was, in fact, shared by many Soviet critics and politicians. In the 1920s and the late 1930s, Blok was regarded as a precursor of postrevolutionary literature who did not survive the revolution. From 1946 onward, he began to be quickly promoted to the status of the first postrevolutionary poet on a par with the celebrated, ostensibly revolutionary, poet Maiakovskii. Quite appropriately, the organizers of the memorial exhibition in

Pushkinskii Dom in Leningrad proudly displayed a copy of *A Cloud in Trousers* (*Oblako v shtanakh*), "personally signed by Maiakovskii," that once belonged to Blok.[60] As will become clear from my discussion of the institution of the Silver Age, the trajectory of its perception by the public coincided with the corresponding developments of its constituent elements such as the already flourishing Blok-related industry.

3

The Russian Silver Age

ITS MAKERS AND UNDERTAKERS

> A failure of historical consciousness occurs when one forgets that history, in the sense of both events and accounts of events, does not just happen but is made. Moreover, it is made on both sides of the barricades, and just as effectively by one side as by the other.
>
> —Hyden White, "Literary Theory and Historical Writing"

Diagnosis of a Fatal Illness

What do we know about the Silver Age? To paraphrase Marina Tsvetaeva's famous statement about Pushkin—"The first thing I learned about Pushkin was that he was killed"—the first thing that I learned about the Silver Age was that it had ended. And I was not alone. A cultural historian, Vitalii Shentalinskii, lamented in 1998:

> The Silver Age . . . As if the flame of inspiration broke out forcefully —not before it got extinguished, no!—but before it had to retreat into the depths, before it had to hide itself amongst the ashes from the hurricane of history. An interrupted thought, a word cut short, an

—45

unfinished song. . . .What did happen, what cataclysm caused Atlantis to sink into the abyss? The year 1917 came to pass with the October upheaval of life that at one stroke turned this life inside out. Soviet power came into being and announced: "with an iron fist will we drive mankind into happiness."[1]

However, the first critical responses to the works of Russian modernists later to be identified with the Silver Age started to appear long before the revolution. Thus, in 1902 a literary critic, Grigorii Novopolin, influenced in his analysis of contemporary literature by the work of Max Nordau, spoke overtly about the cancerous process that ate at the healthy body of Russian literature and made its readers "prone to intellectual sicknesses."[2] According to Novopolin, the intellectually diseased literati had managed to seize almost all of the strategically important positions in cultural institutions, from whence they conveyed a profound disbelief in progress and in the human mind. Like the future critics of the school of socialist realism, Novopolin accused modern writers of being narrow-minded and attacked them for their unwillingness to grasp life in all its immensity and excitement.[3]

Novopolin was not the only critic who fell under the spell of Nordau's theory that sick thoughts are produced by sick bodies and should be treated accordingly. The first Russian translation of Nordau's famous study *Entartung* (in English, *Degeneration;* in Russian, *Vyrozhdenie*) appeared in 1894 and was reprinted two years later. Its first translator, R. I. Sementkovskii stated in his introduction that Nordau's works had long been known and admired by Russian readers.[4] It took only a few years to prepare a twelve-volume Russian edition of Nordau's collected works, which was published in Kiev in 1902 with an extensive introduction by Zinaida Vengerova. Nordau's writings had a profound impact both on Russian literary critics and writers. In 1896, Vengerova's collaborator, the critic Akim Volynskii, criticized Fedor Sologub (then at the beginning of his career) for his inability to portray "the essence of life." He wished that Sologub would experience a "radical breakthrough," so that "morbid decadence, with its empty rhetoric, would give way to" a writer's "self-control, without which no beauty could be attained in art."[5]

Although Nordau completed *Entartung* before Russian *fleurs du mal* had had their chance to blossom, his basic assumptions enlisted numerous supporters in prerevolutionary Russia. His ideas were eagerly embraced by such diverse people as Russian Marxists, "degenerate" intellectuals themselves, conservative critics like Novopolin and Sementkovskii, and Lev Tolstoi, who made similarly dyspeptic pronouncements in his *What Is Art? (Chto takoe iskusstvo?* 1898).[6] Thus, in his introduction to *Entartung* Sementkovskii commended Nordau for his purely scientific approach to modern culture and for shedding useful light on many previously incomprehensible phenomena. "As it turns out, sick artists and thinkers have been gaining so much popularity with the public because the public itself consists of sick individuals," Sementkovskii appreciatively concluded.[7]

In 1908 Russian Marxists (among them Lunacharskii, Gorky, Steklov, Friche, and Iushkevich) also joined forces in criticizing the Russian modernists. In a series of half-baked articles with the unifying title *Decomposition of Literature (Literaturnyi raspad)*, they rushed to expose the shortcomings of contemporary literary works by once again transplanting the main findings of Nordau's analysis (albeit barely acknowledged) from European to Russian soil.[8] According to the Marxist critics, the future of Russian modernism was fairly predictable: they expected the whole movement to die out, more likely sooner than later. The Russian Marxists were not alone. The 1910 collection *Where Are We Going? The Present and the Future of Russian Intelligentsia, Literature and the Arts (Kuda my idem? Nastoiashchee i budushchee russkoi intelligentsii, literatury i iskusstv)* featured responses to a questionnaire put together by the publishing house Zaria. Despite their differences in age, social background, and professional training, the respondents, who included artists, historians, philosophers, literary critics, theater directors, writers, and specialists in social and behavioral sciences, gave a generally negative appraisal of the current political and cultural situation, blaming literature and the arts, together with the politically inert and inept population, for leading Russia to destitution.[9]

In "The Reevaluation of All Values: Decadence and Marxism" ("Pereotsenka vsekh tsennostei: dekadentstvo i marksism," 1914), the celebrated literary historian Semen Vengerov defined modernism as "something fanciful, capricious, flashy, and at the same time beautiful, interesting and often profound in its aspiration to extend to the areas that pure realism has left in the shade."[10] Despite its "art for art's sake" aesthetic, the literature of the Silver Age was nevertheless imbued with the social and political concerns of its time. Likewise, in comparing Russian modernists with their European counterparts, Vengerov stressed that the Russians were far more engaged with the sociopolitical struggles of the day.[11] Like Marxists, many representatives of the so-called Silver Age were longing for radical changes in human nature and the social order, which they associated not so much with political revolt as with "the creative potential of human beings, manifested in two areas of human activity, art and love."[12] Although seemingly apolitical, through their writings the literati of the prerevolutionary period contributed to the general "mood of emotionality, disorientation, and dissatisfaction with the present, in short, a revolutionary mentality that ultimately served to further the goals of the left," writes Bernice Glatzer Rosenthal. "Despite their concern for freedom, many artists tended to a utopian extremism that eschewed compromise, insisted on the hopelessness of parliaments, . . . and denounced all constitutions as farcical. . . . After 1905 especially, art featured mystical and apocalyptic themes. Revolution was exalted in poetry, prose and music; it was 'in the air,' thus intensifying the tendency to defer solutions, to reject piecemeal reform, to wait for the revolution, to destroy, rather than to build."[13]

The 1905 revolution and its aftermath prompted various reevaluations of the Russian intelligentsia and of its contribution to Russia's political and social life. Among the most notable was the collection *Signposts* (*Vekhi*, 1909) that featured essays by such prominent literary critics and philosophers as Nikolai Berdiaev, Mikhail Gershenzon, Sergei Bulgakov, and Semen Frank. In the early 1920s, Berdiaev would simply reaffirm the main theses of his group's critique, this time aiming it primarily at artists and writers rather than the intelligentsia in general. Furthermore, what for the Russian people was a familiar idea—that literature should play a secondary role to ideology and directly serve the goals of social improvement, an idea that became particularly prominent under Stalinism—was first articulated in the Bolshevik tradition not in the 1920s or 1930s but as early as 1905. In "Party Organization and Party Literature" ("Partiinaia organizatsiia i partiinaia literatura"), Lenin contended:

> Away with the non-party literature! Away with the Supermen-writers! The literary enterprise should become *part and parcel* of the all-consuming task of the proletariat, it should become "a cog wheel and a screw" of a single grand social-democratic mechanism that is set in motion by the politically conscious vanguard of the whole working class. The literary enterprise should become an integral part of the well-organized, well-planned, and united work of the social-democratic party.[14]

Between 1900 and 1910 such an extreme approach, as well as the criticism and the berating of modernists, was only a case of wishful thinking among the many extraordinary ideas being expressed at the time. In the late 1920s this wishful thinking started to give way to strict orders for the compulsory imitation of a prescribed canon. The institutionalization of this literary canon, however, was precipitated in the early 1920s by a marked shift in the general artistic preoccupation from the inner sphere to the social sphere.[15] This shift manifested itself in numerous projects in which artists willingly collaborated with the socialist state.[16] As Roman Jakobson, a contemporary, put it, literary evolution "is not so much a question of the disappearance of certain elements and the emergence of others as it is a question of shifts in the mutual relationship among the diverse components of the system, in other words, a question of a shifting dominant."[17] The fact that by 1922 the *dominant* had already shifted irrevocably was succinctly observed by Valerii Briusov in an article on the state of Russian poetry for the journal *Pechat' i revoliutsiia*: "We are not talking here about the reevaluation of the poets' *talents*, rather we are referring to a comparative evaluation of poets' contributions during different periods. If at the end of the nineteenth and at the beginning of the twentieth centuries the works of symbolists had constituted literary milestones, then over the last ten years they have been received as bibliographical curiosities, some of which—alas!—evoked things that we had read before."[18] Briusov echoed Boris Eikhenbaum's assertion about the obsoleteness of Blok's earlier writings: "The latest collections of Blok, such as *Beyond the Boundary of Bygone Days* (*Za gran'iu proshlykh dnei*) and *Gray Morning* (*Sedoe utro*) had the appearance of being published posthumously. They were received with bewilderment. There was nothing in them that many had come to expect after the publication of *The Twelve*. No new direction. Old obsolete poems written from 1898 to 1916 that were excluded from previous publications. Even their very titles were anachronistic. As if Blok had been already dead."[19] Visions of Blok dead or even crucified became widespread through the poems of Akhmatova, Tsvetaeva, Kuz'mina-Karavaeva, Zorgenfrei, and others as early as 1913–1916. Such visions, apart from being informed by a certain literary canon, are symptomatic of transitional periods, when one cultural tradition is replaced by another. Apparently, it is always easier to negotiate such a transition and work out new aesthetic principles while overcoming the legacy of a "dead" author, rather than do the same for a living one. Certainly, many writers who were active during the Silver Age continued writing for many years after the revolution, but their activity fell outside acceptable aesthetic norms. This can be seen in the overwhelmingly negative response—both inside and outside the Soviet Union—to the belated products of the Silver Age, such as Mikhail Kuzmin's masterpiece, *The Trout Breaking through the Ice* (*Forel' razbivaet led,* 1929), Andrei Bely's later novels and memoirs, and the early works of Vladimir Nabokov.[20]

Death and Postmortem

Although in the 1910s there were already signs that the "aesthetic" or the Silver Age tradition would gradually fade from the literary scene, this is not how its closure came to be remembered. This was largely due to the catastrophic shock that was impressed on the Russian populace by the October Revolution. In the late 1910s the long prophesied and welcomed apocalypse turned into a somber reality. In an atmosphere of disorder and depravity, the death of "aesthetic" cultural tradition was no longer just a metaphor, but a fact of everyday life. Either Russian "degenerate" intellectuals were literally dying out one after another, or they fled the country or were forced to emigrate in the fall of 1922. As one contemporary put it in 1923, these people were "the keepers of cultural traditions, the only commodity that the present government has been exporting . . . in abundance and absolutely free of charge."[21]

The human resources of the Silver Age were not the only resources to be put away by the mid-1920s. The Bolshevik Revolution shook all those institutions that had been responsible for the preservation of continuity and the transmission of cultural traditions, such as the church, the schools, the family, and the state. Furthermore, many artifacts, periodicals, publishing houses, exhibition halls, apartments, buildings, estates, restaurants, cabarets, theaters, and even entire cities—all that had been associated with the Silver Age and that constituted some kind of a repository of its culture—would soon change beyond recognition, stop functioning, or cease to exist. Blok's beloved Shakhmatovo would be one of the first estates to be destroyed by rioting peasants, and St. Petersburg would change its name twice within six years to become "the cradle of the Bolshevik Revolution."

Although the years 1917 and, particularly, 1921 (the year of Blok's and Gumilev's deaths) were immediately recognized by many as the closure of an entire epoch in Russian culture, not many people at that time saw it as an irreparable loss. Moreover, when the Bolsheviks started campaigning against the cultural heritage of their immediate past, their iconoclastic slant was in fact shared by a number of intellectuals who were by then greatly disillusioned with Russian literature and culture, blaming it, like the writer and philosopher Vasilii Rozanov, for leading to general confusion and unrest. According to Rozanov, Russian literature, in terms of its main themes, was "such a loathsome thing" because it was traditionally "preoccupied with only 'how they loved' and 'what they talked about'" instead of guiding and educating people.[22]

In his 1919–1920 lectures delivered in Moscow for students of the Vol'naia Akademiia, philosopher Nikolai Berdiaev accused the culture of the nineteenth and early twentieth centuries for paving the road to "the crisis of humanism." Modern art, according to Berdiaev, displaces humanity as the "greatest objet d'art," by tearing man into pieces or merging him with and dissolving him in the material world, as happens in the paintings of Picasso or in Andrei Bely's *Petersburg* (1916). Modern artists undergo bouts of "creative impotence . . . and envy of the more wholesome periods in the history of human culture. . . . Man no longer has wings. . . . He reached the end of modern history by being deeply disillusioned, damaged, fragmented, and creatively exhausted."[23] However, a special feature of Russian culture, according to Berdiaev, is that it reached its decline without passing through the true Renaissance experienced earlier by all other European cultures. Nonetheless, Berdiaev said, the lack of a recent cultural renaissance that can be revisited is not to the disadvantage of the undercivilized Russian people, since—more than Western people, who are so attached to the material world—they recognize their critical situation and can find a way out. In concluding that a golden age is dawning for Russia, Berdiaev joined forces with the Marxists, for his cultural renaissance as well as their golden era of communism were expected to occur in the immediate future.

Vigil and Vigilantes
IVAN IL'ICH

Berdiaev's sharply critical attitude toward the legacy of the immediate past was shared by many other revisionists who attempted to conceptualize the devastating experience of the October Revolution in the 1920s. Thus in his novel *The Sisters* (*Sestry*, 1919–1921), Aleksei Tolstoi paints an unflattering picture of cultural and political life in Russia between 1913 and 1918. Tolstoi's characters are all pleasant but idle people, longing for the cleansing apocalypse, or at least for a much more radical development of the sexual revolution. In the opening section of his novel, Tolstoi revisits and debunks the myth of Petersburg as a mysteriously pernicious and haunted place, an idea entertained in the works of many representatives of the Silver Age. Instead, he shows that the problem with Petersburg, and with the whole of Russia, lay in the indolence and corruption of its ruling classes and in the irresponsible behavior of its intellectuals, who indulged themselves in an artificially aestheticized lifestyle. World War I and the October Revolution are presented as a punishment well deserved by the educated classes for their mishandling of political and social situations.

Although he wrote his novel in Berlin in the heyday of European modernism, Tolstoi demonstrated unexpected loyalty to and affinity with the Russian realist tradition, particularly with the works of Lev Tolstoi. It is not fortuitous that Aleksei Tolstoi's sympathetic character is named Ivan Il'ich (who later became a prominent figure in the Red Army). Lev Tolstoi's famous character of the same name ("The Death of Ivan Il'ich" ["Smert' Ivana Il'icha," 1886]), though on his deathbed, became a truly transformed human being by ceasing to think selfishly about himself and instead starting to care for others. Aleksei Tolstoi painstakingly copied numerous discussions between his heroine Dasha and Ivan Il'ich—including the guessing of words by their first letters—from similar episodes between Kitty and Levin in Lev Tolstoi's *Anna Karenina* (1877).[24]

Unlike Aleksei Tolstoi's later works, *The Sisters* cannot be suspected of having been influenced or supervised by the Bolshevik authorities. In fact, Tolstoi was often reprimanded for not coming up with a sympathetic portrayal of the Bolshevik movement in this novel. In any case, his grotesque description of the life of Russian intellectuals in the 1910s is no different from a similar description found in the work of Vladislav Khodasevich, whose integrity was legendary. Here is how Khodasevich describes this period in 1926:

> We were living in those years that followed the year 1905: these were the years of spiritual fatigue and of pervading aestheticism. In literature [this period was marked] by numerous low-quality imitators of the modernist school, which suddenly became recognized for precisely those aspects that were bad and insignificant. In society, frail girls were resurrecting Hellenism. The bourgeois, who suddenly discovered an appetite for a "daring life," ran up against "sexual questions." The *sanintsy* and *ogarki* were multiplying at the lower level.[25] Decadent buildings were built on the streets. And, without being noticed, electric charges were slowly accumulating above it all. The thunderstorm broke in 1914.... It was difficult to breathe in the hot air of pregnant thunderstorms that characterized those years.[26]

Like Aleksei Tolstoi, Khodasevich came to appreciate if not the style of Lev Tolstoi, then the outlook of his characters. His essay "About Annenskii" ("Ob Annenskom," 1921, 1935) is built on a contrast between the actual life and death of the famous symbolist poet Innokentii Annenskii—particularly how the theme of death was projected into his poetry—and that of Lev Tolstoi's Ivan Il'ich Golovin. Having admitted that Annenskii, by virtue of being a poet, was infinitely more subtle as a person than Tolstoi's character, Khodasevich nevertheless sadly concludes that the miracle experienced by Ivan Il'ich shortly before his death remained unknown and practically inaccessible to Annenskii. Thus "an ordinary man" turns out to be morally superior to "an extraordinary human being, the poet."[27]

A MAN OF THE 1930S

The dull, uneventful life of Lev Tolstoi's "ordinary" and relatively educated Ivan Il'ich, who died in his own bed in the gloomy 1880s (the period traditionally associated with stagnation in Russia's cultural and political life) suddenly became a model to follow for many young emigre writers disillusioned with the alleged ideological impotence of prerevolutionary culture. Although he prefaces his article "A Man of the Thirties" ("Chelovek 30-kh godov," 1933) with an epigraph from one of Aleksandr Blok's poems, the poet and critic Yurii Terapiano attests from the outset to the unbridgeable gap between his own and the older generation, acknowledging that World War I and subsequent revolutions had erected an insurmountable barrier between them:

> A very special feeling, a kind of a touchstone, has been formed in the heart of the modern man as a result of his being put in direct contact with rough and horrible life, with death, with fate, and with the "laws of iron necessity." . . . Any kind of inner falseness and insincerity are immediately detected by this special feeling. Because of such a feeling one can no longer bear even those things that previously had sometimes been taken for the enrichment of the soul, such as rhetoric, scholastics, and the irresponsible playing with the "inexpressible." "I can't," "I don't know how," "I can't talk about it"—are received with more attention now than all of those doctrines about death, God, and human fate, which exhibit so much erudition and so little sincerity. That's why "The Death of Ivan Il'ich" has a greater appeal to a contemporary than Vladimir Solov'ev; the feeling that stopped Tolstoi on the threshold of death is more comprehensible to a contemporary than "words, words, and words."[28]

Terapiano thus denounces the cultural legacy of his immediate predecessors in favor of Lev Tolstoi, propping up his argument with the all too familiar discussion of one's duty to adhere to the "truth" both in life and art, arguing that the man of the 1930s "has learned to distrust himself [and therefore] demands that he himself speak only the truth, [being always] severe and earnest."[29] And since there can be only one truth, Terapiano campaigns against any sign of diversity and richness, while promoting austerity and simplicity both in lifestyle and as an aesthetic principle.

> Modern man is completely poor and naked because he is conscientious. He could have adorned himself with any kind of drapes; as many

times in the past he could have chosen cloth, colors, and hues, but he doesn't want to. I think that this willingness—[that is,] rejection, impoverishment, determination to endure loneliness, and emptiness—is the most important characteristic acquired by the new generation, and God grant that the best of our young poets and writers will resist the temptation of easy and cheap literary success with the crowd.[30]

Terapiano was not alone in his campaign for aesthetic abstinence. Thus in his introduction to Yurii Aikhenval'd's posthumous edition of his literary essays, the critic and philosopher Fedor Stepun also praised Aikhenval'd above all for his "honesty, truthfulness, and spiritual fortitude," explaining that "during the years of the revolution [his generation] lived through so many unprecedented, unusual, impossible, and, one might say, extraordinarily perverted things that [they] are now being inexorably drawn to the genuinely truthful rather than the exceptionally talented, to the real, accurate, reliable and fair."[31] It was almost as if a certain organ that was responsible for accommodating the complexity of styles, methods, and approaches suddenly became atrophied in many "men of the thirties," so that they could no longer appreciate anything that was not simple and straightforward.[32] To paraphrase Clifford Geertz, it seems as if they had suddenly lost the "appropriate skills . . . and experience of living" a Silver Age life and rapidly stopped "seeing things" in a Silver Age way.[33] Thus, another poet and literary critic of that time, Nikolai Otsup, in his 1930 article to commemorate the fiftieth anniversary of Andrei Bely's birth, makes every effort to present Bely as a cultural and intellectual anachronism. Otsup's Bely, dancing wildly in Berlin in the early 1920s, is represented as a peculiar extraterrestrial whose habits, gestures, and especially language are barely comprehensible to his contemporaries. Otsup is particularly critical of Bely's versatility, of his inability to adhere to only one idea:

> There is nothing natural about Bely's behavior. In fact, he can't even move on his chair naturally without a purpose. [He moves] only for the loftiest of considerations. Bely can be called the embodiment of a

transitional epoch. He manages to touch upon everything but is unable to be the master of one idea only or of one emotion. Everything swiftly passes by in front of him. He understands too many people, he is compassionate with too many: he knows how to leave a particle of his ego everywhere but is unable to collect all these dispersed and disparate particles into one place.[34]

While Otsup still cautiously viewed the beginning of the 1930s as a transitional period, Lidiia Ginzburg in a 1930 diary entry attested to the complete dissolution of Silver Age man and to the advent of a physically, psychologically, and socially more adept man of the 1930s:

> I was forced to observe how, from their adolescence, some of my contemporaries had quickly and confidently adopted a certain type of behavior, the behavior of an *intelligent* with lacerations [*s nadryvom*] (spiritual depths, an extreme psychological self-absorption, disruptions of psychological balance, all of which would immediately be aestheticized). [And then I observed] how this inherited mentality turned out to be decisively out of line with [recent] history. Fortunate were those whose historical taste, sophistication, and youth saved them from any further ideologization of these lacerations. A new man with a different set of social characteristics has been superimposed on this potential, half-made human being. Our age has endowed this generation with respect for spiritual and physical health, with respect for activity that leads to results, and with an interest in the public [sphere]: a perception of the world from the social point of view. Our times have endowed this generation with professionalism, a lack of squeamishness toward provisional, day-to-day labor; with a slight disgust for deep psychological introspection, self-preoccupation, and aestheticism.[35]

The upbeat tone of this entry leaves no doubt that Ginzburg was not appalled by these irrevocable transformations that had so changed her contemporaries, but welcomed them wholeheartedly.

The notion of "the 1930s man" was apparently so pervasive that it featured prominently in the new interpretations and reconstructions of the past. The only essay in Khodasevich's *Necropolis* that displays two prominent cultural figures together is "Gumilev and Blok" (1931). One appreciates why this is so. Khodasevich needs a lightweight Gumilev to provide a contrast to an earnest Blok, whom he endows with all the positive characteristics of "the 1930s man." Khodasevich's Gumilev (like Otsup's Bely) is fond of dancing. Being more concerned with his exterior self than with his interior self, he manages to disgrace himself by coming late to the famous 1921 celebration in honor of Pushkin. Blok, by contrast, is self-disciplined, simple, earnest, and above all truthful. In short, he represents all those features that Terapiano would vehemently advocate two years later but were foreign to Silver Age aesthetics and ethics:

> He talked a lot about himself, as if he had been talking to himself, looking deep inside his own psyche, with great restraint, sometimes in a muddled, vague, and confused way; but in his words one could have detected an ascetic and acidic truthfulness. For me, truthfulness and lack of pretension are forever associated with Blok's memory.
> ... He recited very few poems—with a heartfelt simplicity and deep earnestness that could best be described in Pushkin's words [as] "with significance."[36]

Khodasevich's reconstruction and commemoration of Blok as someone who differed radically from his environment was symptomatic of the late 1920s and 1930s. For Soviet critics, Blok was a perfect example of how a man from the old world—a member of the gentry, in Blok's case—could gradually turn himself into a "new" one, albeit at the expense of his own life. The view of Blok as the best representative of his time, perhaps even an anomaly, was also shared by emigre literary circles. Accordingly, Blok's aesthetic confrontation with Gumilev and his cohort in 1920–1921—as depicted by Khodasevich in 1931—acquires the shape of a political struggle between the noble and crystal-clear figure of Blok and the indiscreet acmeists.[37] Moreover, while reminiscing about his symbolist past, Blok confides to Khodasevich that he could hardly understand his own youth, so foreign did the early 1900s appear to him in 1921:

> He was grinning with affection while talking about that time, about their infatuation with mysticism, about Andrei Bely, and about S. M. Solov'ev. One talks about one's childhood that way. He confessed that he could no longer understand many of his own poems written during that time: "I have forgotten what many of those words mean. But at that time they seemed sacred. Now I am rereading those poems as though they were not my own, and I can't always understand what exactly the author was trying to say in them."[38]

To appreciate the drastic changes that took place over the 1921–1931 period, one has to compare Khodasevich's unbending Blok with Bely's protean Blok of 1922, upon whom he—not unlike Dostoevskii with his "Pushkin" of 1880—generously bestows the virtues of "the noble, new, and beautiful man, capable of comprehending everything and everybody" (*vseponimaiushchii*).[39]

By the early 1930s, because of the joint activity of many Russian intellectuals, both those residing in the Soviet Union and those living abroad, the Silver Age was excluded from the currently approved boundaries of Russian culture. It was excluded along with everything for which it stood: an unprecedented degree of experimentation in all spheres of art and life, individualism, and a determined rejection of traditional moralizing. In other words, its legacy was openly rejected both by its very representatives and by its rightful heirs. The many examples of artists claiming allegiance to Pushkin's cultural legacy in the period 1921–1937 might be seen in light of this fervor for shunning the immediate past that consumed the Russian populace at the time. Thus, it is not entirely surprising that Khodasevich was numbered among the most active Pushkinists in the 1920s and 1930s. Khodasevich's approach to cultural evolution was unconventional but consistent. If his Blok became the prototypical "man of the 1930s," then his Pushkin became "the Silver Age man" par excellence.[40] Clearly, one could not blame the Bolsheviks alone for the prevailing critical vision of prerevolutionary culture in the 1920s and 1930s. Such critical appropriations of the past were part of the zeitgeist. Thus, the introductory article by Valentin Asmus to the 1937 volume of *Literaturnoe nasledstvo* devoted to symbolism reads like a laboriously expanded version of the 1928 article by Khodasevich, "The End of Renata," which ten years later opened his collection *Necropolis*.[41] Both Khodasevich and Asmus are particularly critical of the symbolist "life creation" project, which, according to both authors, eventually led to the demise of the whole movement.

Belated Burial and Resurrection

Asmus's 1937 article, however, was already incongruous with the newly emerging image of the Silver Age, as was Khodasevich's *Necropolis*. It follows from his letters that Khodasevich began contemplating writing his *Necropolis* as early as October 1926. However, it took him over twelve years to finish the book. As one critic put it, it was the lack of essential material that stopped Khodasevich from accomplishing his task much sooner.[42] What then was this missing material? To put it bluntly: he needed the dead bodies of his immediate friends and contemporaries. In contrast to those who, like Berdiaev, confined themselves to fortune-telling, Khodasevich chose the more practical role of a mortician concerned with burying the corpses of an exhausted culture.

In the Russian tradition, Dmitrii Merezhkovskii was the first to articulate the idea that a new round of literary evolution is marked by actual deaths of cultural figures. Despite Merezhkovskii's initial strategy of creating a rather blurred boundary between the "old" and "new" literary traditions in his programmatic work *Eternal Companions* (*Vechnye sputniki*, 1888–1897), in 1901 he apparently found it necessary to draw a definitive line between the two. This watershed, according to Merezhkovskii, was exactly parallel to what happened in 1881, the year of Dostoevskii's death and of the beginning of Tolstoi's alleged artistic impotence.[43] In 1907, Andrei Bely echoed Merezhkovskii in his essay "A. P. Chekhov," in which he described Chekhov's literary legacy as a fortuitous combination of symbolism and realism which no living contemporary has been able to achieve, while insisting that Chekhov's death had marked "the completion of a whole epoch in Russian literature."[44] Zinaida Gippius, who did not share Bely's admiration for Chekhov, in 1903 likened the Moscow Art Theater to a "veritable graveyard" and compared its performances to "extravagant burial services" that take place "amid the cheerful adulation of the audience."[45] Not surprisingly, when Gippius needed to debase Briusov in 1923 for his compliance with the Bolsheviks, she also declared him dead both as a human being and a poet:

> Briusov hasn't died physically, but because of his current position in Bolshevik Russia, I can—with a clear conscience—consider him dead as a person, dead for me and for the majority of Russians. There can be no "meeting" between him and me on earth.... I should also add that Briusov is dead as a poet. I find that natural and logical. I don't think it could have been otherwise. I refer those who doubt it to his recently published book of poetry, which is not only bad but also not quite probable [*ne sovsem veroiatnaia*], that is, illiterate [*bezgramotnaia*].[46]

In his reaction to Gippius's essay, an emigre critic, Andrei Levenson, went even further in amplifying the metaphor by suggesting that Briusov's latest works reminded him of "the dead bodies continuing to grow beards and nails, when life in them has long since gone cold."[47]

While the reading public had been adequately prepared for the appearance of such collections as *Necropolis*, Khodasevich's problem was that he had to wait, perhaps too long, for actual corpses before he could accomplish his gruesome task. While in 1926 a collection of beautifully written and carefully chosen obituaries would have been a welcome contribution to the numerous negative reappraisals of the prerevolutionary legacy, in 1939 such a collection was already seen as an anachronism. Thus in the first review of *Necropolis*, a friend and admirer, Yurii Mandel'shtam, felt the need to defend both the title (which Mandel'shtam himself found "confusing") and Khodasevich's approach to the writing of his memoirs. Contrary to the message implied in the title of his collection, Mandel'shtam insisted, Khodasevich saw his task as resurrecting the preceding cultural tradition and not laying it to rest. (Tragically, the "death" of the critical approach to the Silver Age was punctuated by the premature death of its ardent proponent: Khodasevich died within a few months of the publication of *Necropolis*.)[48]

Whatever the truth was, Mandel'shtam's reading of *Necropolis* was in agreement with even newer strategies of appropriation of the Silver Age. For around that time expectations of reaching the golden age—be it the communist paradise or the new spiritual renaissance—had worn thin, and the mythological era of original happiness and prosperity was again identified as having occurred in the immediate past. This idea was developed by the very same Nikolai Berdiaev who had spoken in 1919 about the emasculation of the late nineteenth- and early twentieth-century culture. Already by the late 1920s he had upgraded the prerevolutionary culture to a "time of great intellectual and spiritual excitement." By the late 1930s he had further promoted this period to the status of not only an artistic, but also a religious and spiritual renaissance.[49] Apparently, the twentieth anniversary of the October Revolution in 1937 was all at once identified by many as a point of no return to the prerevolutionary past.[50] In Pierre Nora's terms, it was around that time that the Silver Age had stopped being taken for granted and was beginning to be perceived as a *lieu de memoire*, because there were "no longer *milieux de memoire*, settings in which memory [was] a real part of everyday experience."[51] In such a situation it became more important to preserve what was left than to attack or rebel against it. In the 1930s many Russian intellectuals came to praise and admire the Silver Age and to blame the Bolsheviks for its interruption.[52]

The basic characteristics essential for enhancing and sustaining the commemorative qualities of the age are presented in a nutshell at the end of Konstantin Mochul'skii's biography of Aleksandr Blok (1945). There Mochul'skii attributes the unbecomingly harsh tone of Blok's critique of acmeists to his extraordinary prophetic abilities. For back in 1921 Blok already knew that he was the last representative of the Russian cultural renaissance, and that it was left to him to preserve and defend its legacy after the advent of the boorish Bolsheviks.[53] Mochul'skii writes:

> This tone [toward the acmeists] can be attributed not so much to Blok's personal dislike of the author of "pearls" [Gumilev], but rather to Blok's feeling of responsibility for the fate of Russian literature. Blok understood that the Russian renaissance of the beginning of the century had come to an end; that the level of culture had declined catastrophically; that he himself was the last warrior; and that his battle had been lost before it had even started.[54]

In *The Fallacy of the Silver Age* Ronen demonstrates that the name Silver Age was used to describe certain periods in Russian poetry back in the 1920s and even 1910s. Moreover, at that time the label Silver Age was used by Ivanov-Razumnik in reference to the second half of the 1910s and the early 1920s to denote a period of cultural decline.[55] Ivanov-Razumnik's statements should not come as a total surprise. Nor should it be particularly surprising that the name Silver Age was preserved but reconceptualized a few years later to mark a period of cultural vitality. Such continuity, according to Charles Cooley and Barry Schwartz, is only to be expected if collective memory is to endure.[56] The initial vision of the Silver Age as that of a period associated with decadence and art-for-art's-sake aesthetics has in fact remained intact. What changed was that as a result of its subsequent reconstructions, the Silver Age received a new set of characteristics in addition to the old ones. Among the most important was a strengthened view of its interlocked destiny with the October Revolution. Of course, the Silver Age and the revolution have long been seen as interconnected phenomena. However, if the Silver Age had once been presented as paving the road to the revolution, by the late 1930s it was recharacterized as having been terminated by the revolution. In other words, although the Silver Age is often referred to as "the Russia we lost forever," its "forfeiture" had to be engineered.

The fact that the end of the Silver Age came to be associated with political upheavals gave rise to the long-lasting popular belief in the "unnatural" course of Russia's cultural evolution. Its "expected" course (that is, the continuation of the Silver Age into the 1920s and 1930s) came to be "remembered" as having been brutally interrupted by Bolshevik-controlled social and political developments. This interpretation gained particular prominence among Russian intellectuals residing inside and outside the Soviet Union, and it encouraged, on the one hand, feelings of moral responsibility for the preservation of the prerevolutionary cultural heritage and, on the other, the desire to scrutinize and reevaluate this cultural heritage ad infinitum.

To account for such abrupt changes in the representation of prerevolutionary culture, we have to ask what happened to the image of this period in the 1920s and 1930s that later not only redeemed it in the eyes of its various beholders, but also covered it with a patina of respect and admiration. As I have shown, in only twenty years the overall perception of prerevolutionary culture underwent a crucial transformation. It was no longer perceived by Russians either as "theirs" or as an integral part of the Russian cultural heritage. And it was this quality of "strangeness" which the Silver Age rapidly acquired in the eyes of many that was ultimately responsible for its almost imminent rediscovery and subsequent glorification. As Mikhail Bakhtin perceptively observed, "In the realm of culture, outsideness is a most powerful factor in understanding."[57] We might add that "outsideness" is also the most powerful factor that instigates the creation of cultural memory. The fact that twenty years is indeed an extremely short period with regard to cultural history becomes evident if we recall how many years (centuries, to be more precise) it took for the modern world to rediscover ancient Greece, for the English to rediscover Shakespeare, or for the French to feel the urge to resurrect Joan of Arc.

The main function of what I have called the Silver Age cultural institution in the 1920s and 1930s, therefore, was not to preserve but to purge the cultural legacy of the prerevolutionary period and to push it outside the boundaries of Russian culture. As is often the case, both destruction and preservation proved to be highly beneficial for the creation of cultural memory. I am not suggesting that Asmus,

Aleksei Tolstoi, Berdiaev, Khodasevich, and others had a clear vision of what they were doing or that they were consciously involved in some clearly defined project. I am merely pointing out that their negative re-presentations of the Silver Age in the 1920s and 1930s contributed, in the long run, to the ultimate preservation of cultural memory about this period. If nothing else, they assisted in an erasure of the past that allowed people to better embrace that same past in the future.

4 No "Room of Her Own"

ANNA AKHMATOVA'S TENURE IN SOVIET CULTURE

> The Self . . . like any other aspect of human nature, stands both as a guardian of permanence and as a barometer responding to the local cultural weather. The culture, as well, provides us with guides and stratagems for finding a niche between stability and change: it exhorts, forbids, lures, denies, rewards the commitments that the Self undertakes. And the Self, using its capacity for reflection and for envisaging alternatives, escapes or embraces or reevaluates and reformulates what the culture has on offer. Any effort to understand the nature and origins of Self is . . . an interpretive effort akin to that used by a historian or an anthropologist trying to understand a "period" or a "people."
>
> —Jerome Bruner, *Acts of Meaning*

> "It is all in our hands," [Akhmatova] would say, and: "As a literary critic I know . . ."
>
> —Nadezhda Mandelstam, "Akhmatova"

Although the Silver Age came into being as a result of the collective efforts of many often nameless individuals, one can also detect contributions by outstanding Russian writers, such as Anna Akhmatova, Boris Pasternak, Vladimir Nabokov, and Viktor Erofeev. These contributions deserve closer examination. While continuing to focus on the 1920s, the 1930s, and the early 1940s, I move from the public arena to the private space of Anna Akhmatova's communal apartment. The 1930s marked an important stage in Akhmatova's development as a poet and in her understanding of her role in Soviet society. During those years she went through a period of extended poetic silence, experienced changes in her personal life, and suffered the hardships that befell many Soviet people during the Stalinist purges. From 1927 on, Akhmatova lived with the family of her third husband, Nikolai Nikolaevich Punin (1888–1953). Akhmatova's complex status and life as a lodger in Punin's communal apartment affected her creativity and in large part determined the unique form and manifestations of her anxieties in regard to her immediate predecessors and famous contemporaries.

A Cesspit of a Communal Apartment

"Had he been unfaithful because he preferred another woman? No, he had made no comparisons, no choice. . . . Now he was crushed by the weight of his guilty conscience. 'What next?' He had sometimes wondered, and hoped wretchedly for some impossible, unexpected circumstances to solve his problem for him." These famous lines from *Doctor Zhivago* could easily have been written by Boris Pasternak to describe his contemporary, the celebrated art historian and critic Nikolai Punin. Among others, Anna Akhmatova expressed strong doubts about the viability of a character such as Zhivago in real life, but ironically the recent release of Punin's diaries and letters shows that a Zhivago-like character existed within her own intimate circle.[1]

Notorious Pasternakian chance happenings and coincidences abounded in Punin's personal life. He became acquainted with Nikolai Gumilev and Akhmatova long before he fell in love with the latter, a missed opportunity that subsequently became the subject of scrutiny and the source of reproach in Akhmatova's eyes. In 1921 Punin was arrested at the same time as Gumilev (and on the same charge), and the two men met one another in prison. Punin, however, was one of the very few to be released, as if fate had chosen to spare him and grant him another chance to become completely smitten by Akhmatova only a year after his arrest. Punin was to live through yet another arrest, along with the purges and the siege of Leningrad. He was fortunate to outlive even Stalin himself, despite his third arrest and confinement in a labor camp in Abez'. Like Zhivago, he died unexpectedly from what is thought to have been a heart attack, not in August 1929 but in August 1953. Like Zhivago, Punin lost his mother at an early age and had a penchant for developing entangled relationships with women.

It is with Anna Akhmatova that he appears to have been the least egocentric and most caring. He worshiped talented people and, unlike Akhmatova's previous husband, Vladimir Shileiko, who had been notoriously jealous of her writing, Punin was perplexed when she apparently stopped writing poetry in autumn 1923. "How I love her joyful wonder at a cup, the snow, the sky. She writes quite unconsciously. I was with her, and once again I felt that I have been given very little creativity.... [Anna] has stopped writing verse. Why? What does it mean, here it's been already a year and scarcely a single poem? She says, it is because of me."[2] Despite his evident sensitivity and compassion for other people, Punin was often responsible for causing them as much pain as joy. His inability to break with those he once loved (a feeling entirely understandable in an art collector) resulted in his bringing together several incompatible people in order to lock them up within one communal apartment in the former Sheremetiev Palace (or the Fountain House).

If readers are left ultimately with a distilled product of Zhivago's life, with an epilogue that conveniently separates his complicated and imperfect existence from his artistic legacy, it became Punin's fate to remain buried under the rubble of memoirs about him for many years. As his diary shows, Akhmatova once told Punin that he knew and understood her better than she knew herself. And yet for years Punin was cast in the mold of the uncaring companion of a great poet (that is, Akhmatova) on a par with the other frequently criticized spouses, including Natalia Nikolaevna Pushkina, Liubov' Dmitrievna Blok, and Zinaida Nikolaevna Pasternak. In January 1937, Emma Gerstein, Akhmatova's friend who was in love with her son, went to Leningrad to work in the archives. When introduced to Punin, Gerstein "managed immediately to adopt the right tone with him." In her words, "Aware that he was unbelievably stingy, I realized that I had to shock him somehow, and so when he invited me to dinner and asked what I would like to eat I ordered dishes that were an extravagance at the time (among them pork cutlets)." Gerstein attended a number of family gatherings, which gave her plenty of opportunity to study Punin's unusual household:

> The very first day, I was invited to eat with the family. At the table sat Punin, his wife, Anna Yevgenievna, their daughter Ira, Akhmatova, and Lyova [Lev Gumilev]. . . . Ira and her mother sat at one end of the very long table with Lyova and Akhmatova at the other. In silence, Anna Yevgenievna would periodically down a small glass of vodka and only rarely, like a knife thrust, utter some remark in her low smoker's voice. . . . On another occasion, there was . . . talk of idlers. Anna Yevgenievna suddenly announced: "Who the hangers-on are here, I don't know." Lyova and Akhmatova stiffened at once. For several minutes, I could see nothing but two proud and offended profiles, seemingly linked by an invisible thread. . . . During one of my visits, a very animated [Pavel] Luknitskii dashed in. . . . A dish of carved slices of meat was brought in. All were to serve themselves. "Pavlik! Lyova!" Punin cried. He was not urging them to take what they wanted, but was "apprehensive" that they would forget themselves and put too much on their plates. Punin had a large family to support! . . .With his tic and his domestic dramas, the effusive Nikolai Punin was like no one else I knew.[3]

Gerstein was not the only one to comment on the strained relationships among the various lodgers in Punin's apartment. Similar remarks on the difficult and sometimes unbearable situation Akhmatova found herself in after moving in with Punin abound in accounts by Pavel Luknitskii, Nadezhda Mandelstam, and Lidiia Chukovskaia, as well as in the memoirs of other visitors and admirers. Besides all that, as Akhmatova herself revealed to Lidiia Chukovskaia in 1940, Punin and his study, the room that Akhmatova shared with him from 1927 to 1938, were not conducive to writing poetry:

> Strange that I lived with Nikolai Nikolaevich for so long after it had ended, isn't it? But I was so depressed that I didn't have the strength to leave. I was very low, because I hadn't written any poetry for thirteen years, just think: thirteen years! I tried to leave him in 1930. Sr[eznevskii] promised to get me a room. But Nikolai Nikolaevich went to see him and said that for him, my [staying or] leaving was a matter of life and death.... Sr[eznevskii] believed him, grew scared, and didn't get me a room. I stayed.[4]

Nevertheless, when Akhmatova parted with Punin in 1938, she simply left his study and moved into the former nursery. Despite his several attempts to convince her to move out, Akhmatova was determined to stay.[5] Her unwillingness to move may be explained by her attachment to the former grandeur, history, and central location of the Sheremetiev Fountain House, her irregular income, her well-documented lack of domestic skills, and the endemic housing crisis in Leningrad, but only in part. In January 1940, Akhmatova joined the Soviet Writers' Union, which allowed Aleksandr Fadeev, the union's secretary, to petition on her behalf and get a separate room for her. She was also given a state stipend *(pensiia)* and was invited to publish her poetry in Soviet periodicals.[6] Despite the offer of such a favorable resolution of her problems, Akhmatova chose to stay with the Punins and continued to live with them in two different places, long after their forced departure from the Sheremetiev Palace, until her death in 1966.

By the time Akhmatova moved into the former nursery, the Punins had lost part of their apartment to another family, the Smirnovs, with two small children. With inadequate wall partitions, Akhmatova's guests were often exposed to the noises made by the drunken Smirnov or by his wife beating one of the boys. In August 1940, Akhmatova read to Chukovskaia her new poem, "The Neighbor from Pity Might Go Two Blocks" ("Sosedka iz zhalosti—dva kvartala"), which was directly inspired by her crude surroundings and by a premonition of her own death. Chukovskaia was deeply moved and marveled at Akhmatova's ability to turn "a cesspit of a communal flat" into "a solemn and touching funeral hour."[7] Like Lidiia Chukovskaia, other memoirists took pains to underscore Akhmatova's unique ability to rise above her environment. Invariably she exhibited remarkable self-control in the face of unbelievably petty opposition, which only enhanced Akhmatova's beauty and her regal behavior. "Like a nun," the translator Nancy Andersen asserts, Akhmatova "saw herself as having a vocation that required her either to live on the charity of others or to go without. She consciously entered the Punin household in the vulnerable position of a dependent."[8]

These recollections and interpretations speak more to their authors' general disgust with the communal apartment as a Soviet institution than to Akhmatova's actual relationship with her surroundings. The cursed cesspit of a communal apartment presented Akhmatova with a set of strategic possibilities that she exploited to alleviate the anxieties she apparently experienced from 1923 to 1935, the period she found least conducive to writing poetry.[9] One obvious solution was to put all the blame for her seemingly inexplicable creative hiatus on Punin and his entourage. However, this simple explanation, which most of her friends, like Lidiia Chukovskaia, found satisfactory in the late 1930s, did not sound convincing in the 1950s. By then, her failures in her private life had become largely irrelevant for a poet of her stature.

In general, few writers' homes have been accorded so much scrutiny and have left such a complete record as Akhmatova's. Yet the intricate relationship between these dwellings and the intellectual work of writing deserves further examination and explanation. What was it about Punin's study that enabled Akhmatova to write her penetrating analyses of Pushkin's works there but was at the same time lethal to her own creativity?

Akhmatova was not the only woman writer who fell silent in mid-career.[10] Jane Austen was silent for nine years, followed by a very productive period during which she wrote her last three novels. "This long silence, in the middle of a relatively short life is bewildering," Carol Shields writes. "It is a silence that drives a wedge between her first three major novels and her final three: *Mansfield Park, Emma,* and *Persuasion*. The silence asks questions about the flow of Jane Austen's creative energies and about her reconciliation to the life she had been handed. She lived in a day when to be married was the only form of independence—and even then it was very much a restricted liberty."[11] Jane Austen did not marry and lived her life mostly as a dependent of her parents; later she relied on support from her wealthy brother Edward. When her parents decided to sell Austen's beloved family home at Steventon and moved to Bath, she had to oblige. "There can be little question," Shields contends, "that Jane Austen's rather fragile frame of creativity was disturbed following the move to Bath."[12] Not until years later, after Jane Austen and her relatives had finally settled in Chawton Cottage, was she able to resume her writing. Shields would have liked Jane Austen to have become independent at an earlier stage—either through marriage or through inheritance. Either resolution might have translated into a larger quantity of books, as with Virginia Woolf, who was lucky in having both an inheritance, which gave her financial independence, and a loving husband devoted to promoting her career. Ironically, to create her writing space, Akhmatova had to dispose of her possessions and rearrange her private life in order to accommodate not only spousal jealousy but also textual infidelities and the anxieties of literary influence.

A Room of One's Own

In *A Room of One's Own* (1929), Virginia Woolf contends, "A woman must have money and a room of her own if she is to write fiction." Woolf's statement, however correct in general, proved to be wrong when applied to successful women writers of Stalin's and even Khrushchev's Russia. In fact, evidence of their talent seemed to be in inverse proportion to the amount of privacy they were able to enjoy and the amount of living space they were free to occupy. Liubov' Dmitrievna Blok (1881–1939), in one of her later additions to her memoirs, described the new interior of her room:

My living quarters are fitted out at last. They reflect my soul, as they should. There are a lot of primitive, home-made, and unfinished items, but my living space isn't devoid of inventiveness, it doesn't look philistine and aspires after the future, emulating Europe, despite the unavoidable limitations. Having a radio is just great. The bathroom is comfortable and fitted out meticulously, as in Europe. The walls are painted a light color and don't dwarf the space. Blok's portrait lives here—it's larger than the natural, human size. The art objects aren't numerous but they always catch your eye. The window commands a view of the sky stretching away over the flowers, roofs, and chimneys. The armchairs and couches for friends are soft and comfortable. That this is a woman's dwelling is suggested by the multicolored pillows and the scent of perfume. Here I am.[13]

According to many memoirists, Liubov' Dmitrievna Blok always sought to make her home with Aleksandr Blok as "cozy" as possible, filling it with photographs, pictures, and other mementos of their life together.[14] Unfortunately for her, most of their married life was spent in the company of members of her husband's family, in particular, his mother. As a result, she not only had the stress of living with these relatives but also had to face up to the pressures of developing her own career as an actress, which was not easy alongside a famous and demanding poet.[15]

It is clear, however, that by the time L. D. Blok embarked on writing her memoirs in the late 1930s, she had achieved the independence for which she had struggled so long. She was able to analyze her life with her husband, recognizing both its positive and negative aspects, and to realize her professional aspirations as a teacher and writer on the world of European ballet. As her numerous references to Freud suggest, she was so empowered by the recent developments in psychoanalysis that she felt obliged to tell the "truth" about her marriage without sparing the reader any embarrassing details. In a sense, the reference to the window in the above-quoted passage is reminiscent of the famous final scene in Mikhail Kuzmin's *Wings* (*Kryl'ia*, 1906), where an open window signifies Vanya Smurov's decision to embrace his homosexuality; or of the chapter from *Eternal Companions* (*Vechnye sputniki*, 1897), in which Dmitrii Merezhkovskii marvels at the simplicity and ingenuity of the Laurentinum, the famous villa built by Plinius Junior in the second century in the vicinity of Rome. In his renditions of Plinius' letters Merezhkovskii celebrates him for his attention to detail and for his ability to appreciate both the joys of nature and personal comfort:

> The villa is comfortable, and maintenance costs are low. The atrium, unpretentious but not without elegance, is at the front. Behind it, there's an arc-shaped portico, resembling the letter "D," that encloses a cute little courtyard, a delightful shelter from the elements. . . .
> Up ahead, an inner courtyard, bright and cheerful. From there one can proceed to a beautiful dining room jutting out over the sea. . . . Next door is a lavatory and a warm bathroom with a walled-off steam compartment. . . . The hot-water tubs are set up so cleverly that one can enjoy the view of the sea from them while taking a bath.[16]

In fact, the similarities between L. D. Blok's memoirs and Kuzmin's and Merezhkovskii's texts are so striking that they suggest that her recollections, called *Facts and Fables about Blok and Myself* (*I byli i nebylitsy o Bloke i o sebe*), were informed not only by her real-life experience but also by the Russian fin de siècle cultural tradition with its acclaimed penchant for individualism and exhibitionism.[17]

The search for and the acquisition of a room of her own was not only a symbolic gesture for Liubov' Dmitrievna. In the mid-1930s, a relative visited her when she was sharing her apartment with Blok's aunt, Mariia Andreevna Beketova (1862–1938). "At that time," her visitor recalled, "the enfilade of rooms was divided between the two of them: on Liubov' Dmitrievna's side, everything was subordinated to her work. She was writing a book about classical dancing and was giving ballet lessons to dancers of the Kirov and Maly theaters—G. Kirillova, N. Dudinskaia, V. Chabukiani, and others. All the furniture had been removed from the room and large mirrors and a ballet practice bar had been installed. The only untouched little island was

Aleksandr Blok's couch with his portrait by Tatiana Gippius over it and an animal skin on the floor near it."[18] Ten years earlier, however, in March 1925, Lidiia Chukovskaia's father, Kornei Chukovskii, observed L. D. Blok desperately searching for a job:

> I saw Liubov' Dmitrievna Blok yesterday. . . . Either she's pretending to be poorer than she actually is [pribedniaetsia] or she's really in dire poverty. A wretched threadbare fur coat, a missing tooth, she was standing at the entrance to Kubuch [the Committee for Improving the Living Conditions of Scholars] in the frightful crush, offering her translations from the French. The widow of one of the most famous Russian poets, the "Beautiful Lady," and also Mendeleev's daughter.[19]

A year later, Chukovskii recorded another meeting with Liubov' Dmitrievna. By then, her position had improved, but only nominally: "Two days ago I ran across the 'Beautiful Lady,' Liubov' Dmitrievna Blok, on the staircase of Gosizdat [the state publishing house]. She works at Gosizdat as a proofreader, a big bloated forty-five-year-old woman. Out on the landing for a smoke. Slitlike eyes. A fringe across her forehead. Blathering with other proofreaders."[20] Although Chukovskii wept inconsolably when he heard of Blok's death in 1921 and subsequently contributed to the promotion of Blok's legacy, he was entirely unsympathetic to his widow, to the extent that she is notably absent from his diary entries from the year 1927 until his death in 1969. Chukovskii was not alone. Any information about L. D. Blok's life in the late 1920s and the 1930s is extremely scarce. It therefore remains a mystery how exactly, in the early 1930s, she had found her new vocation—"the rare gift of a historian of the classical ballet"[21]—and succeeded, despite her weak heart and meager income, in finishing her 500-page magnum opus, *Classical Dancing: History and Modernity* (*Klassicheskii tanets: istoriia i sovremennost'*).[22]

After L. D. Blok's sudden death in 1939 from a heart attack, all her letters to Aleksandr Blok, together with her private memoirs, which were not intended for publication, became the property of the newly founded State Literary Museum. As a member of the Aleksandr Blok

Literary Heritage Committee, Kornei Chukovskii studied the memoirs and shared his indiscriminately negative impressions with the members of Blok's immediate circle. Although the actual memoirs were not published in Russia until 2000, before that time many people either had a chance to see them in the archives or, like Anna Akhmatova, heard about their content from Chukovskii.[23] "K. I. [Chukovskii] was telling me about Liubov' Dmitrievna's *Diary*," Akhmatova reported to Lidiia Chukovskaia in August 1940. "He says it's such muck that you have to wear galoshes. And [only a few days ago] I was feeling sorry for her, I thought it was a diary from her youth. Not at all, it contains recent recollections. . . . Just think, she writes: 'I cast aside the blanket and he admired my voluptuous body.' My God, how awful! And she is so petty, so nasty about Blok, all his illnesses are listed."[24] Akhmatova told Chukovskaia on another occasion, "Just think of it, she could have remained, for the rest of her life, the Beautiful Lady, Sophia the Wise. All she had to do was keep silent. Instead, she wrote some pornographic reminiscences that disgusted everybody."[25] Akhmatova's negative assessment of Liubov' Dmitrievna Blok as an unfit widow and a malicious chronicler was very popular among her close friends and acquaintances and has been the prevalent view among the general public, despite recent publications of L. D. Blok's theoretical works and their wide acclaim among specialists.[26] To a considerable extent, such an unfairly critical reaction to L. D. Blok's private recollections, which overshadowed her many other achievements, can be explained by the Soviet practice of granting memoirists the privileges of being keepers and guarantors of Russian collective memory.

Until recently, the periods immediately preceding and following the Bolshevik Revolution were routinely misrepresented in official Soviet narrative. The main sources of reliable information about these periods were private records and memoirs kept by social outcasts such as Nadezhda Mandelstam or Lidiia Chukovskaia.[27] At a time when private recollections so often differed from historical records, memories (and memoirs) could no longer be regarded as purely private phenomena. Instead, they became a powerful weapon in social, political, and cultural struggles. Thus, paradoxically, while bemoaning the loss of personal privacy imposed on them by the Soviet regime, many intellectuals were in fact engaged in recycling their very private affairs in order to represent them later as deeds of public importance. Such memoirs were also heavily censored (if only by the memoirists themselves or by members of their entourage), and facts were conveniently bent to fit a "truthful" account of the time. What Chukovskii, Akhmatova, and other intellectuals seem to have found particularly upsetting about L. D. Blok's memoirs was the very "private" quality of her writing. Incidentally, Akhmatova and Nadezhda Mandelstam were equally shocked by Sergei Rudakov's all-too-personal accounts of his meetings with the Mandelstams in Voronezh.[28] Likewise, they anticipated finding something truly "monstrous" in Mikhail Kuzmin's personal diary if it were to appear in book form in the 1940s.[29] Although Nadezhda Mandelstam has had a reputation of a true rebel whose behavior was impulsive and unpredictable, there is nothing spontaneous about her rendition of the past in her first book of memoirs. Not surprisingly, *Hope Against Hope (Vospominaniia, 1970)*—in which Nadezhda Mandelstam, unlike L. D. Blok, was less preoccupied with telling the truth than with manipulating the reader—quickly acquired the status of not only an objective historical document but also a means of deconstructing Stalinist institutions.

In his obituary for Nadezhda Mandelstam, Joseph Brodsky recalled various dismal dwellings that she occupied in the 1960s. In 1962, he visited her in the town of Pskov, where she lived in a room "eight square meters large," or roughly "the size of an average American bathroom," he explained to readers unfamiliar with the metric system. "Most of the space was taken up by a cast-iron twin-sized bed; there were also two wicker chairs, a wardrobe chest with a small mirror, and an all-purpose bedside table, on which sat plates with the leftovers of her supper and, next to the plates, an open copy of *The Hedgehog and the Fox* by Isaiah Berlin."[30] Another frequently quoted testimony to the writer's poor living conditions comes from Chukovskaia's *Notes on Anna Akhmatova [The Akhmatova Journals]* (*Zapiski ob Anne Akhmatovoi*), in which she describes her first visit to Akhmatova in 1938:

> I climbed the tricky back staircase that belonged to another century, each step as deep as three. There was still some connection between the staircase and her, but then! . . . The general appearance of the room was one of neglect, chaos. By the stove an armchair, missing a leg, ragged, springs protruding. The floor unswept. The beautiful things—the carved chair, the mirror in its smooth bronze frame, the lubok prints on the walls—did not adorn the room; on the contrary, they only emphasized its squalor further.
>
> The only thing that was genuinely beautiful was the window onto the garden, and a tree gazing right in at the window. Black branches.
>
> And, of course, she herself.

Without much ado, Akhmatova informed Chukovskaia that she had recently separated from Punin and at that particular moment was wondering whether to "hang pictures on the wall," or whether it was "no longer worth the trouble."[31]

What Chukovskaia observed was in fact truly special: Akhmatova was putting final touches to the "room of her own." In this room in 1938–1941, she composed some of her best-known works, including *Requiem, The Way of All the Earth, In 1940,* and a larger portion of the first (Tashkent) version of *Poem Without a Hero*. From that time on, Akhmatova's poetry poured out in one uninterrupted flow. Eventually, Akhmatova changed rooms as well as locations, but the decor of *her* room remained relatively the same.[32] When Chukovskaia had a chance to visit Akhmatova in December 1959, the sight of the familiar furnishings brought her to tears:[33]

> I'm at her place in Leningrad, for the first time after the war. It's [also] my first time [in her new apartment] on Krasnaia Konnitsa Street.
> . . . The staircase is pitch dark and filthy. Akhmatova's staircase! It's so much like Akhmatova that it makes me want to cry! . . . I suddenly find

myself in a different time and amid the things I have long since forgotten: the same smooth frame of the cloudy mirror, the same armchair with a broken leg. As well as the same little mahogany table that used to stand in the room in the Fountain House twenty years before.

Overwhelmed with nostalgia, Chukovskaia rationalized her emotions by investing Akhmatova's shabby surroundings with intransient properties. For her, they functioned simultaneously as a reminder of national traumas and as a material signifier of Akhmatova's creative energy: "For Anna Andreevna the things in her room are, most likely, filled with the year 1913; for me, they are out of 1937. . . . I only saw them in 1938 but they, like myself, witnessed the creation of *Requiem*, the greatest monument to that epoch, . . . which is now called 'the year thirty-seven.'" Without realizing it, Chukovskaia made Akhmatova's room look like a memorial museum, where every new exhibit needed to be accounted for. Not surprisingly, she immediately spotted "a portrait of [Olga] Sudeikina on the wall," which she did not "remember seeing in that other room, in the Fountain House." Subconsciously, Chukovskaia did not want to see significant changes in Akhmatova's habitat, and apparently neither did Akhmatova.

As many memoirists have recorded, Akhmatova showed little interest in her private possessions except for her small suitcase, in which she kept her manuscripts and which rarely left her sight. "Her close friends," Kornei Chukovskii recalled, "all knew that once they presented her with, say, a rare engraving or a brooch, in a day or two, she would have given them away." Chukovskii readily compared Akhmatova to other celebrated "homeless" writers, such as Coleridge, Gogol, Apollon Grigoriev, and "her friend" Osip Mandelstam. However, Akhmatova's disregard for comfort seemed so unique to him that he devoted another page of his memoirs to this particular subject:

> She had no creature comforts around her, and I can't think of a period in her life when her surroundings could be called comfortable.
>
> The very words "furnishings," "coziness," or "comfort" were intrinsically alien to her—both in her daily life and in her poetry.

> Both in life and poetry, Akhmatova was more often than not homeless [bespriiutna].
>
> Of course, she valued beautiful things and was a connoisseur of them. Old candelabra, oriental fabrics, engravings, caskets, old icons, and so on would appear in her modest quarters on a regular basis, only to disappear a few days later. . . . She didn't part only with those things that held some truly sentimental value for her. Those things were her "eternal companions"—a shawl given her by Marina Tsvetaeva, a drawing by her friend Modigliani, or a ring she received from her late husband—and, being what was considered "luxury items," they only put into graphic relief the squalor of her everyday life and furnishings—her threadbare blanket, a couch with holes in it, or a worn-out patterned dressing gown which for years served as her only at-home clothing.
>
> That was habitual poverty that she never tried to get out of.[34]

This remarkable inventory of items both wanted and not needed, among other things attests to Akhmatova's real or perceived dependency on her immediate surroundings. Moreover, her compulsive urge to get rid of any new item within a day or two suggests that this relationship was predicated on the supremacy of the object over its owner and not the other way around.[35] In my opinion, Mandelstam's "homelessness" was different from Akhmatova's: for him it was a matter of gracefully accepting what fate had handed him; for her, more significantly, it created a new writing venue and therefore was a matter of choice.

Deus Conservat Omnia

Although it was Osip Mandelstam who famously declared his group's attachment to material culture in "The Morning of Acmeism" ("Utro akmeizma," 1910, 1913), it was not his but Akhmatova's poetry (as well as her personal life) that was constantly being read against the backdrop of culturally codified domesticity.[36] Following the Bolshevik Revolution, the classic nineteenth-century oppositions of private versus public, and interior versus exterior, acquired a distinctly political connotation. Depending on the critics' various agendas, Akhmatova's poetry was routinely compared either to the stuffy atmosphere of a cluttered bedroom or to the cell of a nun. Most notably, in 1936, Elizaveta Kuz'mina-Karavaeva (the renowned Mother Maria, 1891–1945) described the early 1910s as a period of cultural decline and political stagnation. She recalled the first Poets' Guild and its founding fathers as being "priggishly serious, somewhat dull, and full of posturing."[37] That was the time when "Gumilev and Akhmatova were each beginning to make their distinctive mark." While Gumilev "ranged a long way off from the Russian plains, in foreign exotic lands," Akhmatova "hardly ever ventured outside her stuffy room cluttered with bric-a-brac." Gumilev's study, in which he exhibited his African collection, also smelled "strangely" of the rhinoceros, whose fat the Abyssinians used to preserve their paintings. "Neither [Gumilev] nor [Akhmatova] had much to offer," she concluded.[38]

For Kuz'mina-Karavaeva in 1936, Akhmatova's room clearly functioned as a trope for the failure of the acmeist preservationist project to avert the calamity of WWI and of the Russian revolutions that followed. In fact, as she perceptively observed in her earlier article, "The Last Romans" ("Poslednie rimliane," 1924), in their art the acmeists were motivated first and foremost by the preservation of "the *dying* world."[39] Therefore, "their loving attitude toward the surrounding world" was informed and conditioned by the inevitability of its ultimate destruction. The poets eagerly worshiped such potentially endangered items as "some little whip, a pair of gloves, every trifling thing, every stray object," as if, while sitting in the comfort of their rooms, they all had "glimpsed something terrible and frightening" through their windows. This "ever-present . . . horror" made one "look constantly back over one's shoulder at the window" and "lent a special significance to Akhmatova's poems by enhancing the mystery" of her otherwise ordinary existence.[40]

Kuz'mina-Karavaeva's insightful criticism runs counter to the popular view of the acmeist movement as being founded on the supremacy of cultural traditions and unbounded continuity, but it makes a lot of sense when applied to its particular representatives.[41] More specifically, it sheds useful light on Akhmatova's somewhat unusual reaction to the news of Olga Glebova-Sudeikina's death in 1945: "When I learned that Olga had died, I was, of course, saddened. But the next morning I woke up and thought: What was that good thing they told me about Olia yesterday?"[42] In November 1940, the thoughts of her old friend (who was then still alive) inspired Akhmatova's famous recollection "You Came to Russia out of Nowhere" ("Ty v Rossiiu prishla niotkuda"), which was the impetus for her future *Poem Without a Hero*. When read on its own, this passage sounds like an obituary: Akhmatova describes Sudeikina as a "poets' beloved friend" and immediately declares herself to be her heir:[43]

> O poets' beloved friend,
> The fame you once [enjoyed] is now my own.

The narrator's appropriation of her friend's prime possession anticipates the disturbing logic of the *Poem*'s opening lines:

> . . . .
> . . . and since my paper has run out,
> I am using your rough draft for writing.

Readers are usually enthralled by the beauty of these lines, intensified by compassion for the poverty-stricken author, and rarely take notice of the heartlessness of this transaction. Numerous scholars and admirers have been concerned with establishing the identity of the mysterious author of the rough draft rather than commenting on the moral aspects of the idea of stealing from the dead (by then all likely candidates were dead). Akhmatova was no keeper. She was an undertaker. In February 1936, puzzled by Akhmatova's extended period of silence, Osip Mandelstam compared her to a "carnivorous seagull" *(plotoiadnaia chaika)*, whose voice is heard only during "historic events" such as "war" and "revolution," while "steady and deep-flowing periods in life do not stir her to poetry."[44] Akhmatova's silence was broken when she wrote "I Drink to My Ruined Home" ("Ia p'iu za razorennyi dom"), followed by "From You I Hid My Heart" ("Ot tebia ia serdtse skryla"), epitaphs to her deteriorating relationship with Punin, along with a number of poems inspired by historical figures and her own contemporaries, most of whom were by then dead. In the late 1930s, she also worked on *Requiem*, a testament to the Stalinist terror and its victims.

Evidently, Akhmatova's productivity in the late 1930s amazed Punin and also hurt his feelings.[45] She confessed to Chukovskaia in March 1940, "Nikolai Nikolaevich has now discovered a new reason for taking umbrage at me: why didn't I write when we lived together, when I write so much now?"[46] If Akhmatova's poetic world thrived only when its interiority was being threatened, as Kuz'mina-Karavaeva suggested, then her beleaguered existence in the communal apartment, particularly after Akhmatova and Punin separated, may well have had a restorative effect and assuaged her anxieties rather than creating them, as many memoirists seem to imply. By the late 1930s, the Akhmatovian room-window paradigm, as defined by Kuz'mina-Karavaeva, had been turned around. As Chukovskaia's recollection of her first visit to Akhmatova suggests, the existential horror no longer originated in the outside world, but in the writer's own room, with the window serving as a reminder of unattainable normalcy and beauty: "The only thing that was genuinely beautiful was the window onto the garden, and a tree gazing right in at the window." It so happened that even the acmeists' propensity for conserving absolutely everything *(kazhdaia sluchainaia veshch' . . . konservirovalas')*, which Kuz'mina-Karavaeva found particularly objectionable and somewhat senseless in 1924, by the late 1930s had acquired a definitely positive significance in the eyes of Akhmatova's culture-conscious readers and admirers.[47] That, again, was in part related to her actual living quarters. The famous motto of the Sheremetiev family was *Deus Conservat Omnia*. Every visitor to the Fountain House had to go first through the gates inscribed with this motto and only then entered the communal apartment. Not surprisingly, Akhmatova chose this motto as an epigraph to the *Poem Without a Hero*. Although Akhmatova joked that the inscription simply meant:

"Dear God, protect my supplies of canned food" *(Bozhe, sokhrani moi konservy)*, she saved such jokes for her very young interlocutors.[48] Following the disappearance of the prerevolutionary material culture, Akhmatova's poetry was read by many as a manifestation of cultural resilience and as a bridge linking many centuries of Russian history.

A Nun in Love

Unlike Jane Austen, who entered her period of silence a decided spinster, in the early 1920s Akhmatova was beginning her lasting relationship with Punin. Her stunning appearance certainly gave her an advantage over less attractive or older female intellectuals, such as L. D. Blok, who struggled to promote their careers or simply to make ends meet. On December 15, 1922, Kornei Chukovskii recorded his impressions of a visit to Akhmatova:

> Yesterday I stopped by to see Anna Akhmatova. . . . The staircase was dark and dusty—a typical back entrance. I knocked on the door and heard a voice say, "It's open!" In the small kitchen a watery soup was on the stove. Anna Andreevna was not there. Then she walked in with Nikolai Nikolaevich Punin. We went into the living room with icons hanging on the walls formerly belonging to the Sudeikins and began to talk—about personal, not worldly, matters. I saw her once as a hungry and ascetic nun (when she was living on Liteiny in 1919); I saw her later as a woman of the world (three months ago); and now she was . . . just a young woman from a very ordinary family. The crowded rooms, kitchen entrance, the mother, cook . . . who would have thought that this was the same Anna Akhmatova who today has surpassed in fame Gorky and Lev Tolstoi and Leonid Andreev, who is the subject of dozens of articles and books, whose poetry is known by heart by the entire province?[49]

Chukovskii caught Akhmatova in one of her happier moments and the Kuleshov-like montage sequence of "watery soup," "crowded rooms, kitchen entrance," "mother," "cook," and "icons" conveyed the idea of an unadorned but fulfilling womanhood. Chukovskii left Akhmatova "with a good feeling." A few months later, when he found Akhmatova and her friend, Olga Sudeikina, sitting alone in their apartment, the sight of two women "without husbands" and "without money" filled his heart with pity and compassion. "I was so moved by their lot," Chukovskii admitted, "that I took them both to the theater to see [Maeterlinck's] *The Miracle of St. Anthony*."[50]

Although in real life Chukovskii apparently wished for an uncomplicated and prosperous existence for Akhmatova, in his interpretive schemes she conveniently belonged to a nunnery.[51] Her "words, intonations and gestures," he revealed to his audience in 1921, "betray a nun in love—one who simultaneously kisses and makes the sign of the cross over you. . . . But her kisses are about to end because many of her latest poems say that she has all but died with regard to earthly things, . . . [and] that silence has descended on her." Akhmatova "is a poet of orphanhood and widowhood." Unlike other poets, Chukovskii submitted, Akhmatova had a "strong predilection for squalor. . . . The upholstery of her armchairs is 'threadbare,' the rug is 'worn-out,' the head scarf 'has holes in it,' her wallet is 'empty,' the flag is 'faded,' the shoes are 'down-at-the-heel,' and the statue is broken and lying down. Everything has been belittled and found deficient, but that's exactly why Akhmatova finds those things dear to her." Her poetry, for that reason, lacked graphic descriptions of passionate kisses and embraces; "everything boils down to the barely noticeable." Akhmatova's "world is small and narrow—delectable, poetic but small." In fact, her world is so small, Chukovskii kept warning his readers, that "a light touch of somebody's hand acquires, in the mind of the cautious and reserved woman, an unforgettable significance. . . . I can imagine the confusion in Akhmatova's white nun convent," Chukovskii intimated, "if [some] overly enthusiastic giant of a man knocked on their door. A moment ago, there was quiet and prayer and sanctity there, and now this . . ." This muscle-bound male is none other than the poet Vladimir Maiakovskii (1893–1930), renowned for his revolutionary zeal and unqualified support for pro-Bolshevik developments. The difference between these two poets, in Chukovskii's eyes, lays bare the basic rift between the pre- and postrevolutionary cultures:

> Akhmatova and Maiakovskii are as hostile to each other as the two hostile epochs that produced them. Akhmatova is a solicitous keeper of the most precious prerevolutionary riches of Russian verbal culture. . . . By contrast, every line and letter of Maiakovskii's poetry embody the current revolutionary period—he himself is the embodiment of the epoch's beliefs, its noise, failures, and climaxes. He has no ancestors. He is a would-be ancestor himself, and whatever strength he may have lies in his progeny. There are ages of the magnificent past behind her. There are ages of a magnificent future ahead of him.[52]

Despite the apparent tension between the two poets, Chukovskii argued for their future reconciliation:

> I think it's time for these two elemental forces to synthesize. . . . This synthesis has long been predicted by history, and the sooner it materializes, the better. . . . All of Russia has been yearning for it. The two phenomena are not to survive independently of each other. They're relentlessly gravitating toward a confluence. In the future, they can only exist as one—otherwise both of them are destined to perish.[53]

Although Chukovskii's comparative study laid a foundation for much of the unjustified criticism of Akhmatova's work for years to come, it also presented a utopian resolution to the crisis of the postrevolutionary mentality.[54] If Blok's death was interpreted by many in 1921 as evidence of the unbridgeable gap between the pre- and postrevolutionary cultures, then Akhmatova's remarkable appearance, her perpetual "widowhood" and "homelessness" provided an outlet for fantasies about the possibilities of most unthinkable unions and reconciliations. Arguably, the communal apartment with its mismatched lodgers was one such place to turn those dreams into reality. With gossip being the main source of information about the writers' private lives during the Soviet period, Akhmatova was claimed to be either in love or to have had some kind of a romantic relationship with a number of celebrities, including Pasternak, Mandelstam, Maiakovskii, Aleksei Tolstoi, Zamiatin, and Blok.[55] "Is this the very same Akhmatova who made Blok kill himself?" Chukovskaia recorded a female student asking in January 1961.[56]

The Intimacy of Anxiety: Akhmatova and Other Women

In the early 1920s, Akhmatova's perplexing homelessness and pennilessness was aggravated by the heavy burden that fell on her shoulders following the emigration or deportation of many representatives of the Russian cultural and intellectual elite, preceded by the premature deaths of Aleksandr Blok and Nikolai Gumilev. "You have a difficult job now—you are Gorky, and Tolstoi, and Leonid Andreev, and Igor Severianin—all in one," Chukovskii claims to have said to Akhmatova on February 14, 1922. "It's frightening," he concluded. "She is at the height of her fame. Yesterday the Free Philosophical Association organized a recital of her poetry, and the editors of different magazines are calling her from morning till night: 'Give us something, anything.'"[57] A month later, Chukovskii found Akhmatova seriously disturbed by the new article about her in the magazine *Novaia Rossiia*. "Read the criticism. It's about me. They really berate me!" Akhmatova uttered indignantly. Although the article came up with a rather positive overview of Akhmatova's work, her exaggerated reaction to it only demonstrated to Chukovskii the extent of her vulnerability and insecurity: "I developed a great pity for this suffering woman. She showed me her large square notebook of new poems. There is enough there for a new book. But the critics will say once again: 'Akhmatova is repeating herself.'"[58]

Such pressure from the editors alone, together with the heightened expectations of the reading public, may have been responsible for her subsequent inability to write poetry and should have activated her angst about her contemporaries and her forefathers.[59] And yet, Akhmatova's devotion to Pushkin, Dante, Dostoevskii, and Blok, as well as her friendship with and loyalty to Mandelstam and Pasternak, are well known. In his letter to Lidiia Chukovskaia, her friend David

Samoilov, a poet, commented on Akhmatova's amazing lack of anxiety about her famous predecessors: "She . . . was never afraid of influences and she liked this quality in Pushkin, too. It is the modernists like [the poet Andrei] Voznesenskii, who are scared of influences; they don't like culture—they like only themselves."[60] The acmeists have traditionally been considered the least susceptible to literary jealousy of other writers and poets. With a few exceptions, literary scholars have rarely challenged this popular image of Akhmatova. One such exception is John Malmstad, who has perceptively identified Akhmatova's lacerating remarks about Kuzmin's *The Trout Breaking through the Ice* (*Forel' razbivaet led*, 1929) as a clear manifestation of her anxiety of influence. On September 5, 1940, Chukovskaia asked Akhmatova what she thought about *The Trout*. "Everything in it is derived from German expressionism," Akhmatova replied. She praised certain parts of the poem but insisted that its "obscenity" left her "with a very heavy heart." In her words, "I'd like to have put ellipses in many places. . . . It's too exclusively for those with peculiar tastes: 'practicing nincompoops.' Kuzmin has always been homosexual in his poetry, but here he has gone beyond all reasonable bounds. . . . It's most repulsive."[61]

Soon after making these negative statements about Kuzmin, Malmstad points out, Akhmatova began writing *Poem Without a Hero*, "which polemicizes with the first cycle of Kuzmin's collection, where he made a personal myth of the triumph of love between two men that is threatened by the destructive passion of one of them for a woman."[62] Malmstad continues, "There is something very sad about [Akhmatova's] remarks. . . .There is nothing at all explicit in [Kuzmin's] book or any of his others, and nothing remotely 'obscene,' unless for Akhmatova it was the fact that Kuzmin addresses, as usual, same-sex love. That had not shocked her when he lived under her roof in 1912, nor in the years 1921 to 1923, when she shared an apartment with Sudeikina (sparking rumors of a lesbian relationship), where Kuzmin, usually accompanied by his lover, was a constant and welcome visitor." Akhmatova's change of heart toward Kuzmin occurred sometime in the mid-1920s when, according to Malmstad, Akhmatova lived "in growing enforced isolation," while Kuzmin, also a persona non grata, still managed to get his books into print and continued to "play a certain role in [Leningrad's] cultural life. All that," Malmstad infers, "may help explain the sourness and the tone of prudish moralizing in her statements about him throughout the thirties and after, when most of her contemporaries felt the lash of her tongue, although none to the extent of the puritanical vindictiveness of her portrait of Kuzmin."[63]

In fact, Akhmatova's persistent references to the unethical behavior of a younger poet, Georgii Ivanov (1894–1958), whom she condemned as a "totally ignorant pederast," and to the famous symbolist Viacheslav Ivanov (1866–1949), whom she invariably described as a "traitor" and a "charlatan,"[64] were no less vicious and arguably even more damaging to their reputations. By the late 1930s, when Chukovskaia arrived on the scene to trigger and record Akhmatova's recollections of many representatives of prerevolutionary culture, such as Kuzmin, Blok, Gippius, and Ivanov, to name but a few, Akhmatova had started to devise her own strategies for dealing with anxieties about her illustrious contemporaries. Instead of addressing the strengths and weaknesses of their oeuvre directly, she vented her frustrations by gossiping about artists' private lives and their unusual domestic arrangements.[65] The Russian Silver Age, with its proliferation of disastrous life-creation projects, could not fail to provide ample support for her criticism.[66]

"What a terrible life they had!" Akhmatova exclaimed one day. In her *Notes*, Chukovskaia explained that Akhmatova referred to Blok and his wife, a popular subject of their many discussions in the summer and autumn of 1940. "Real bedlam *[balagan]*, there is no other word for it.[67] He has one affair after another. She keeps packing her cases all the time and going off somewhere with her latest young man. He sits alone in the flat, angry, missing her. He writes in his *Diary*: 'Liuba! Liuba!' She returns—he is happy—but by that time he's having an affair with Delmas. And so it went on."[68] Akhmatova asked rhetorically, "Why didn't they divorce?" Chukovskaia was stunned by Akhmatova's liberal approach to the institution of marriage, which, as it turned out, was very similar to her own. "I am always for divorce," Akhmatova reassured her. "It is very difficult to stay together once it is over. What you get is bedlam, like we have in [this] flat." To support her allegation, Akhmatova "tapped lightly on [Punin's] wall." Chukovskaia understood. "I believe Blok generally treated women badly, disrespectfully," Akhmatova lectured Chukovskaia. "I never had even a trace of an affair with Blok . . . but by chance I know a bit about his affairs. . . . Two women at different times told me about their relationships with him—essentially, it was the same story. . . . Both were young and beautiful. . . . One visited him late, in his empty flat . . . the other at the Stray Dog. . . . Both were the femme fatale type. . . . But he pushed them away at the last moment: 'My God . . . it's dawn already . . . farewell . . . farewell . . .'" When Chukovskaia interjected that it was the two women that were at fault rather than Blok, Akhmatova once again drew Chukovskaia's attention to her own experience of living with Punin as the ultimate proof of her right to judge and interpret the lives of other people: "'Sometimes there are chance infidelities, and then everything rights itself again, but that is rare. . . . But such an accumulation of wives'—once again she tapped Nikolai Nikolaevich's wall lightly—'is utter nonsense.'"

Chukovskaia eagerly listened to Akhmatova's every word and prompted her to talk more about Liubov' Dmitrievna Blok. Was she beautiful? In response, Akhmatova broke into a long monologue:

> Come on, L. K., with a back like that! Not only [wasn't] she beautiful, she was hideous! I met her when she was thirty. That woman's main feature was her back—immensely broad, round-shouldered. And her bass voice. And thick large arms and legs. Inwardly, too, she was hideous and malevolent, as if something had broken her. . . . But he, always, all his life, saw in her a girl with whom he had fallen in love. . . . And he loved her.

As if such an unflattering characterization was not enough, Akhmatova followed it with her portrayal of the singer Liubov' Delmas, with whom Blok, according to most memoirists, including his own wife, had a lasting and fulfilling sexual relationship. Delmas, Akhmatova stated, was "decent, kind, but not clever. She had freckles, red hair, an unattractive, flat face, but beautiful shoulders and she was plump. ... Apparently [Blok] liked his women to be well covered," Akhmatova concluded.

The entry for August 19, 1940, covers several pages of printed text and is one of the longest in the *Notes*. Chukovskaia's phenomenal memory and her obsessive love of Akhmatova's spoken word are well documented. Chukovskaia, Beth Holmgren points out, was an "ideal helper-caretaker."[69] From their very first meeting, she willingly combined the roles of self-effacing transcriber and zealous editor while heeding Akhmatova's numerous urgent calls for help with her daily chores. Admirers of Chukovskaia's *Notes* usually praise her for her courage and impartiality when chronicling Akhmatova's life. Her enemies, conversely, accuse her of being so petty as to record Akhmatova's every word, even her most insignificant or malicious remarks, thus underscoring her weaknesses rather than her strengths. Chukovskaia is often held responsible for provoking Akhmatova's outbursts of embarrassingly unfair criticism by means of her somewhat naive questions about the private life of Akhmatova's predecessors and contemporaries. What is one to make of Chukovskaia? Evidently, in her editorial duties, Chukovskaia (whether consciously or subconsciously) went further than just tending to Akhmatova's poetic texts and publications.

I have already mentioned that Chukovskaia met Akhmatova in November 1938, shortly after Akhmatova and Punin separated. Although Akhmatova put on a brave front, she did not take her third divorce lightly. In fact, she was so confused that (like L. D. Blok) she had to consult Freud in order to identify the exact cause of Punin's inability to sustain a lasting relationship with a woman. When Chukovskaia suggested that Freud was annoying, Akhmatova responded, "Don't say that. I wouldn't understand many things about Nikolai Nikolaevich to this day if not for Freud."[70] Despite Chukovskaia's lack of appreciation for Freud, she was undoubtedly instrumental during the 1938–1942 period in helping Akhmatova to create a story of her life that reflected Akhmatova's new familial circumstances as well as contemporary cultural developments. In psychoanalytic terms, Akhmatova, with her self-righteousness and eagerness to convey her own account of the past, was the analysand, while Chukovskaia, with her unassuming attitude and desire to learn as well as to record, acted as the analyst. Following Roy Schafer's findings, the narrative psychologist Jerome Bruner says that "the analysand's Self" is "a maker of tales" that has "a distinctive style" of his or her own. "Under the circumstances, the analyst, it would seem, comes increasingly to serve in the role of helpful editor."[71] The objective of such collaborative projects, Bruner reveals in his summation of David Polonoff's work, is not in discovering some hidden archaeological treasures or in uncovering the truth about the analysand's past, but in the analysand's achieving "external and internal *coherence, livability,* and *adequacy.* . . . Self-deception was a failure to achieve this, not a failure to correspond with an unspecifiable 'reality.'"[72]

Akhmatova was not a malicious gossiper, as some critics imply; rather, she was a "serious" gossiper. As Patricia Meyer Sparks explains, "serious" gossipers "use talk about others to reflect about themselves, to express wonder and uncertainty and locate certainties, to enlarge their knowledge of one another." The serious gossip "takes place in private, at leisure, in a context of trust. . . . The relationship such gossip expresses and sustains matters more than the information it promulgates; and in the sustaining of that relationship, interpretation counts more than the facts or pseudo-facts on which it works."[73]

The well-read Chukovskaia, born in 1907, with only precious childhood memories of her father's home to draw upon in her accounts of the prerevolutionary cultural scene, was an ideal interlocutor for Akhmatova. In a sense, she was one of those mysterious "guests from the future" whose arrival was somewhat deflated by her gender and by the unsentimental nature of her first visit: "Yesterday I was at Anna Andreevna's on business."[74] As her *Notes* indicate, Chukovskaia revered Akhmatova as a victim of Stalinist repressions, as an outstanding poet, and simply as a strikingly beautiful woman with a richly mysterious love life. A writer in her own right, Chukovskaia glowed in Akhmatova's presence and did everything in her power to prolong their discussions without questioning the validity of Akhmatova's accounts. When Akhmatova insisted that she "never had even a trace of an affair with Blok," Chukovskaia was surprised, but she saved her reservations for the bracketed commentary in her Notes.[75] With Akhmatova, Chukovskaia entered a disciple-master relationship similar to the imaginary friendship between Dante and Virgil. In this case, however, Akhmatova led Chukovskaia through the Inferno of the Soviet communal apartment.

Despite criticism of the individualistically narrow "home-and-family" quality of her poetry, by the 1940s Akhmatova herself had successfully appropriated her critics' tools and idioms and routinely made negative comparisons of other poets to various interior styles and designs. For example, in March 1940, she announced to Chukovskaia that Sergei Yesenin's poetry "reminded [her] of an apartment during NEP: the icons are still up but the place is already overcrowded, and there's someone drinking and pouring his feelings out in front of strangers."[76] Likewise, in August 1940, Akhmatova interpreted Blok's drama *The Song of Fate (Pesnia Sud'by,* 1908) as a projection of "the spiritual context of his flat" with its "bentwood chairs, art nouveau [and] the northern modernist style," on the one hand, and a notoriously tangled relationship between Blok, the actress Natalia Volokhova, and Liubov' Dmitrievna, on the other.[77] In May 1942, Akhmatova further accused Blok of having had "a communal apartment mentality" because all he cared for in life, according to her, were his "mom," "auntie," and his "unrefined, bourgeois" wife.[78] Apparently Chukovskaia (who loved Blok's poetry even more than Akhmatova's) found such diatribes against Blok justified, given the context of Akhmatova's firsthand experience of living in a communal apartment, particularly since in her criticism Akhmatova targeted not so much Blok himself as his immediate family.

Although Akhmatova repeatedly implied to Chukovskaia that she had known all along that Blok was a repulsive person who "got disoriented by the feud of two coarse females—his wife and his mother" —and when she met him in 1911 "no longer made any effort whatsoever to conceal his contempt for people," that was not necessarily how she felt about Blok a decade or two earlier.[79] Thus in 1926, upon reading Sviatopolk Mirskii's article in which he suggested that Akhmatova was "a fan of Blok's in the most intimate sense of the word," she declared that she was not "offended at all." She told her biographer Pavel Luknitskii, "Blok was so sweet and nice that it's quite all right with me if people think I had an affair with him!"[80] Except for several memorable meetings with Blok and persistent but unfounded rumors about their love affair, Akhmatova's knowledge of Blok's private life was in fact very limited.[81] She eagerly awaited each new publication of Blok's works, diaries, and notebooks in order to inform herself about his attitude toward her poetry and about his impressions of her as a woman.[82] In her discussions with Chukovskaia, Akhmatova accordingly referred to Blok's diaries as the main source of her discontent.

Akhmatova was not the only reader who was appalled by the nightmarish quality of Blok's life or by his uncharitable and immoderate observations about other literati, most of whom had considered themselves to be his friends. "What can I say? In a nutshell, I was reading them and yelling," was Andrei Bely's first reaction in 1928 to the publication of Blok's *Diaries*. "There's a measure of mendacity and there's a measure of stupidity," Bely wrote in his letter to Ivanov-Razumnik, "but where was 'the wife,' where was 'the auntie,' and where was the 'Blok Academy'?"[83] In his response, Ivanov-Razumnik came to Blok's defense by attributing Blok's vindictive remarks about his contemporaries to the "pernicious influence of the Beketovs" [*Beketovshchina*] and the demoralizing effect of his wife. He also blamed himself for loosening his hold on Blok's legacy and for letting him slip under the control of such literary critics as Pavel Medvedev, who was romantically involved with L. D. Blok in the mid-1920s and was largely responsible for several hastily prepared publications of Blok's works, including his *Diaries*.[84] Because of Blok's ambiguous position within the Soviet cultural hierarchy, along with their personal and professional investment in the Blok industry, both Bely and Ivanov-Razumnik rushed to absolve Blok of any liability for his nonpoetic works by making his wife and relatives responsible for his objectionable remarks. As

Bely pointed out in another letter to Ivanov-Razumnik, "Blok's decadence, inherited from [his father], could only flourish on the fertile soil provided by the Beketovs and 'Liuba.'"[85]

Like Beethoven, who in 1804, upon hearing the news that Napoleon had proclaimed himself emperor of the French, famously tore up the title page of his Napoleon-inspired symphony, the *Eroica*, Andrei Bely plunged into rewriting his memoirs about prerevolutionary Russia in order to make them conform to the newly acquired information about Blok. He felt that in *The Beginning of the Century* (*Nachalo veka*) he failed in portraying Blok. "But I faced a hard task," he explained to Ivanov-Razumnik in 1931. "The 'hero' of *Reminiscences* had to be inserted into a swarm of characters without making him stand out; he had to be recycled to conform to the general tenor of the book describing the period from 1901 to 1905."[86] Bely's lifelong project of reexamining his past was driven by his insatiate desire to be loved and understood by new Soviet readers with no previous experience of the turn-of-the-century culture. (This will be discussed later.) Blok's diaries, imbued with the sentiments and frustrations of a sick degenerate intellectual, which Bely aspired to analyze and expose, certainly fortified his determination to continue with his revisionist project. "Maybe my third version is going to be more successful," he reassured Ivanov-Razumnik.[87]

While Bely was primarily preoccupied with the personal aspects of his relationship with Blok, with his feelings fluctuating from those of a devoted "brother" to those of a jilted lover and misunderstood friend of the family, for Akhmatova (nine years younger) Blok was above all Harold Bloom's "strong" poet, whom she had to dismantle for her own good. If Bely and Ivanov-Razumnik readily blamed L. D. Blok for her husband's idiosyncratic behavior and in fact tried retrospectively to separate him from his family, Akhmatova, on the contrary, treated L. D. Blok as a word-made-flesh extension of his soul, thereby providing evidence of the deficiency of his creative endeavors.[88] While Bely and Ivanov-Razumnik would have preferred to see more ellipses in certain published passages from Blok's diaries, Akhmatova, conversely, wanted everything spelled out without any omissions. She stated authoritatively to Chukovskaia on August 19, 1940, "Incidentally, they say there are some terrible things in the *Diary* about [L. D. Blok]—[Vladimir] Orlov didn't publish them, but people who've read the manuscript told me."[89]

Between 1938 and 1942, Akhmatova freely drew upon Blok's personal life in her interpretations of her relationship with Punin and of their stressful cohabitation, but, more important, she used Blok's private life as an excuse and an opportunity to criticize him on terms acceptable to literature-loving intellectuals such as Chukovskaia. In fact, with her childlike curiosity and desire to please Akhmatova, Chukovskaia was equally responsible for the shape and tenacity of this discourse. If in 1940 her recollections of L. D. Blok were in a state of flux, with Akhmatova still maintaining a delicate balance between her feelings of compassion and a strong urge to disparage Blok at all costs, then by the late 1950s they had acquired the solidity of one of her famous "records." Thus when the general conversation flagged at a friendly gathering in April 1964, someone obligingly asked Akhmatova whether Liubov' Dmitrievna Blok was beautiful. "This was familiar, well-trodden ground," Chukovskaia recorded with relief. Akhmatova's response came "in a quiet voice, syllable-by-syllable":

> "She looked like a hippopotamus standing up on its hind legs." Then in greater detail: "Her eyes were slits, her nose was a boot, and her cheeks were pillows. Her legs were this big, and her hands were this size.... Apparently, they all had a mental image of her, based on Blok's delightful poetry, where she is the Fair Lady, Sophia, God's wisdom.... Liubov' Dmitrievna's plainness made me think about the beauty of another lady—Natalia Nikolaevna Pushkina. Was she really beautiful? She was also perceived through poetry: she was Psyche, et cetera, et cetera. But that was the way she was seen during *his* life. When she returned to high society, she was just thirty-two years old—a woman's prime!—but for some reason not a word was ever said of her beauty. The letters tell us this and that about her but nothing at all about her being beautiful."[90]

Lidiia Ginzburg observes that Akhmatova "had a personal relationship with Pushkin and his circle that bordered on the idiosyncratic. She judged, loved, and hated these people as if they were still [around]. She had a peculiar jealousy of Natalia Nikolaevna and of all the women in Pushkin's life. . . . This made her judgements biased and undeservedly cruel."[91] Akhmatova's numerous unreasonable attacks on Natalia Nikolaevna (like questioning her well-documented beauty), whom many Russians still hold responsible for her husband's tragic death in a duel, are usually attributed to her remarkable devotion to Pushkin, whom she revered all her life both as Russia's greatest poet and as a human being. However, it seems that her attitude toward Natalia Nikolaevana was no different from her attitude toward L. D. Blok (in fact, she drew this parallel herself in the above-quoted passage at a dinner table) or toward Zinaida Nikolaevna Pasternak and many other writers' wives and widows.

What is the point, one may ask, in analyzing all this gossip and how does it further our understanding of Akhmatova's creativity? In my view, Akhmatova's frequent seemingly unmotivated attacks on writers' companions (even the most inarticulate ones) stemmed from the unique form that her anxiety of influence assumed in the 1930s. Since many writers met tragic deaths, were persecuted, banned like Dostoevskii, or forced to live in cultural and political isolation, it would have been unethical to fight against them directly.[92] Consequently, Akhmatova directed her anxiety-fueled anger not so much at her forerunners or her talented contemporaries as at their wives and companions, such as Blok's, Dostoevskii's and Pushkin's widows, Maiakovskii's love of his life, L. Yu. Brik, and Pasternak's wives and mistresses.[93] In the cases of Kuzmin and Marina Tsvetaeva (who had no female companions to be critical of), she resorted to the same technique of transferring the weight of her defamation from their writings to Kuzmin's homosexuality and Tsvetaeva's unkempt appearance and unfortunate love life.[94]

The reason Akhmatova's relationship with Pasternak (who, like Akhmatova, was a "prisoner of his time") remained unclouded for the almost forty years of their friendship is that until the late 1950s she managed to conceal her anxiety about his fame and productivity by conveniently casting him in the role of a misguided and unfortunate husband.[95] Most frequently, Akhmatova blamed Pasternak's second wife, Zinaida Nikolaevna, for being "coarse and shallow" and for constantly showing disrespect for her husband's talent by making him prepare barrels for the cucumbers, plant potatoes, and listen to her gibberish while she played cards with her equally mediocre friends. "Maybe I find this book unpleasant because of Zina's presence in it," commented Akhmatova, analyzing her negative response to Pasternak's collection of poems in 1940. "*Second Birth* is the poetry of a bridegroom. It is written by a flustered bridegroom. . . . And what unpleasant poems to his former wife! He apologizes to one and runs to the other with a little nosegay—surely there you have a flustered bridegroom?"[96]

In the early 1950s, when Pasternak was finishing *Doctor Zhivago* and appeared likely to achieve world recognition sooner than Akhmatova, she repeatedly declined his invitations to come to any of his famous readings from the novel, explaining to Chukovskaia that she did so because she disliked the general atmosphere in his house:[97] "Boris Leonidovich called to invite me to their place on Monday. . . . [He said,] 'Whether or not life is worth living depends on this day.' That meant reading the novel, buckets of champagne, caviar, and actors. . . . I didn't go." When in 1956 she finally agreed to visit Pasternak at his country house in Peredelkino, she left him with "an unpleasant, heavy feeling." She explained her impressions to Chukovskaia: "I grew tired of his ambiguous relationship with his wife: 'mommy, mommy.' . . . I could have understood those endearments if they meant a breakup with that thief [Olga Ivinskaia] . . . but they meant nothing of the kind. I was totally confused. . . . I grew tired of all that wealth and I grew tired of being unable to guess who the informer was," she concluded with no apparent connection. She not only accused Pasternak's mistress, Olga Ivinskaia, of ruining his family and stealing money from political prisoners, but even blamed her for alleged weaknesses of *Doctor Zhivago,* claiming that Ivinskaia had written some of the supposedly flawed passages herself: "I finished reading Boris Leonidovich's novel. Some of its pages are written absolutely unprofessionally. I suppose they were written by Olga. Don't laugh. I'm serious. As you know, Lidiia Korneevna, I've never had any editorial aspirations, but in this case I felt like snatching a pencil and crossing out one page after another."

With time Akhmatova came to distrust all writers' companions. "She looks like a divine apparition but she acts like the devil," Viacheslav Vs. Ivanov recalled Akhmatova saying in the 1960s about the female friend of a "talented poet."[98] Despite the differences in their social backgrounds and experience, Akhmatova made all writers' wives appear like faceless dummies. All these women, with their broad backs, big feet, and haggard faces, Akhmatova seemed to imply, faked their femininity by wearing wigs (like Zinaida Gippius), dyeing their hair (like L. Yu. Brik) and concealing their true age (like most women, including Irina Odoevtseva and Glebova-Sudeikina). In other words, they all wore masks to hide their true intentions, to appear less threatening, even vulnerable, and ready to be taken advantage of by gullible male literati.[99]

Although Akhmatova repeatedly criticized Lev Tolstoi for his unfair treatment of women in his novels, particularly for making Anna Karenina suffer for her adultery and for throwing her under the train,[100] in her own descriptions of women she drew heavily on Tolstoi's misogynistic masterpiece, *The Kreutzer Sonata* (*Kreitserova sonata,* 1889).[101] Her love-hate relationship with Tolstoi was typical of Akhmatova. She vehemently attacked only those writers whose works were particularly important for her own development.

The only writer's wife who escaped Akhmatova's lacerating scrutiny was Nadezhda Mandelstam. The precise nature of their relationship remains a mystery.[102] While Akhmatova was alive, Nadezhda Mandelstam acted as an obedient younger sister or a poor relative. "All she wanted was to die in her bed," Brodsky recorded in his obituary.

"And, in a way, she looked forward to dying, because 'up there I'll again be with Osip.' 'No,' replied Akhmatova, upon hearing this. 'You've got it all wrong. Up there it's now me who is going to be with Osip.'"[103]

A Family Romance

Akhmatova became interested in writers' companions in the mid-1920s, when she had difficulty writing poetry and busied herself with Pushkin studies and the preservation of Gumilev's memory. Akhmatova had married Nikolai Gumilev in 1910, and they were officially divorced in August 1918. By all accounts, it was not a very happy marriage. At the time of his imprisonment and execution in 1921, he was already married to Anna Engelgart (1895–1942), while Akhmatova continued living with her second husband, Vladimir Shileiko. Why Gumilev, then? Nancy Andersen suggests that Akhmatova accepted "the politically risky honor of being Gumilev's widow" out of her unparalleled loyalty to the dead. "At a time when many people were doing their best to reinvent themselves and to play down their connections with disgraced figures from the past, Akhmatova conspicuously made herself Gumilev's literary executor and the representative of his memory."[104] Although Akhmatova, indeed, did not "play down" her relationships with her persecuted or executed contemporaries, this did not necessarily stop her from "reinventing herself." Ironically, to become the celebrated keeper of cultural traditions, she had little choice but to reshape her past, including extramarital affairs.

Akhmatova's interest in Gumilev's life was rekindled by her friendship with her future biographer, Pavel Luknitskii (1900–1973). A budding poet and a devoted student of Gumilev, Luknitskii appeared on Akhmatova's doorstep in December 1924. As his recently published *Diary* reveals, he soon became her lover.[105] In her preface to this remarkable document (in which Luknitskii carefully enciphered all geographical and personal names, including that of Shileiko's dog), his widow (nearly thirty years his junior) suggests that Akhmatova manipulated the young and sensitive Luknitskii to promote her own image as that of an unquestionable authority on Gumilev's legacy and to develop a romantic friendship that was different from her increasingly complicated relationship with Punin. As his *Meetings with Akhmatova* (*Vstrechi s Annoi Akhmatovoi*) indicates, Luknitskii was completely smitten with Akhmatova. He cheerfully ran numerous errands for her and delighted her with his findings about Gumilev's personal life, not least with his predictably negative impressions of his brief affairs with Gumilev's former lovers. Akhmatova, apparently, encouraged Luknitskii's sexual exploits because they added authenticity to his scholarly accounts and spiced up their endless conversations. According to Vera Luknitskaia, Luknitskii fitted beautifully the role of an erotic mediator between the dead Gumilev and Akhmatova, giving her an opportunity to relive her disappointing relationship with Gumilev on terms very much her own:

> Being the kind of person she was, Akhmatova couldn't let anybody have Gumilev to himself or herself. That's why she drew in Luknitskii. The main thing was not to let go of Gumilev. A student—Akhmatova—Gumilev. A second rewarding life with Gumilev. Such an opportunity just couldn't be passed up. . . . Especially now, when the "Fountain House" was beginning to show what her new family life [with Punin] had in store for her—promising to be so hard, complex and exhausting. . . . And here—if only temporarily—a breathing space. And Gumilev.[106]

Whether, as Andersen implies, Luknitskii was employed by the secret police to submit reports on Akhmatova or simply fell prey to her feminine charms, their joint work on Gumilev's biography in the mid-1920s undoubtedly enhanced Akhmatova's awareness of the important role the female companions play in writers' lives both before and after their deaths.[107] I suggest that until she resumed her writing in the mid-1930s, Akhmatova resigned herself to her respectable position of Punin's companion and Gumilev's "estranged" widow.[108] Likewise, in her biographical studies of Pushkin she focused on his family happiness and on his fateful duel.[109] Pushkin, according to Akhmatova, longed to be loved and to start his own family yet feared that his marriage to Natalia Nikolaevna would be a disaster. In her Pushkinian projection, Gumilev (who fought a duel in 1909 and who was executed by firing squad in 1921) was equated with Pushkin, while Gumilev's second wife, Anna Engelgart (whom both Luknitskii and Akhmatova rated as mediocre and selfish) was conveniently cast in the role of the guilty Natalia Nikolaevna.[110] It seems that the key to Akhmatova's bitter confrontation with Punin in the late 1930s, which she repeatedly advertised for the sake of her eager chroniclers, may lie in her dramatic reconceptualization of her own position with regard to Punin in particular and to Russian literature in general. Whereas previously she had seen herself as a dependent of Punin, whom she willingly assisted with his research and preparation for lectures, beginning in the mid-1930s, she came to look upon herself as the more important figure in that union.[111] Once she had shed doubts about her own talent, Punin started to look more like one of those crude female companions that, as she herself demonstrated, were both a burden and a trademark of every true artistic genius. The beginning of this process can be traced to 1927, when in a letter to Punin in Japan, she explicitly compared herself to Pushkin and him to Natalia Nikolaevna: "I kiss the tips of your wings, as Voltaire used to tell [his friend, the count of] Argental, and as Pushkin [used to tell] Natalia Nikolaevna."[112]

Akhmatova's interest in Pushkin in the mid-1920s was stimulated by her desire to dissect his poetry by establishing the exact sources of his inspiration.[113] Akhmatova, according to Luknitskii, avoided talking about her own poetry and apparently was disturbed by her own silence, which made her keep an eye on other temporarily silent poets, such as Pasternak, Mandelstam, Nikolai Aseev, and Nikolai Tikhonov; at the same time, she looked up to already accomplished poets, such as Pushkin, Gumilev, and Innokentii Annenskii for guidance in finding a suitable niche for herself. She felt triumphant each time she managed to establish a subtle link between various poets, claiming that she was much happier since her thoughts had been completely absorbed by her new research. When Luknitskii suggested that she devote herself solely to writing Gumilev's biography and become its single author,

Akhmatova turned down the idea by pointing out that she would be embarrassed to discuss Gumilev's affairs in public. Instead, she promised to write an article "about all other poets that had an influence on him."

In fact, Akhmatova failed to keep Gumilev's private life and his relationships with his precursors and contemporaries apart. And this was totally to be expected, since most of the objects of his infatuation and fascination (most important, Akhmatova herself) were either poets in their own right, such as Yelizaveta Dmitrieva, Irina Odoevtseva, and Larisa Reisner, or people intimately related to the world of art and literature, such as the member of Kuzmin's circle, the artist Olga Arbenina-Gildenbrandt. This highly inbred literary world may have led Akhmatova to conceive of literary competition as a struggle within a small group of closely related people sharing some common space, similar to that of a communal apartment. This interpretive strategy, for example, allowed Akhmatova in 1940 to portray Erikh Gollerbakh—whose articles and recollections she found particularly objectionable in the 1920s—as guilty of "taking possession" both of his wife and of Akhmatova's personal letters. "'This is what he did,' said Anna Andreevna, 'he married the second wife of my late sister's husband. And got possession of [*ovladel*] my letters and my sister's diary.'"[114]

Unlike Bloom's theory of a "family romance" which, in fact, rejects kinship in favor of highly coveted discontinuity, Akhmatova's way of reconfiguring poets' relationships with one another was literally based on the idea of one extended, yet close-knit family, with every poetic influence being accounted for by marriage, friendship, sympathy, or extramarital affairs.[115]

When they quarreled about something trivial and in order to hurt Gumilev's feelings—Akhmatova admitted to her friend Natalia Roskina—she would tell him that she was by far a better poet than he.[116] Previously, when she was at the start of her career and Gumilev was already considered a mature poet, people often inquired about her husband's opinion of her poetry. Did he approve of it?[117] Blok, conversely, had a low opinion of Gumilev, to the point of berating

Akhmatova for his faults. "[I] was putting on [my] boots in some cloakroom," Akhmatova recalled, "while Blok stood behind me mumbling 'You know, I don't like your husband's poetry.'"[118] Akhmatova worked on an agreeable story of her relationship with Gumilev for forty years. "I believe we were engaged for too long," she confessed to Chukovskaia in 1940. "I was in Sebastopol, he was in Paris. When we got married in 1910, he had already lost his passion."[119] While in the 1920s and in the 1930s she had admitted that their relationship was tainted by their incompatibility and mutual infidelities, in the 1960s, the sole reason she gave for divorcing Gumilev was her alleged desire to break away from his gripping authority. Consequently, in 1965 she left the following instructions for the future biographers of Gumilev:

> I would advise you to rewrite Gumilev's messed-up biography *in a most detailed way* in order to show what he meant to young people already in the 1930s. It's surprising that the poet that influenced whole generations after his death didn't have the slightest influence on the young girl that was next to him and to whom he was attached by his enormous, tragic love for such a long time. (Come to think of it, perhaps, his love was the [main] reason). . . . That's a subject worth working on.[120]

In the 1960s Akhmatova praised herself for being present, even if only inadvertently, in the main body of Gumilev's poetry. He, on the contrary (according to her), left almost no trace in hers. Thus, in Akhmatova's versions of her past, with time, textual impenetrability substituted for unrequited love and erotic desires.

Akhmatova also insisted that her looks, talent, and personality did not fail to produce a profound effect on both Mandelstam and Pasternak, who—apart from Tsvetaeva—were arguably her two most important poetic rivals. In fact, Mandelstam, as she reminded Chukovskaia, was at some point in love with Tsvetaeva. Then "Osip tried to fall in love with me twice, but both times it seemed to me to be such an insult to our friendship that I immediately put a stop to it."[121] Pasternak "proposed to me three times," Akhmatova revealed to a surprised Chukovskaia after Pasternak's death. "But what use would he have been to me? . . . I was married to Punin at the time, though that didn't seem to matter to Boris. As for Marina [Tsvetaeva]," she continued thoughtfully, "they had an affair abroad."[122] Even with Annenskii, who died in 1909 and whom she honored as her "teacher" and a major source of influence, Akhmatova claimed to have had a more personal relationship, to the extent that he would have married her if given a chance. Akhmatova "knew him only slightly," one chronicler dutifully wrote describing her relationship with Annenskii in the 1960s. Annenskii "was the principal of a grammar school for boys, and Akhmatova was a student in a girls' school. . . . When a relative of his married Akhmatova's elder sister, Annenskii remarked, 'I would have chosen the younger one.'" Although Akhmatova was no doubt aware that her anecdote was redolent of the famous exchange between Pushkin's Lenskii and Onegin,[123] she, as her chronicler pointed out, valued every word in Annenskii's suggestive remark.[124]

Pushkin was not the only source of inspiration for Akhmatova. With time, her relationship with Gumilev started to look less like the relationship between Pushkin and his wife and more like that between Dante and Beatrice. "I made a long and frightening trip through Gumilev's poetry, both lighting my way and in complete darkness, with the assurance of a sleepwalker making his way along the very edge of something," Akhmatova recorded in her notebook on May 9, 1965.[125]

Akhmatova's Inferno

Akhmatova's strategies for controlling her anxieties were related to her work on the first, so-called Tashkent, version of *Poem Without a Hero*. Akhmatova wrote its longest part, "The Year 1913," in one sitting in Leningrad on December 27, 1940. As I have shown, the year 1940 was remarkable because she voraciously read (often reread) various works of her Russian predecessors and contemporaries and voiced her discontent not so much about the actual texts as about their authors' private lives. To understand why Akhmatova treated other writers in such a way, one might recall her interest in Dante's life and work that reached its peak in the late 1930s and particularly in 1940, when her friend Mikhail Lozinskii was working on a translation of *The Divine Comedy* and shared with Akhmatova his findings as well as his literary and historical sources. "The whole of last night she [was] reading Dante, comparing it to the literal French translation," Chukovskaia recorded in her *Notes* on September 17, 1940. Although Akhmatova had read Dante all her life, as she revealed to Chukovskaia, there was something special about this particular reading: "Italians think that all Italian poetry derives from the *Comedy*, which is true, of course. But the interesting thing is this: with Dante everything was domestic, almost familial."[126] She was referring to the first part of *The Divine Comedy* in which Virgil leads Dante through the nine circles of the Inferno.

What Akhmatova most likely meant by the "domestic, almost familial" quality of Dante's work is his evident compassion toward most of the sinners, who were all known to him because they were either his friends and contemporaries or easily recognizable literary and historical figures. Dante's intended audience was also expected to identify most of his characters, which may have created an impression similar to that of flipping through a family album. Dante's idea of presenting his illustrious contemporaries as repenting sinners must have appealed to Akhmatova and informed the initial stages of her work on the *Poem* as well as her general approach to presenting both men and women as embodiments of one specific vice or characteristic—as can be seen in her general treatment of other women as ugly creatures, in calling Kuzmin a "sodomite," or in references to Viacheslav Ivanov as a sorcerer and a traitor. As is well known, the sodomites and various types of traitors and seducers feature prominently in Dante's *Inferno*.

Like Dante's *Inferno*, the *Poem* is populated by famous people, but in Akhmatova's case these are the poets, actors, artists, and musicians who left an imprint on the turn-of-the-century Russian culture. In "The Year 1913" the elaborate structure of the Inferno is reduced to the space of a communal apartment, where the "author" is visited by the shadows from her past on the eve of 1941 and together with them relives the dramatic events that took place in Petersburg before WWI and the revolutions.[127] Although Dante's name is conspicuously missing from the elaborate network of the *Poem*'s literary allusions, his presence is nevertheless discernible. Each character wears a mask, which makes it easy to reduce him to a single role. More so, each character is associated with a certain sin, thereby assigning its bearer to a particular circle within Akhmatova's Dantean Inferno. Here are some of the most obvious parallels: Sudeikina-Columbine, like Dante's Francesca, embodies the vice of lust; Kniazev, the poet who committed suicide, represents violence against himself; Kuzmin-Ivanov-Cagliostro represents traitors, seducers, and sodomites. No wonder that Petersburg, where the action takes place, is described as a cursed place "where one can hear a rumble, a distant warning sound" of the imminent catastrophe. With time, the *Poem* grew in size, and "The Year 1913" became one of its larger parts. Despite her manifest compassion for most of her characters, the author, like Dante's pilgrim, moves on into contemporary Leningrad, leaving her friends and acquaintances behind in the year 1913. They are forever captives of that turbulent time.

5   The Winged Eavesdropper

KUZMIN AND NABOKOV

> To take a deep breath and up to the shoulders
> place my stretched arms in the *Wings,*
> [then] from the windowsill to slide into the air
> and fly despite [the laws] of science [. . .]
> I am afraid I'll not survive the flight . . .
> No, I've survived. I sit on the floor in darkness,
> I am dazzled, and there is a buzzing in my ears,
> and a blissful ache in my shoulders.
>
> —Vladimir Nabokov, 1929

In one of the episodes of the literary television broadcast *The School for Scandal* (*Shkola zlosloviia*, May 2005), the writer Sergei Gandlevskii suggested that Vladimir Nabokov was far better at keeping Russian cultural traditions alive than Akhmatova, who was only interested in herself. Although Gandlevskii did not substantiate his claim with any concrete examples, he was certainly right in one respect: Nabokov's position within the pantheon of Russian cultural custodians is indeed different from that of his older contemporaries. Unlike Anna Akhmatova (1889–1966) and Boris Pasternak (1890–1960), Vladimir Nabokov (1899–1977) did not write during the so-called Silver

Age. Because he started to write seriously only after his emigration to Europe following the Bolshevik Revolution and the civil war, he was often challenged to prove his worth as a Russian writer. According to Aleksandr Dolinin, "Nabokov's lack of [a pre-Soviet] literary past put him at a disadvantage as compared with the other former residents of Petersburg—Georgii Adamovich, Nina Berberova, Georgii Ivanov, or Irina Odoevtseva, whose high esteem among young emigre authors rested, in large part, on their semilegendary biographical regalia, such as having been acquainted with Innokentii Annenskii or Blok, or having been friends with Mandelstam, Gumilev, and other celebrities."[1]

In his autobiographical *Speak, Memory* (1966), Nabokov presents a sympathetic portrayal of his younger self, the author Sirin, whom he describes as "the loneliest and the most arrogant" Russian emigre, whose "work kept provoking an acute and rather morbid interest on the part of the critics."[2] As suggested by his numerous openly hostile attacks on various writers, including Dostoevskii, Nabokov was not as preoccupied with the ethical implications of denigrating the prematurely dead or persecuted Russian writers as Akhmatova was. However, as a perpetually rootless author, Nabokov became notoriously secretive about which works truly influenced him in the course of his career. Unlike Akhmatova and Pasternak, who inspired several volumes of memoirs, Nabokov succeeded in maintaining a reclusive life even during his later years, when he became an international celebrity. His literary texts, therefore, are the most reliable testaments to his intricate bonds with his predecessors and contemporaries. This chapter is about a turning point in Nabokov's literary career, which, I believe, coincided with his writing his lesser-known novel *The Eye* (*Sogliadatai*, 1930).[3]

In the late 1920s and early 1930s, although steadily turning into one of the most prominent Russian emigre writers (and definitely one of the most published), Nabokov was nevertheless subjected to severe criticism. Uncertain how to classify his works, critics labeled them poor imitations of French and German originals. Nabokov, who used the pseudonym "Sirin," rapidly gained the reputation of a trickster, seeking cheap success with his readers. Georgii Ivanov, whose review of "Sirin's" *Mary; King, Queen, Knave; The Defense;* and *The Return of Chorb* appeared in 1930 in the first issue of the Parisian journal *Chisla*, described these works as "trite, banal, not lacking in virtuosity, however," and lamented about "our wretched critics" and "undemanding reading public" who contributed to the success of the "Sirins" of this world.[4] Ivanov portrayed Nabokov as "an impostor" and an outcast who could not possibly belong to the great Russian tradition.[5] If in the earlier years of his career, suffering from the imposed loss of his motherland and the tragic death of his beloved father, Nabokov found refuge in writing patently imitative works of poetry,[6] in maturity he claimed decidedly unconventional sources of inspiration. Thus, in *The Gift (Dar*, 1938) Nabokov's alter ego, the writer Fedor Godunov-Cherdyntsev, insists on borrowing his "wings" of artistic inspiration "from conversations with [his] father, from daydreams in his absence, from the neighborhood of thousands of books full of drawings of animals, from the precious shimmer of the collections, from the maps [and] from all the heraldry of nature and the cabbalism of Latin names."[7] Notwithstanding these claims, one should not ignore another possible supplier of Nabokov's "wings," namely, the famous fin de siècle writer and poet Mikhail Kuzmin (1872–1936), whose novel *Wings (Kryl'ia*, 1906) was successfully appropriated by Nabokov in *The Eye*. I will show how various thematic blocks, collisions, and motivations for the actions of the characters in *Wings* were melted down by Nabokov into *The Eye*. Moreover, his literary "affair" with Kuzmin gave birth to Nabokov's archetypal character—an ambivalent, sexually inverted, emigre loner—whose strivings and misfortunes became the main focus of most of his subsequent works.

Why Kuzmin?

When Kuzmin's novel *Wings* appeared in the literary journal *Vesy* in 1906, it brought its author "instant fame and notoriety."[8] This was not fortuitous. Kuzmin not only failed to portray homosexuals as doomed and tragically misunderstood, as might have been expected, but also came up with a picture of a homoerotic paradise readily accessible to those who so desired it. Having gone through a number of trials, the young homosexual Vanya Smurov is gradually led to understand that there is nothing inherently unnatural or perverse in any activity: "What is important in every action is one's attitude toward it, its aim, and also the reasons behind it; actions in themselves are merely the mechanical movements of our bodies and cannot offend anyone, much less the Good Lord."[9] Smurov's maturation is presented as a spiritual journey, at whose end he comes to appreciate love and beauty.[10]

The publication of *Wings* became a significant event in the cultural life of Russia in the 1900s and gave rise to various debates and discussions. The impact of the novel on the reading public was equivalent to that of Chernyshevsky's *What Is to Be Done? (Chto delat'?* 1862).[11] Thus, upon his return to Russia from France, the artist Aleksandr Benua attributed the disturbing changes that he found in his friends—they were no longer concealing their homosexuality—primarily to the influence of "new young people" like Kuzmin.[12]

However, despite his popularity—often scandalous—Kuzmin was largely misunderstood by his contemporaries; because of the deceptive "lightness" (or as Vladimir Markov puts it, "non-vodkalike quality") of his poetry and works of prose, he was often assessed as a second-rate author whose works belong to the literary salons.[13] For many of his readers, Kuzmin became the symbol of "art for art's sake"—an unrewarding position within a literary tradition whose main virtue has been seen as that of educating and guiding its readers rather than entertaining and amusing them. Interestingly, the husks of these accusations were articulated twenty years later by the very same Georgii Ivanov who criticized Nabokov in his pseudoautobiographical *Petersburg Winters* (*Peterburgskie zimy*). This collection of "feuilletons" was published in Paris in 1928, and it is very likely that Nabokov was familiar with it. Kuzmin is presented as a lightweight author whose talent came in handy when the "progressive" reading public got weary after the outburst of Russian symbolism and demanded simplicity. Ivanov's Kuzmin is more concerned with his wardrobe than with what to write or how to write; he writes effortlessly and mindlessly and sends off his works to the publisher immediately—"why bother rewriting them—my handwriting is impeccable," he confides to Ivanov.[14]

As noted earlier, Ivanov's critique of Kuzmin was part of a larger campaign against the prerevolutionary cultural legacy and everything it stood for that was launched by Vladislav Khodasevich and was carried on by the younger literati such as Yurii Terapiano and Nikolai Otsup. If Khodasevich in "The End of Renata" ("Konets Renaty," 1928) attested soberly to the ultimate failure of the symbolist "life-creating" project, then Otsup, Terapiano, and their group were much more aggressive in advocating simplicity and truthfulness both in life and in art.[15] In such an austere environment, one openly hostile to any artistic activity that was not pursuing identifiable ideological purposes, the "lightweight" Kuzmin (with his legendary inability and unwillingness to adhere to any particular school or movement) should have appeared a perfect father figure to a seemingly fatherless and rootless aesthete like Nabokov. There was also a family connection in Nabokov's latent identification with the author of the first Russian novel about homosexuals. In the early 1900s Nabokov's father, Vladimir Dmitrievich, a recognized authority on criminal law, argued on many occasions for the decriminalization of homosexuals, maintaining (not unlike Kuzmin) "that homosexuality was neither inherently abnormal nor morally reprehensible."[16]

Nabokov and Kuzmin were first paired by Andrew Field and later by Gennadii Shmakov, Vladimir Markov, and Olga Skonechnaia.[17] The similarities perceived between these two authors are, however, very general in nature. Kuzmin and Nabokov are matched either because of their mutual disregard for the didactic, ideological function of literature or because of common stylistic innovations. Nabokov himself never made any open statements of his attitude toward Kuzmin's oeuvre. Kuzmin's name is not listed in the indexes of books written by or about Nabokov. The links between Nabokov and Kuzmin are, however, much closer than would appear at first sight.

John Barnstead has exposed a complicated system of references to Kuzmin's various works in Nabokov's short story "Lips to Lips" ("Usta k ustam," 1929, 1931). In a footnote he also mentions that the name of Kuzmin's protagonist in *Wings*, Vanya Smurov, reappears in Nabokov's *The Eye* but is split between two characters: Smurov, the protagonist, and the girl he loves, who bears the nickname Vanya.[18] In fact, the surname of Kuzmin's protagonist comes from Dostoevskii's *The Brothers Karamazov* (*Brat'ia Karamazovy*, 1881): Smurov is a little left-handed boy befriended by Alyosha.[19] His first name is never revealed to the reader, so the combination "Vanya Smurov" is unmistakably Kuzminian. Nabokov cunningly preserves references to both literary sources: his Smurov is described by one of the characters as a "sexual lefty" (*seksual'nyi levsha*).[20]

Allusions to Kuzmin in *The Eye* can be discerned, but they are camouflaged, which probably explains why Kuzmin's name is rarely mentioned in connection with this novel. In giving the name Vanya to the object of Smurov's unrequited love, Nabokov provides it with etymological explanations. The girl is reported to be nicknamed Vanya as a result of her demanding "to be called 'Mona Vanna' (after the heroine of some play or other)."[21] Another allusion that is intentionally left open to different interpretations may be observed when Smurov's mistress, Matilda, invites him home to borrow a book entitled *Arianne, Jeune Fille Russe* (*O kakoi-to russkoi devitse Ariadne*) (15). Barton Johnson identifies this work as a novel written by Jean Schopfer, but it "does not seem to have thematic implications for *The Eye* as a whole."[22] The pairing of Matilda and Ariadne, however, brings to mind Kuzmin's *The Gentle Knight* (*Tikhii strazh*), written in 1915 and reprinted by the publishing house Petropolis in 1924.[23] In this work, the longing of a dying Matilda Petrovna for her son is mockingly compared to the suffering of the mythological Ariadne deserted by Theseus.[24] Each of the three opening paragraphs of *The Gentle Knight* starts with the name Matilda, which is rare to a Russian ear. This section tells of Matilda's burdensome love for her son. Nabokov evokes the general mood of Kuzmin's original in the following passage that appears near the beginning of *The Eye*: "Matilda, who would inquire coyly if I wrote poetry; Matilda, who on the stairs or at the door would artfully incite me to kiss her, only for the opportunity to give a sham shiver and passionately whisper, 'You insane boy . . . '; Matilda, of course, did not count."[25]

Nabokov's depiction of the relationship linking Smurov, Matilda, and her husband Kashmarin (which frames the "main" story) also sets *The Eye* in an unmistakably Kuzminian context. Here is the gist of what happens. Having learned of Matilda's infidelity, Kashmarin loses control and beats Smurov up. Humiliated, Smurov attempts suicide. Kashmarin, however, finds out that Smurov was not his wife's first—or even her last—lover, divorces her, and puts his energy into looking for his former rival. Not only does he succeed in locating Smurov, he also offers him his guidance and protection, with the possibility of future trips to Italy. Smurov accepts Kashmarin's proposal with gratitude. A similar situation is described by Kuzmin in his novel *Travelers by Land and Sea* (*Plavaiushchie-puteshestvuiushchie*, 1915), in which the two former rivals for the attention of a woman finally see through to her "shallowness" and develop a special relationship between themselves.[26] In Kuzmin's fictional world a conventional love triangle (two men competing for one woman) is turned upside down, and it is usually a man and a woman who both fancy one man.[27] Similar love triangles are outlined in *Wings*. Vanya has to compete for Stroop's attention first with the "absolutely revolting" Nata, and then with the more sophisticated Ida Goldberg.

One of the striking things about *The Eye* is the photographic quality of its fictional world. Either the characters are shown as if posing for the taking of a picture or they are perceived by the narrator as static photographic images. In *The Eye* the world of the photograph takes precedence over "real" life. It is not the photograph that reflects everyday life but vice versa. For example, Smurov breaks into Vanya's apartment in order to see whether she still cherished the picture that shows them together. He begins to suspect that his love is unrequited not because common sense tells him so but because he finds himself missing from that picture—Vanya has carefully cut him out. Incidentally, Georgii Ivanov remarked in 1928 that Kuzmin's "treacherous 'beautiful clarity' [prekrasnaia iasnost'] was responsible for imparting a lifeless-photographic quality to the meaningless 'jabber' of his uninteresting characters."[28]

As this brief analysis shows, the Kuzminian subtext in Nabokov's *The Eye*, although obscured, is nevertheless recoverable. Although Nabokov was most likely unaware of this, the title of his novel—*Sogliadatai* (translated by Nabokov himself as *The Eye*)—comes from Kuzmin's vocabulary. In May 1906—a few months prior to the publication of *Wings*—Kuzmin wrote in his diary about one of the soirees at Viacheslav Ivanov's: "I suddenly felt weary of not loving anyone here (not really being in love) and, most important, of nobody loving me, and of my being a sort of unwanted eavesdropper [*chto ia kakoi-to lishnii sogliadatai*]."[29] Nabokov's Smurov combines the distinctive characteristics of both writers. Like Nabokov he is a Russian emigre and works as a tutor for a Russian family in Berlin. Like Kuzmin he presents an effeminate appearance; "his frailness, his decadence, his mincing gestures, his fondness for eau de cologne, and, in particular, those furtive, passionate glances" that he allegedly directs at men, convince one of the characters that Smurov is a homosexual (85).

Both Kuzmin and Nabokov contributed—not without the help of others—to the creation of the myth about their doppelganger personalities.[30] Kuzmin, for instance, claimed that his "I" comprised three different personae.[31] With Nabokov's Smurov the myth of the elusive soul reaches its apogee; there are as many different Smurovs as there are different people that come into contact with him. Each of the passers-by goes away with his own unique image of Smurov. Nabokov's bildungsroman tells about Smurov's learning to cope with his scattered personality.

The Bildungsroman

Like *Wings*, *The Eye* also belongs to the genre of the bildungsroman.[32] A typical bildungsroman recounts the story of the moral development of an initially unsophisticated protagonist, often an orphan, who eventually finds his place in life. Following the literary pattern, each Smurov unexpectedly finds himself in an unknown, even hostile, environment. The mother of Vanya Smurov in *Wings* dies suddenly, and he is looked after first by his dull relatives from St. Petersburg, next by some Old Believers, then by a teacher of Greek, and finally he is left under the protection and guidance of the Russified Englishman, Stroop. Nabokov's Smurov not only loses all of his relatives but also is forced to emigrate, must live among indifferent Germans, and is in touch with equally detached and suspicious compatriots.

Kuzmin's bildungsroman was written in the heyday of the symbolist movement and was informed by the conception, popular among Russian symbolists, that the ultimate goal of enlightened men and women should be not procreation but continuous striving toward spiritual rebirth or resurrection. In this context, homoerotic love (which denies procreation) was seen as an effective vehicle for accelerating this rebirth.[33] In agreement with this theory, Vanya's advancement in life is shown metaphorically as the development of a fetus within the mother's womb. The novel opens with Vanya traveling from the provinces to St. Petersburg in a train car with "misted windows" and concludes with his famous opening of the window in Canon Mori's house. The open window shows the reader that Vanya is reborn as a "completely transformed being" who accepts the role of Stroop's companion and beloved one. Throughout much of the book, however, Vanya sits snugly in rooms with windows closed or even moves into a dark cellar with the Old Believers. This apparently stems from Vanya's unwillingness to part company with the comfortable protection of the womb; the second birth—admission of his homosexuality—is not all roses.

At the beginning of the story, Nabokov's Smurov also feels the need to return and hide himself in a well-sheltered space. Having been severely beaten by Kashmarin, Smurov decides to take his own life. He delays his decision, however, and resolves "for five minutes at least, to sit in safety" and goes "to his former address" *(tuda, gde zhil ran'she)* (25). Smurov's desire to return to the place where he had lived previously, together with the description of "the familiar room" cluttered with various vessels that the landlady keeps filling up with water for no particular reason, is suggestive of his craving to reenter his mother's womb.

Nabokov's Smurov commits suicide in the outer darkness, and the last thing he remembers is "a delightful vibrating sound." He describes the event in terms reminiscent of the breaking of uterine water: "It was immediately replaced by the warble of water, a throaty gushing noise. I inhaled, and choked on liquidity; everything within me and around me was aflow and astir" (28). Subsequent mention of Smurov's "incomprehensible sensation of tight bandages" and the fact that he finds himself surrounded by neighbors ("mummies like [himself]") brings to mind not only "the semblance of a hospital" but, more precisely, a maternity ward (29). Nabokov, however, stages the "resurrection" of his Smurov in the first chapter, and not the last, as might be expected. By doing this, he strips this act of its symbolic and philosophical implications. The second birth is presented not as a desired culmination, the outcome of the character's moral revival, but only as a motivation of the plot.

The Platonic Theme

As Donald Gillis shows, Kuzmin's discourse on homoerotic love echoes the second speech of Socrates in Plato's *Phaedrus* about the relationship between the lover and his beloved.[34] For the sake of simplification, Socrates describes the soul of the lover as a charioteer in charge of two horses.[35] One horse is beautiful and always obedient: "it is a lover of honor. . . . It needs no whip but is driven simply by a word or command." The other—the epitome of lust—is therefore "crooked in conformation . . . deaf and barely responds to a combination of whip and goad." When the lover first sees the beloved, he is overcome with lust and the charioteer has a difficult task taming his obstinate horse. Gradually, however, the lover learns to rid himself of his unbecoming, base emotions, and his efforts are amply rewarded. The lover is allowed to take "care of all his darling's needs and treats him like an equal of gods . . . and the darling himself naturally becomes a friend to the one who cares for him."

Socrates speaks mainly about the actions of the lover, who first starts growing wings himself as a result of contemplating the beauty of his darling and then returns "the stream of beauty" to the beloved one, thereby helping his soul to regain its wings too.[36] In *Wings* Kuzmin chooses to elaborate on the story of the beloved, which is only briefly outlined by Socrates. In Socrates' speech, we learn that the beloved was initially convinced by his friends that it is shameful to be associated with his lover.[37] Similarly, Vanya Smurov also has to see through all the "false" accusations against Stroop (for instance, Stroop's alleged responsibility for Ida Goldberg's suicide), "and as time goes along destiny and increasing maturing lead him to accept" Stroop as his lover.

The relationship between Smurov and Kashmarin in Nabokov's story has all of the necessary Platonic ingredients. Kashmarin is at first described as "savagely jealous" and as a likely owner of rolling eyes who "gnash[es] his teeth and breath[es] heavily through the nose" (16). His portrait evokes the description of Plato's "bad" horse with its "bloodshot eyes." (Nabokov wittily describes Matilda's obsessive references to her husband's jealousy as her "hobbyhorse"). Smurov's only recollection of their first encounter was Kashmarin's "heavy bright-knobbed cane with which he would tap on the floor" (14). When they meet for the second time, Kashmarin allows his emotions to overtake him; he refuses to shake hands with Smurov and beats him up instead. Kashmarin's repeated thrusting of a "thick black cane" at Smurov in the presence of the two boys eagerly condoning his violence is suggestive of a gang rape with the stick as a phallic instrument: "There he was, teeth bared, cane upraised, and behind him, on either side of the door, stood the boys" (23).

In the last scene, however, we are introduced to a totally different Kashmarin. Not only has he parted company with his gruesome stick, but he humbly begs Smurov for his forgiveness: "I'm trying to apologize for my vile temper. I couldn't live at peace with myself after our—uh—heated discussion. I felt horrible about it" (101). Encouraged by the silent approval of Smurov, who blushes like a schoolgirl, hiding his face in a bunch of flowers, Kashmarin invites Smurov to see him the next day at the Hotel Monopole to discuss their future arrangements.[38] This episode is almost an exact replica of a similar scene between Stroop and Vanya in the concluding portion of *Wings*. The "lovers" express their gratitude to their "beloved ones" in almost identical words: "I am so grateful that you agreed to come," Stroop says (107); Kashmarin exclaims, "I'm so glad, so very glad I ran into you" (102). Both Stroop and Kashmarin urge their "beloved ones" to give them the definite answers by the next afternoon and morning, respectively; and while Stroop and Vanya are already living in Italy—a Mecca for Russian homosexuals—Kashmarin reassures Smurov that "trips to the Riviera and to Italy are not to be ruled out" (102).

Kashmarin, despite all evidence of his spiritual growth, is however nothing but a parody of a genuine platonic lover like Stroop. He appears briefly only at the very beginning and the very end of the novel and, in Smurov's words, is important only as a bearer of "yet another image" of himself (102). One-third of the way through *The Eye*, however, we learn from the narrator that he is seriously engaged in spying on Smurov. He sits back in the same room as Smurov and eyes him shamelessly. Smurov produces a strong and lasting impression on the narrator:

> He was not very tall, but well proportioned and dapper. His plain black suit and black bow tie seemed to intimate, in a reserved way, some secret mourning. His pale, thin face was youthful, but the perceptive observer could distinguish in it the traces of sorrow and experience. His manners were excellent. A quiet, somewhat melancholy smile lingered on his lips. He spoke little, but everything he said was intelligent and appropriate, and his infrequent jokes, while too subtle to arouse roars of laughter, seemed to unlock a concealed door in the conversation, letting in an unexpected freshness. (40)

The enchanted narrator resolves to continue spying on Smurov, and his eyes tell him that Smurov was "obviously a person who, behind his unpretentiousness and quietness, concealed a fiery spirit" (43).

The statements of the "observing" narrator betray at first that he is not totally indifferent to Smurov—"I definitely liked him" (44)—then, that he becomes addicted to his "espionage" to the point of admitting that he has been experiencing "an excitement new [to him]" (59). The narrator creeps behind Smurov like a shadow. He peeps at him in the bookstore, "I see him . . . behind the counter in his neat black suit, hair combed smooth, with his clean-cut, pale face" (49); then he listens to Smurov's breathtaking adventures in the Crimea. Even after learning of Smurov's deficiencies—Smurov is a proven liar—he cannot stop regarding him with affection.

The bizarre behavior of Nabokov's narrator is explicable in the light of the same theory that informed the behavior of Kuzmin's characters, that is, Plato's theory of love. Contemplation of any form of beauty—particularly that of a beloved one—is an essential means of achieving immortality in Plato's myth of the winged soul, "for sight is the keenest of the sensations coming to us through the body."[39] At the sight of his beloved, the lover

> is awestruck, as though he were gazing upon a god. . . . He is warmed by the effluence of beauty he receives through his eyes, which naturally moistens the wing-feathers. As he grows warmer, the follicles, which had earlier hardened and closed so that the feathers could not sprout are softened; and as the nourishing moisture flows over them, the shafts of the feathers swell and begin to grow from their roots over the entire form of the soul, which was feathered all over before. . . . The soul of the one who is beginning to sprout feathers itches and is irritated and excited as it grows its wings.[40]

It does not take too long for the reader to realize that Smurov and the narrator are, in fact, one and the same person.

Smurov-Narcissus

The narrator's love for Smurov is called narcissism. As Irina Paperno has shown, the story of the Greek fair-headed youth Narcissus, who fell in love with his own reflection, was popular with Kuzmin.[41] At the beginning of *Wings* Vanya's behavior is clearly reminiscent of that of

Narcissus. Twice he is shown absorbed in examining his own reflection in the looking-glass, and each time it coincides with someone's mentioning the name of his future lover, Stroop, who at this point remains a complete stranger to Vanya. Later, with the development of their mutual attachment and attraction to each other, he stops looking in the actual mirror and relies on Stroop to provide him with the needed reflection, for, in Plato's words, the beloved "is seeing himself in his lover as in a mirror."[42] Psychoanalysts would describe Vanya's narcissism as "primary," typical of any child's normal development.[43] When Vanya matures, his feeling of self-sufficiency gives way to the growing need for another male person—Stroop. As we are told, Stroop "values [Vanya's] heart's noblest aspirations, [and] will never deny [him] his understanding and affection" (74).

With Nabokov's protagonist, the situation is totally different. Being a penniless and friendless Russian emigrant in Berlin, he lives under constant stress. He lacks confidence and is lonely. He looks in the mirror once, but the sight of a "wretched, shivering, vulgar little man in a bowler hat" is repulsive to him (26). The little man commits suicide, giving birth to the mysterious Smurov and his shadowy admirer. Not being adequately loved, Smurov goes through yet further fragmentation. The fact that the name of Kuzmin's character, Vanya Smurov, is broken down by Nabokov into two names—that of an attractive girl, Vanya, and Smurov-the-narrator—can be seen as a typical instance of Nabokov's playing games with his readers. On the other hand, it can be viewed as the ultimate proof of Smurov's self-fragmentation. In the long run, it is not the reader who is deluded, but Smurov himself, who—because of the missing or misleading mirrors—remains unaware of his outlines, confusing Vanya with his missing half. At the end of the story, however, both men are happily reunited: "As I pushed the door, I noticed the reflection in the side mirror: a young man in a bowler carrying a bouquet, hurried towards me. That reflection and I merged into one. I walked out into the street" (97).

Only his falling in love with himself finally makes Smurov invulnerable to the threats of the outside world: "What does it matter that I am a bit cheap, a bit foul, and that no one appreciates all the remarkable things about me—my fantasy, my erudition, my literary gift. . . . I am happy that I can gaze at myself." Thus he conveniently readjusts Plato to his own needs (103).

It is no accident that Nabokov's bildungsroman about Narcissus's quest for identity was fashioned after Kuzmin's *Wings*, the story about the moral development of a homosexual. What Nabokov's "emigrant" and Kuzmin's "homosexual" have in common is their isolated position with regard to the rest of society.[44] In many ways, Nabokov's Smurov is the same Vanya Smurov from *Wings*, but placed in the context of an emigrant. While Kuzmin's Smurov gradually comes to grips with his estrangement from society by reaching out to similarly oriented people; in order to survive in extreme conditions (like being uprooted and living in a foreign country), Nabokov's Smurov directs his love totally toward himself. If for Kuzmin's Smurov narcissism is only an intermediate stage in his growing up, then for Nabokov's Smurov it is the only state that allows him to sustain his integrity and survive. Smurov's behavior is in agreement with Freud's observation that a person's "narcissistic attitude" increases his or her resilience and diminishes "susceptibility to influence."[45]

Narcissism—love of oneself—is in many ways similar to homoerotic love, because in both situations the lover and the beloved are of the same gender. In his seminal study "On Narcissism" (1914) Freud suggested that narcissism often accompanies what he terms "other disorders," like homosexuality.[46] Freud was not alone in this assumption. In the 1910s and 1920s a number of scholars (Lowenfeld, Rank, and Sadger, among others) believed in a direct correlation between homosexuality and narcissism. Sadger, for example, described homosexuality as "the narcissistic perversion *par excellence*."[47] It is unlikely that Nabokov could have been unaware of these discussions. It is noteworthy that in discussing narcissistic traits scholars drew their conclusions both from their work with actual patients and from analyses of literary texts.[48] Science and literature were going hand in hand in their construction of the twentieth-century myth of Narcissus.[49] It will suffice to mention that in *The Eye* Nabokov explored the traumatic effects of emigration on the mental state of a young person—which he knew only too well himself—long before the famous revelations of Heinz Kohut, who showed that any "external shifts, such as moves from one culture to another; from private life into the army; from the small town to the big city" are traumatic to one's ego and serve as a precondition for a growing need of exaggerated love for oneself.[50]

As my findings show, *The Eye* is in many ways a product of Nabokov's transferal of Kuzmin's *Wings* into the cultural environment of the late 1920s and early 1930s. Both authors were exploring a similar theme—alienation—but in different contexts: the context of Russia at the turn of the century for Kuzmin, and the context of emigration for Nabokov. By creatively appropriating one of the important cultural texts of the preceding tradition, Nabokov was able not only "to write back" to its opponents but also to rid himself of imitative features, unavoidable at the stage of apprenticeship, and glide smoothly into a more gratifying craftsmanship. *The Eye* is a perfect example of what Thomas Greene terms "heuristic imitation": "Heuristic imitations come to us advertising their derivation from the subtexts they carry with them, but having done that, they proceed to *distance themselves* from the subtexts and force us to recognize the poetic distance traversed."[51] Hence, Nabokov's discourse on alienation was informed not only by the prerevolutionary cultural legacy (via Kuzmin), but also by the contemporary discourse on narcissism as a scientific phenomenon and by his own experience as an emigrant. The result of such amalgamation was a literary character who later became the hallmark of Nabokov's fiction.

Smurov is the first lonely "sexual lefty" among Nabokov's numerous "perverted" characters. The happy homosexual couple from *Mary* (*Mashen'ka*, 1926) is an exception rather than the rule. Latent or evident perversion of any kind in Nabokov's characters—such as Sebastian Knight, Charles Kinbote, Humbert Humbert, to name but a few—appears to be a product of their social isolation, and not the other way around. For certain, in *The Eye*, Smurov's narcissism and alleged homosexuality are unequivocally presented as a direct consequence of his enforced emigration and alienation. Suffering from finding himself in the unrewarding position of a rootless Russian emigrant in a hostile Berlin, Smurov does not feel himself at home in the company of his compatriots. His pupils openly dislike and despise him. The owner of the bookshop, Weinstock, seriously believes that Smurov is a Soviet spy, while Vanya's family strive to expose him as a liar or a petty thief. It is only after having been irrevocably rejected by Vanya that Smurov throws himself under Kashmarin's protection. Latent homosexuality therefore becomes for Nabokov an additional marker of the emigre-outsider, signaling his exceptional position vis-à-vis an unfriendly environment.

It is usually assumed that Nabokov intended to portray Smurov as a failure, both as an artist and as a human being.[52] I disagree. By carefully piecing himself together, Smurov-Narcissus attains a degree of integrity and peace within himself that is favorable to creativity. Smurov, as a character at any rate, did not fall into oblivion. He came back to life in the happily self-centered Fedor Konstantinovich Godunov-Cherdyntsev of *The Gift* (unlike the "nameless" Smurov, this character is given not only a name but also a patronymic and a double-barreled surname), who, by the end of the book, is a picture of real happiness and confidence: "It is easier for me, of course, than for another to live outside Russia, because I know for certain that I shall return—first because I took away the keys to her, and secondly because, no matter when, in a hundred, two hundred years—I shall live there in my books—or at least in some researcher's footnote."[53] Apart from the fact that both narratives are recounted by the interchanging Ich/Er-narrators, the protagonists in both novels are young Russian emigre writers and both novels also take place in the Berlin of the mid-1920s. The mysterious Marianna Nikolaevna from *The Eye* reappears in *The Gift* as Marianna Nikolaevna, Zina's mother. Fedor's latent homoerotic attachment to Koncheev—the scene of the naked Fedor meeting with the dressed up "Koncheev" with a stick in the Grunewald (part 5) is particularly suggestive—is usually overlooked by the critics. Fedor's lonely sunbathing in the Grunewald may have been informed by similar scenes of Michel's suntanning from André Gide's novel *L'Immoraliste* (1902). In this novel Michel resorts to naked sunbathing in a secluded spot (leaving his devoted wife at home) as a means of recovery from tuberculosis, the disease that (according to Susan Sontag) was only an outward manifestation of his inner suppression of homosexual desires.[54] It is not fortuitous that Nabokov's Sebastian Knight (*The Real Life of Sebastian Knight*, 1941) also suffered from a mysterious disease that eventually drove him away from his girlfriend, Clare Bishop. Gide's groundbreaking work was well known to Kuzmin and apparently also to Nabokov.

In Kuzmin's Shadow

The question of whether *The Eye* was intended as a parody of Kuzmin's *Wings* is a tricky one. Even if it had been meant as such, Nabokov's contemporaries certainly failed to recognize its "target text," and Nabokov did not assist them in this endeavor.[55] Unlike Akhmatova, who couched her poetic rivalry with Kuzmin in expressing her discontent with Kuzmin's personal life, Nabokov chose complete silence regarding his relationship with this particular predecessor. It would seem, however, that Nabokov took a long time to rid himself of Kuzmin's influence.

Kuzmin's presence can be detected not only in *The Eye* and in *The Gift*, but also in the strangely homoerotic poem "How I Love You" ("Kak ia liubliu tebia," 1934), which bears a striking resemblance to corresponding portions of Kuzmin's long poem *The Trout Breaking through the Ice* (1929). "Kuzmin" can be also recognized in Konstantin Ivanovich Chateau (*Pnin*, 1953), "a subtle and charming scholar . . . [with] mild melancholy caribou eyes, the auburn goatee . . . [and] long frail fingers" whose article Pnin forwards to his Akhmatova-like future wife in the 1920s. In his article Chateau (not unlike Kuzmin in *Wings* and Nabokov in *The Eye*) "brilliantly refutes . . . [the] theory of birth being an act of suicide on the part of the infant."[56]

Maybe it was only in *Pale Fire* (1962), whose main theme is apparently what Bloom terms "the anxiety of literary influence," that Nabokov managed to shed Kuzmin's influence and any other influence, for that matter. In this later parodic rewriting of *The Eye*, Charles Kinbote fails spectacularly in his endeavor to influence and enliven the artistic imagination of his illustrious neighbor, the poet John Shade, in spite his frenzied activity involving incessant discussions, eyeing, spying, and eavesdropping. Not only does he not see any trace of his personal story in Shade's last poem (the only word that resonates throughout the work is "shade"), but even his perceived physical resemblance to Shade is completely bogus. Shade looks not like Kinbote but like Judge Goldsmith, a resemblance that costs him his life in the end. Shortly before the tragic accident, Kinbote—not unlike Kuzmin's lyrical hero from *The Trout Breaking through the Ice*—rescues his "dearest friend" Shade from the influence of his "mediocre" wife by inviting him to his house to recite his completed poem. Like Kuzmin's protagonist, he literally leads Shade (whose feet are numb) to his house. Not surprisingly, he brings him death, instead of life.

6 The Silver Age in Translation

BORIS PASTERNAK'S *DOCTOR ZHIVAGO*

> There is a sense in which Akhmatova and her contemporaries Gumilev and Marina Tsvetaeva are the last great voices of the nineteenth century—perhaps Pasternak occupies an interspace between two centuries.
>
> —Isaiah Berlin, "Conversations with Akhmatova and Pasternak"

Unlike Nabokov, Andrei Bely, Konstantin Fedin, Maxim Gorky, Aleksei Tolstoi, and many others, Pasternak failed in the 1920s and 1930s to produce the major prose work that he longed to do or to transport his intellectual characters (with a few exceptions, such as those of "Aerial Ways" and "Malady Sublime") across the watershed of World War I or the Bolshevik Revolution. This is not to say that Pasternak really did not want to write about contemporary issues. He did, but his big prose work, which he kept announcing in his letters to friends and colleagues, for a long time had remained nothing but a handful of disjointed fragments till he finally embarked on writing *Doctor Zhivago* in 1945.[1] By confining the time frame of his fictional work to pre-Bolshevik Russia, Pasternak apparently sought to avoid highlighting and testing prerevolutionary aesthetic and moral ideals against the new postrevolutionary background. In his autobiographical *Safe Conduct (Okhrannaia gramota*, 1931), Pasternak similarly shunned any serious revisions of the legacy of his predecessors, claiming that all along he desired to repeat their findings—albeit "more swiftly, heatedly and wholly"—rather than supplant or depose them:

> It was the youthful art of Scriabin, of Blok, Komissarzhevskaia and Bely, enthralling, advanced and original. And it was so striking that not only did it evoke no thoughts of its own replacement. On the contrary, to increase its durability one felt like repeating it from the very foundation, only more swiftly, heatedly and wholly. One wanted to retell it all again in a single burst—and that was unthinkable without passion. But passion leapt to one side, and this way something new was created. Only the new did not come to replace the old, according to the usual idea. Quite the contrary, it arose from a rapturous reproduction of its model.[2]

Although in this excerpt Pasternak reports the feelings that he allegedly experienced in the 1910s, his mere recollection of them reinstates their relevance to his outlook in the 1930s. In the 1950s, Pasternak once again reclaimed his aversion to innovation by hinting that the search for new means of expression and the death of the searcher were bound by a cause-and-effect relationship: "People who died early, such as Andrei Bely, Khlebnikov, and some others, prior to their death immersed themselves in a search for new means of expression and in a dream of a new language, groping for its syllables, vowels, and consonants. I never understood those searches."[3]

Symptomatically, Pasternak endowed his favorite artistic figures and his later character Yurii Zhivago with a similar reluctance to oust their predecessors and impress their audience with an innovatory style or techniques. Thus, the work of Chopin, according to Pasternak, was "original throughout not because of its being different from the work of his rivals, but because of its kinship with nature," which Chopin strove to emulate in his music.[4] Similarly, we are told that Yurii Zhivago in the 1920s aspired "to achieve an unnoticeable style" that would free him from the reputation of a trickster and jarring innovator and would "enable the reader or hearer to master the content without noticing the means by which it reached him."[5] As is well known, Nabokov was infuriated when Pasternak was awarded the Nobel Prize for Literature in 1958, criticizing *Doctor Zhivago* for its melodramatic quality, stylistic backwardness, and even Sovietophilia. However, Nabokov might have been pleased to see the picture of Pasternak in the *Big Soviet Encyclopedia* (1975) squeezed between that of Louis Pasteur (1822–1895), the famous French biologist and physician, and that of Enrique Pastorino (b. 1918), leader of the Uruguayan Communist Party and recipient of the Lenin Prize for Strengthening Peace Between Nations. Ironically, the photograph captures Pasternak's precarious position as an intermediary between prerevolutionary and postrevolutionary cultures, which might have accounted for his unremitting reluctance or inability to reevaluate Russia's cultural past.

It was only in the 1950s, when the Silver Age started to wedge its way back into Russian culture, that Pasternak found it possible to criticize its representatives. For instance, when asked in 1958 which of his fellow writers managed to weather nicely the 1920s, Pasternak (at that time himself the author of a full-length novel) spoke negatively about Andrei Bely, whom he accused of being always "too hermetic and too limited." He told an interviewer, "Everything he wrote may be compared with chamber music—and that's his limit. If he had really suffered, he could have written a great book—he was capable of that. But he had never come into conflict with real life."[6]

Apart from political and moral pressures, the belated or protracted nature of Pasternak's rebellion against his predecessors is explicable also in the light of his personal relationship with his father, a recognized artist in the realist vein, Leonid Osipovich Pasternak (1862–1945). Despite the many kilometers separating them after 1921, the authoritarian figure of Leonid Pasternak remained a looming presence in his son's life. Even at the age of fifty-one Boris Pasternak still claimed to feel crushed on measuring his achievements against those of his father.[7] This overwhelming feeling of self-doubt and insignificance seemed to subside immediately after Leonid Pasternak's death in May 1945.

In 1945 Pasternak suddenly felt the urge, and, more important, the ability, to write his major work of prose, which grew into the novel *Doctor Zhivago* (1945–1955):

> I'm frantically writing a lengthy narrative in prose, which covers the years of our life, from Musaget to the last war; it's the world of *Self-Conduct* again minus the philosophizing, it's in the form of a novel, but it's wider and more mysterious, it's filled with events and dramas, and it's closer to the essential things, to the world of Blok and to my own poems to Marina [Tsvetaeva].[8]

As this excerpt reveals, particularly pertinent to Pasternak's newly acquired attitude toward the past was his involvement in preparations for the 1946 jubilee to commemorate the twenty-fifth anniversary of Aleksandr Blok's death. To enhance public understanding and appreciation of Blok's legacy, a new two-volume edition of his writings was scheduled to appear in 1946–1947. As a member of the editorial board, Pasternak had occasion to examine Blok's texts closely and was asked to write an article on the poet, for which he immediately started gathering material, mainly by slowly redigesting the Berlin Alkonost edition of Blok's writings (1923). The article, however, was never finished and no part of it was published in Pasternak's lifetime. As he explained at a public gathering in the spring of 1947, he abandoned the project in favor of working on *Doctor Zhivago:* "In the summer, I was asked to write something on the occasion of Blok's anniversary. I wanted to write an article about Blok very much, but then I thought to myself that I was writing the kind of novel that was already a substitute for an article about Blok."[9] Furthermore, in 1953 when his work on *Doctor Zhivago* was half-finished, Pasternak, whose main source of income at the time was his translations from English and German, rationalized it as yet another exercise in translating the prerevolutionary epoch into the modern language of the late 1940s and early 1950s, rather than as innovation or even a continuation of the Blokian tradition.

> Everything has changed since that time. Even the language that was used at the time is gone. So it is no wonder that, having abandoned many things, risky passages, extremes, and the distinguishing features of the arts of that time, I'm trying to provide a present-day translation, in the language used today, which is more ordinary, mundane and serene, of at least a small part of that world, of at least its most precious things.[10]

Pasternak's humility notwithstanding, his project was indeed innovative. To appreciate the novelty of Pasternak's approach to the appropriation of the prerevolutionary cultural legacy, one needs to recall similar undertakings by his immediate predecessors and contemporaries, including those of Sergei Diaghilev and the World of Art Movement, of Mikhail Kuzmin, Valerii Briusov, Dmitrii Merezhkovskii, Andrei Bely, Maxim Gorky, Aleksei Tolstoi, Konstantin Fedin, and Sergei Eisenstein.

On the Border of Two Centuries

The aesthetic principles of mediating between different cultural situations were worked out by Merezhkovskii in his *The Eternal Companions* (*Vechnye sputniki*, 1888–1897). In this collection of essays, Merezhkovskii found features of decadent aesthetics in the writings of such diverse people as Goethe, Calderon, Flaubert, Pliny the Younger, Marcus Aurelius, Ibsen, Euripides, Turgenev, Maikov, Pushkin, and Dostoevskii, which allowed him to inaugurate them all as the forerunners of the emerging literary trends in Russia of the 1880s and 1890s. By promoting such diverse cultural figures to the status of his readers' "eternal companions," Merezhkovskii not only made their writings more accessible to his contemporaries but also gave them license to interpret the works of the great writers of the past in accordance with their personal needs and the needs of any given historical and cultural situation: "What makes great people great is the fact that time does not destroy but renews them: each new age gives them a new body and a new soul in its own image, as it were . . . , because every age and every generation calls for an explanation of the great writers of the past in their *own light*, in their *own spirit*, and from their own perspectives."[11] Konstantin Fedin's own *Eternal Companions* (*Vechnye sputniki*, 1937–1953), in which he invited his fellow writers to follow Gogol's lead with regard to his vivid descriptions of the "enemy [of the people]," were apparently modeled after Merezhkovskii's work of the same title:

> Gogol! The eternal companion of an adolescent, a young man, a mature man, and a mature woman, a school pupil who has just learned to read and write, as well as an old man who has gained wisdom having lived his life. . . . The wonderful genius of Gogol transcends time, extends a helping hand to contemporary writers, and calls on them to master the high art of depicting the enemy in all his guises—the way he called on the great writers of Russian classical literature.[12]

In a similar vein, Maxim Gorky in *The Life of Klim Samgin* (*Zhizn' Klima Samgina*, 1925–1936), Fedin in *Early Joys* (*Pervye radosti*, 1944–1946) and in *No Ordinary Summer* (*Neobyknovennoe leto*, 1948), and Aleksei Tolstoi in *Road to Calvary* (*Khozhdenie po mukam*, 1919–1943) reinterpreted the cultural life of prerevolutionary Russia from the vantage point of the 1920s, 1930s, and 1940s by plunging their intellectual protagonists into the heart of revolutionary activity. In doing so, these writers joined the ranks of Soviet compradors, in Katerina Clark's apt definition:

> By comprador I mean that special institution that emerged in the era of European economic domination in Asia. The comprador was the non-European who mediated between the local people and the European commercial enclave. He spoke two languages, the vernacular (his own language) and that of the particular European community he served. Originally, he spoke the European language only haltingly. Over time, he became increasingly fluent in it. By the 1930s, the typical Soviet intellectual had become a comprador in that his task

was to mediate between the language of high culture, which he spoke "natively," and that of his masters, the language of ideology and power. At first, he might speak the latter imperfectly, but in time the successful comprador passed more and more for a member of the elite group. He could enjoy many of its privileges (cream cakes), but only as long as his linguistic skills proved useful.[13]

Not every mediator was seduced by Soviet cream cakes or not by them alone. The generally acknowledged gap between pre- and postrevolutionary cultures encouraged intellectuals to plug this gap if not with their own bodies, then with the body of their artistic work. Thus in November 1927 Pasternak expressed his admiration for a recent installment of Gorky's *The Life of Klim Samgin,* which he read both as a manifestation of the existing cultural divide and of Gorky's unique ability to bridge it with his writing. "It is strange to realize," Pasternak confessed to Gorky, "that the period you describe needs excavation as if it were some kind of Atlantis. This realization is strange not only because most of us still have a clear recollection of that period but especially because at one time it was portrayed directly from life by you yourself and other like-minded writers as everyday reality," he concluded. "The upshot is that the period becomes all the more virginal and unexplored in its new, present-day state as the forgotten and lost foundation of the present-day world or, in other words, as the prerevolutionary prologue penned by a revolutionary writer *[kak dorevoliutsionnyi prolog pod revoliutsionnym perom]*."[14] By 1928, a number of politicians, artists, and linguists on numerous occasions were suggesting that young people of the late 1920s were virtually unable to understand the language of prerevolutionary intellectuals.[15] The active vocabulary of Russian speakers was on the one hand significantly depleted because various words were no longer recalled in everyday situations, since the notions and objects that they denoted had become obsolete; on the other hand, the language was continuously enriching itself with new words denoting the new realia unknown to older generations. The generation gap, the need for translation from one language into the other, as well as the relativity of any experience—including cultural experience—was immediately recognized by some representatives of the prerevolutionary cultural tradition such as the writer Andrei Bely (1880–1934).

In his succession of postrevolutionary memoirs (1922–1934), Bely attempted to justify his contemporaries in the eyes of Soviet readers by portraying them either as alleged Marxists or as romantic rebels who, as such, contributed to the advent of the Bolshevik Revolution.[16] Andrei Bely's project of depicting intellectual life in Russia some thirty years before the revolution was a truly evolving one. It was conceived in 1921–1922 as a monograph devoted solely to the life of the recently deceased Aleksandr Blok (*Recollections of Blok* [*Vospominaniia o Bloke*], 1922–1923), but the work quickly outgrew the genre restrictions of hagiography that Bely initially imposed on himself. By 1934 it had grown to three volumes, each corresponding roughly to a period of less than ten years: *On the Border of Two Centuries* (*Na rubezhe vekov*, 1930), *The Beginning of the Century* (*Nachalo veka*, 1933), and *Between Two Revolutions* (*Mezhdu dvukh revoliutsii*, 1934). "Bely may have caricatured his contemporaries," Lazar Fleishman wrote in the 1980s, "but at least a later generation could learn of their existence. In this perspective, Bely's memoirs stand a unique witness to the symbolist era in Russian cultural history."[17] In his drive to explain his own life and that of his generation for the modern reader, however, Bely fell into the trap of filling a position midway between the Soviet establishment and intellectuals who came of age at the dawn of the twentieth century. Hence, in his memoirs Bely looked back at his past through the eyes of his supposedly young, morally and physically fit readers, and from their perspective he suddenly saw that his illustrious peers were seemingly "brought up in such traditions that stink, in an antihygienic environment, without physical culture, normal leisure, or joyful songs and camaraderie, and never stood a chance of devoting [themselves] to what healthy natural instincts drew [them] toward." He concluded, "They all started [their] lives half crippled." He even identified himself with his potential readers in stating that what he was depicting in his memoirs was "neither close to *us*, nor contemporaneous."[18]

Despite his considerable concessions to the tastes of various readers, Bely failed to meet their expectations. On the one hand, his detailed subjective descriptions of a variety of cultural figures and literary movements remained foreign to the average reader, while on the other hand, many intellectuals were appalled by his cavalier treatment of the earlier cultural tradition. Similarly, Vladimir Maiakovskii's willingness in the 1920s to tune his poetic voice to the ears of his less sophisticated contemporaries provoked outbursts of displeasure among some critics. "Maiakovskii gave the mob what it wanted," Vladislav Khodasevich observed after Maiakovskii's death in 1930. "He hauled the treasures accumulated by human thought out into the marketplace, where the exquisite was debased, the complex was simplified, the subtle was coarsened, the profound was made shallow, and the lofty was lowered and trampled into the mud."[19] As someone who was at various stages close to both Bely and Maiakovskii, Pasternak was well aware of the pitfalls awaiting any cultural mediator. This emerged in these comments written in the 1950s:

> The 1920s brought widespread falsity and transformed vibrant creativity into mechanical skills and schemes. The period was destructive and depersonalizing for me, but even more so for Maiakovskii. It was also bad for Yesenin. This was the time when Andrei Bely, for instance, deluded himself into thinking that he would remain an artist and save his art provided he preserved the distinctive features of his technique, even as he wrote things contrary to what he thought.[20]

As Pasternak's earlier letters reveal, he was equally unimpressed by the undertakings of Aleksei Tolstoi and Sergei Eisenstein, who exerted themselves in portraying Peter the Great and Ivan the Terrible as tragically misunderstood precursors of Stalin.[21]

Like his contemporaries, Pasternak recognized the gaping chasm between prerevolutionary and postrevolutionary cultures and endeavored to bridge it by his own up-to-date "translation." Like Bely, too, Pasternak chose the life and art of Aleksandr Blok as a pivot for this project. Even one of the provisional titles for *Doctor Zhivago* (*On the*

Border [*Na rubezhe*]) is reminiscent of Bely's memoirs, *On the Border of Two Centuries* (*Na rubezhe vekov*). Nevertheless, in his "translation" Pasternak chose not to follow in Bely's wake, and his strategies of appropriating the past were essentially different from those of Bely. This was only to be expected, given the difference in their ages and the fact that Pasternak, unlike Bely, lived into the 1940s and the 1950s. I submit that unlike numerous contemporaries, who in their effort to preserve the past saw a need to "modernize" it, Pasternak chose the opposite procedure. The story of the Silver Age poet Yurii Zhivago is presented not as an initial blueprint for the story of a future builder of communist society, but as a projection of events that took place over the previous nineteen hundred years, including the biblical story of Jesus Christ, the legend of Faust, and the tragedy of Hamlet. Instead of bringing his story of an artist closer to contemporary events, Pasternak related it to the events of the past where, in his view, it had originated.

Blok in Translation

In the novel that, according to Pasternak himself, was inspired by Blok's personal life and art, his named presence was reduced to a bare minimum, however. We are told that "young people in both capitals were mad about Blok" (80); Yurii Zhivago is described as having promised Gordon an article about Blok for his journal (which he would never write); and later, shortly before his death, he recalls Blok's writings. But there are no more detailed mentions than these, and in fact Yurii is the only literary figure portrayed in the novel. Apparently, Pasternak was particularly dependent on Blok in the initial stages of his work: it was originally conceived as the story of Innokentii Dudorov, the unfortunate son of a revolutionary terrorist and a Caucasian princess. A similar character is briefly outlined in Blok's "Confession of a Heathen" ("Ispoved' iazychnika," 1918), in which this character dies in a boating accident. Although a few sentences from Blok's story grew into a whole section in part 1 of *Doctor Zhivago*, as work progressed Dudorov ceased to be the main character and was only occasionally highlighted, mainly in negative contrast to the protagonist. Pasternak's composite image of Zhivago-cum-Blok-cum-Christ-cum-Faust-cum-Hamlet may have been related to Bely's earlier memoirs of Blok (1922), in which he constantly drew parallels between Blok and other universal literary characters, such as Hamlet, Faust, and Christ.[22]

When Pasternak insisted that *Doctor Zhivago* was written in lieu of an article about Blok, he was telling the truth. One fails to see Pasternak's indebtedness to Blok immediately because of Pasternak's "backward-oriented" strategy that, I believe, he developed with regard to the legacy of his immediate predecessors. This backward-oriented translation is particularly noticeable in his treatment of Blok's early poetry when integrating it into his novel.[23] The following passages from Blok's poetry of 1902 and from *Doctor Zhivago* suggest a reverse relationship between Blok's verse and Pasternak's later prose, in that Pasternak's text does not seem to be derived from Blok as would be expected, but that Pasternak inspired Blok's poetry. Pasternak seems to restore the situation that initially prompted Blok's otherwise obscure poems of the fall of 1902, providing a context from which they might have been derived and thus clarifying their meaning for contemporary readers. The passage from *Doctor Zhivago* tells about Yura's first encounter with Lara and Komarovskii, when Lara's mother attempts to take her own life and Yura's guardian, a doctor, is summoned to render medical assistance. He takes young Yura along with him.

First, the work of Aleksandr Blok from 1902 (for original text of these selections, please see the appendix):

> He appeared at a stately ball
> In a glitteringly intimate circle.
> Lights flickered ominously,
> And his gaze described an arc.
>
> All night they whirled in a bustling dance,
> All night along the walls their circle narrowed.
> And at dawn—in the window's glare
> His silent friend appeared.

He stands now, lifting his owl-like gaze,
And watches—intent, alone—
The place where a jingling Harlequin
Has dashed after a pale Columbine.

While there, in the corner, beneath the icons,
In the motley bustling of the crowd,
Rolling his childlike eyes,
Trembles a disheartened Pierrot.
October 7, 1902[24]

❊ ❊ ❊

They made merry in the yellow light,
All night along the walls their circle narrowed.
The rows of dancers doubled,
And I seemed to see my relentless friend.

Desire lifted the ladies' bosoms,
Sweltering heat showed in their faces.
I made my way, fantasizing about a miracle,
Tormented by others' lust . . .
September 1902[25]

❊ ❊ ❊

. . . Yellow flames would flicker,
Along with electric candles.
And he would join her in the shadows,
While I watched and sang their encounters.

If they were suddenly alarmed
By a premonition of something,
The blank, dark gates would keep me
Hidden in their recesses.

> And I, unseen by anyone,
> Would follow the man's graceless profile,
> Her silver and black fur,
> And their whispering lips.
> *September, 1902*[26]

Boris Pasternak writes in *Doctor Zhivago* (for the original text of this selection, please see the appendix):

> It was not Tyshkevich who came out from behind the screen, but a thickset, portly, self-confident man. Carrying the lamp above his head, he went over to the table and replaced it in its bracket. The light woke up the girl. She smiled at him, squinting her eyes and stretching. . . . Meanwhile a silent scene took place between the girl and the man. Not a word passed their lips, only their eyes met. But the understanding between them had a terrifying quality of magic, as if he were the master of a puppet show and she were a puppet obedient to his every gesture.
>
> A tired smile puckered her eyes and loosened her lips, but in answer to his sneering glance she gave him a sly wink of complicity. Both of them were pleased that it had all ended well—their secret was safe and Madame Guishar's attempted suicide had failed.
>
> Yura devoured them with his eyes. Unseen in the half darkness, he kept staring into the circle of lamplight. The scene between the captive girl and her master was both ineffably mysterious and shamelessly frank. His heart was torn by contradictory feelings of a strength he had never experienced before.
>
> Here was the very thing which he, Tonia, and Misha had endlessly discussed as "vulgar," the force that so frightened and attracted them and which they controlled so easily from a safe distance by words. And now here it was, this force, in front of Yura's very eyes, utterly real, and yet troubled and haunting, pitilessly destructive, and complaining and calling for help—and what had become of their childish philosophy and what was Yura to do now? (64)

As these texts suggest, Blok's early poems and Pasternak's mature prose are related.[27] In the drafts for his unfinished article on Blok, Pasternak copied these lines: "They made merry in the yellow light, / All night along the walls their circle narrowed" *("Pri zholtom svete veselilis', / Vsiu noch' u sten szhimalsia krug")* and remarked that their theme was echoed in a number of Blok's poems from the same cycle.[28] In *Doctor Zhivago* Pasternak on the one hand preserves the aura of mystery shrouding Blok's youthful poetry, and on the other makes it comprehensible to his own contemporaries.

The fact that even Blok's mature poetry (not to mention his earlier work) could benefit from some updating was apparent even to devoted readers of Blok such as Lidiia Ginzburg, who as early as 1932 stated in a diary entry that Blok already seemed out of date. "The other day I read Blok (volumes 2 and 3)," Ginzburg recorded in her diary. "I opened the book with mistrust, cautiously, the way you open an old diary. It turned out that his poetry still affected me, and rather forcefully. Only it gets across the way Appolon Grigor'ev's poetry does—it has a distinct flavor of Blok's style and historical period."[29] Symptomatically, in 1928 some peasants with whom the educator Adrian Toporov discussed Blok's poem "As Soon as the Velvety Blackness of the Sky Begins to Twinkle" ("Lish' zaiskritsia barkhat nebesnyi") found the poem difficult to follow because the poet allegedly failed to spell out what "he" thought and felt, and what the woman "he" longed for thought, and why "they" had so much "trouble." Among their responses were the following:

> "Even the girl's face he didn't depict properly. This poem is frozen. Fet's 'Whisper' ['Shepot'] is different. There's love and nature in it." . . .
>
> "In general the poem makes one happy, but it expresses no thought. What the man suffered is never described."
>
> "It seems 'he' never came up 'to her' and talked 'with her.' It's not shown in the poem like it should have been." . . .
>
> "It's a tad incompletely described."[30]

In the same collection Toporov published an account of how certain sophisticated peasants reacted to Pasternak's long poem *Spektorsky* (1924–1930). They were ultimately unable to stomach more than the eight opening lines because they were so appalled by their fuzziness and incomprehensibility.[31] Some of their comments follow:

> "There ain't nothin' clear in it. There ain't no sense in nothin'. The whole verse is like a shorn hen—somethin' awful. He better not write such stuff. The book is done soiled by these verses. What the author wanted to say I didn't get."
>
> "The words are Russian, understandable, but they have no substance in them."
>
> "There ain't no coherent words." . . .
>
> "I'm simply in a frenzy. I cannot get a grip on myself. I'm so deranged with irritation that I could strangle the author with my bare hands right now."[32]

As Evgenii Dobrenko demonstrates, it was readers like Toporov's peasants who were ultimately responsible for the shaping of the canon of socialist realism. Their opinion was crucial in determining which literary works were worth publishing and which should be taken out of circulation.[33] From the late 1920s on, Pasternak was very much aware of his failure to write easily accessible literary works—a "shortcoming" which, as his numerous letters show, he increasingly tried to rectify in the 1930s and 1940s.[34] In 1947 he confessed to Vsevolod Ivanov that "accessibility" *(dokhodchivost')* was one of the key qualities he pursued in *Doctor Zhivago* and that he hoped the work would be read "in one gulp by anyone" *(vzakhleb liubym chelovekom).*[35]

Hence, what Blok left intentionally oblique and elusive received a form of "substantiation" in Pasternak's *Doctor Zhivago*. For instance, the ball scenes (the mysterious background of Blok's poetry of autumn 1902), apart from the above-quoted scene at the Chernogoriia Hotel, were further developed by Pasternak in the subsequent Christmas party episode at the Sventitskiis' house. At this party Lara attempts to murder Komarovskii, and Yurii observes the two of them from a distance, having previously been denied admission to their magic "circle."[36] If for Blok a "circle" *(krug)* usually meant a circle of light mysteriously separating the observer from the objects of his "espionage," Pasternak managed to preserve and explore its various connotations. Thus, the chapter where Yurii first sets eyes on Lara is called "A Girl from a Different World/Circle" ("Devochka iz drugogo kruga"). The first implication of this title, fully supported by the narrative, is that Lara comes from a middle-class, petit bourgeois background that is different both from Yurii's upper class and Pasha Antipov's proletarian world. Still, as we find out, Yurii's (and Pasha's) problems in his relationship with Lara eventually arise not from their social differences but from her inability to break out of Komarovskii's "enchanted circle" of magical sexual powers.

A very revealing instance of how Blok's poetry was digested and assimilated by Pasternak's prose comes in the scenes that show Yurii Zhivago at the funeral service for Tonia's mother, Anna Ivanovna. The "source" text for the following episode I believe to be the two poems written by the young Blok on the occasion of his grandfather's death in July 1902 (for the original text of these selections, please see the appendix):[37]

"ON THE DEATH OF GRANDFATHER"

Together we waited for death to come, or sleep.
Anguishing moments came and went.
Suddenly a breeze blew from the window,
And a leaf fluttered in the Holy Book. . . .

But it was sweet to catch sight of the soul
And to spy its cheer as it departed.
The hour had come for us to remember and to love,
And to celebrate a different housewarming

July 1, 1902

❊ ❊ ❊

Don't be afraid to die in your travels.
Don't be afraid of either enmity or friendship.
To cross the borders of fear,
Listen to the words of a church service.

She will descend to you unbidden.
No longer will you beckon the laughing sunrise
In mortal bondage,
In aspect poor and docile.

She and you are a single law,
A single dictate of the Supreme Will.
You are not eternally doomed
To desperate and mortal agony.

July 5, 1902

Boris Pasternak writes in *Doctor Zhivago* (for the original text of this selection, please see the appendix):

> Sorrow, standing for many hours on end, lack of sleep, the deep-toned singing and the dazzling candles by night and day as well as the cold he had caught, filled Yura's soul with a sweet confusion, a fever of grief and ecstasy.
>
> When his mother had died ten years earlier, he had been a child. He could still remember how he had cried, grief-stricken and terrified. In those days he had not been primarily concerned with himself. He could hardly even realize that such a being as Yura existed on its own or had any value or interest. What mattered then was everything outside and around him. From every side the external world pressed in on him, dense, indisputable, tangible as a forest. And the reason he had been so shaken by his mother's death was that, at her side, he had lost himself in the forest, suddenly to find her gone and himself alone in it. . . .
>
> Now it was quite different. In his twelve years at gymnasium and university, Yura had studied the classics and Scripture, legends and

poets, history and natural science, which had become to him the chronicles of his house, his family tree. Now he was afraid of nothing, neither of life nor of death; everything in the world, all the things in it were words in his vocabulary. He felt he was on an equal footing with the universe. And he was affected by the services for Anna Ivanovna differently than he had been by the services for his mother. Then he had prayed in confusion, fear, and pain. Now he listened to the services as if they were a message addressed to him and concerning him directly. He listened intently to the words, expecting them, like any other words, to have a clear meaning. There was no religiosity in his reverence for the supreme powers of heaven and earth, which he worshipped as his progenitors. (86–87)

Pasternak's text is clearly far more "complete" and exhaustive than Blok's. The poet's lines, "But it was sweet to catch sight of the soul / And to spy its cheer as it departed," are not only "recycled," but also fully motivated in Pasternak's "derivative" text. The sensations of sweet merriment and peacefulness that overcome Yurii during the funeral are first meticulously explained by his state of delirium resulting from influenza and a general state of exhaustion; then they are accounted for by his education and a recently acquired philosophical outlook, whose formation the reader is allowed to follow. Hence, just as Blok "prescribed," Yurii manages to negotiate the barriers raised by his fear of death and to heed the actual message of the funeral service.

Pasternak's treatment of Blokian texts is not so much a process of adaptation and simplification as a studious effort to recreate the situation that gave rise to this or that poetic impulse and by doing this to gain understanding of Blok's poetic work and to help others understand it.[38] One should not underestimate Pasternak's own appreciation of the innovative nature of his project. When in the early and mid-forties Pasternak devoted much of his creative efforts to translation, he insisted that his translations (mainly of Shakespeare) should be considered as original works in their own right. His translation of *Hamlet*, Pasternak insisted, "must be accepted as an original Russian drama because, besides its accurate rendering of the original text, its having the same number of lines as the original, and other things, it is an ultimate expression of conscious freedom without which no approximation to great things is possible."[39] It is also well known that for most of his later life Pasternak felt drawn toward prose writing and was perpetually dissatisfied with his poetic achievements. As he explained to Varlaam Shalamov in 1954, poetry by definition could not stand on its own. It had to be accompanied by works of prose to achieve its fullest comprehension and recognition:

> Why is it important for a poet to write prose? The poet Pushkin is perceived together with his prose; he is appreciated against the background of his prose. Poetry cannot express everything. Lermontov's poems are understood and experienced in a more subtle, or rather, better way if you keep in mind his prose. Prose itself is material for a better understanding of poetry. By contrast, Verlaine, who didn't write prose, can only be fully appreciated in the context of the contemporary French paintings.[40]

Therefore, Blok, who wrote little prose fiction, might have appeared to need a novel or a long story to his credit.[41] One might indeed suggest that *Doctor Zhivago*—particularly the passages discussed above—was precisely the prose work that Blok never wrote himself but probably (according to Pasternak) should have written to ensure that his legacy would be preserved for posterity.

The Silver Age in Translation

Blok's legacy was not the only one "translated" in Pasternak's novel, however. For example, his detailed description of the shopkeeper Olga Galuzina (who is introduced for no apparent reason and later disappears without trace) may account not only for Blok's but also for the painter Boris Kustodiev's mysterious predilection for the color lilac.[42] Kustodiev (1878–1927) was famous for his portraits of the wives of merchants and shopkeepers, whom he dressed up in strikingly rich lilac clothing against a lilac background. So if anybody in the 1950s wondered about the reason for all this lilac color, Pasternak gave a plain explanation:

> There, in the middle of the row of shops, was Galuzina's large grocery store with its three windows. Its bare, splintery floor was swept morning, noon and night with used tea leaves; Galuzin and his assistants drank tea all day long. And here Galuzina, as a young married woman, had often and willingly sat behind the cash desk. Her favorite color was a violet-mauve, the color of church vestments on certain solemn days, the color of lilac in bud, the color of her best velvet dress and of her set of crystal goblets. It was the color of happiness and of her memories, and Russia, too, in her virginity before the revolution, seemed to her to have been the color of lilac. She had enjoyed sitting behind the cash desk because the violet dusk in the shop, fragrant with starch, sugar, and purple blackcurrant sweets in glass jars, had matched her favorite color. (281)

Although Galuzina subsequently vanishes from the narrative, her image, like that of Blok's Eternal Feminine, proves a guiding light for her dim-witted son Terentii, saving him miraculously from almost certain death.

A thrifty "translator," Pasternak transports his watermelon to the Chernogoriia Hotel from an equally dismal hotel in Anton Chekhov's "The Lady with the Lapdog" ("Dama s sobachkoi," 1899). In this story the aging Lovelace Gurov seduces an unhappy and vulnerable young woman, Anna Sergeevna, in her hotel room. When the lovemaking is over, Anna Sergeevna feels crushed by the new experience, while Gurov finds the whole situation awkward and a bit boring. Instead of talking his partner out of her gloomy mood, he starts eating a watermelon. These nuances in the characters' contrasting moods and behavior are conveyed in a few laconic sentences. In *Doctor Zhivago* not only does the watermelon grow in size, but the text devoted to its consumption also increases in length.

> In their hotel room [Lara] was staggered at the sight of a watermelon of incredible size. It was Komarovskii's housewarming gift and seemed to her to be a symbol of his power and wealth. When he thrust a knife into this marvel and the dark green globe split in half, revealing its icy, sugary heart, she caught her breath in alarm, but she dared not refuse a slice; her nervousness made the fragrant pink mouthfuls stick in her throat but she forced herself to swallow them.
>
> Just as she was intimidated by expensive food and by the night life of the capital, so she was later intimidated by Komarovskii himself—this was the real explanation of everything. (92)

Although it is Lara who eats the watermelon while Komarovskii is portrayed as the owner of a ferocious bulldog, the pattern of her (submissive) and his (dominant) behavior in this episode is recognizably Chekhovian. The sensual description of the cutting of a watermelon (first a deflowering and then forced oral sex) prefigures Lara's future relationship with Komarovskii. Pasternak, however, left no chance for feminists to treat themselves to his watermelon scene (as has often been the case with Chekhov). He not only produced a far more impressive account of the dangers harbored by a juicy watermelon, but also forestalled any attempt to savor this scene at his expense by exposing Komarovskii as a blatantly pompous and uncaring male (in case the reader has not grasped this already) who uses his power to exploit and dominate fragile and often naive women.

On a broader scale, Pasternak's novel about the fate of an artist at a time of political and cultural uncertainty and upheaval seems partly indebted to one of the key texts from the Silver Age, namely, Dmitrii Merezhkovskii's novel *The Romance of Leonardo da Vinci* (*Leonardo da Vinchi*, 1901). Both Leonardo and Yurii are portrayed not only as free-spirited intellectuals consumed by a lofty passion for art, but above all as human beings who often have to resort to rather menial jobs in order to provide for their near and dear ones. Both are extremely lonely figures, although surrounded by occasional and even devoted disciples. Most of Leonardo's major scientific discoveries remain unappreciated by his contemporaries, and many of his works of art (like some of Yurii's) are lost in war, fire, flood, or some other natural disaster. Both characters move from one geographic location to another, opting to stay out of politics, but when they must have it, they do not shun financial support and protection from powerful benefactors. They also both lack willpower and lose their lovers either through death or some unidentified cause, and in any case they both prefer to immortalize them in art rather than take care of their actual needs. As is often the case with Lara, Mona Lisa is isolated from her lover by the "charmed circle *[zakoldovannyi krug]* which separate[s] contemplation from life." Leonardo is tempted to go over this barrier, but each time he suppresses his desire. He rationalizes his behavior by insisting that unlike the real-life Mona Lisa, her "spectral image upon the canvas—an image he had evoked—would become still more imbued with life, still more actual."[43] Merezhkovskii's memorable description of Leonardo's ultimate failure to bridge the gap between life and contemplation may have informed Blok's early poetry and Pasternak's novel.

Closer to the end of the novel, in book 15, "The Most Holy Inquisition," Merezhkovskii tells briefly of Leonardo studying anatomy in Milan in association with a certain Marc Antonio, "one of the first savants of Europe."[44] This Marc Antonio "had consecrated himself to the service of science when scarcely a youth. . . . Neither the games of childhood, nor the passions of youth diverted him from this strict service. He had come to love a maiden; but, deciding that it was impossible to serve two masters—love and science—had given up his bride and definitely forsaken the world. Even in his childhood he had impaired his health with excessive studies."[45] In many ways, the character of Marc Antonio reads like a blueprint for a chain of similar characters in Pasternak's narrative verse and prose, culminating in the character of Pavel Antipov.

Like Zhivago and Antipov-Strel'nikov (and to a certain extent, Gordon and Dudorov), Leonardo and Marc Antonio are antipodes. If Leonardo "at the outposts of knowledge . . . sensed a mystery, which, throughout all the manifestations of the universe, drew him to it," Marc Antonio only

> feared it. The learning of Leonardo was directed toward God, the learning of Marc Antonio was directed against God, and his lost faith he was fain to supplant with a new [faith]—a faith in the reason of man. ... The one was only a scholar, the other both a scholar and an artist. Leonardo knew and loved—and his love deepened his knowledge. His drawings were so exact, and at the same time so beautiful, that it was difficult to decide where art ended and science began; the one entered into the other, blending together into one indivisible whole.[46]

Like Antipov-Strel'nikov, Marc Antonio is zealously fanatical. "Leonardo felt that [Marc Antonio], were he to be given power, would send men to be burned at the stake in the name of reason, even as his enemies the monks and the churchmen burned them in the name of God."[47] No wonder that the tale of Marc Antonio serves as an introduction to the deeds of the "Most Holy Inquisition."

What Merezhkovskii sketched out only briefly develops into one of the major themes in *Doctor Zhivago*—the conflict between a true artist, highly sensitive to all mysteries of nature, and a rigid proponent of a single scientific or political doctrine. However, although Antipov-Strel'nikov is endowed with Marc Antonio's fanaticism and an all-consuming devotion to his course, his behavior is also fully motivated and well grounded in the circumstances of his life. Pasternak furnishes him with a believable, if elaborate, metamorphic chain: giggling Patulia is transformed into the serious and diligent student Pavel, then into Lara's hypochondriac husband Antipov, and finally into the grim revolutionary Antipov-Strel'nikov.

Here I cannot discuss Pasternak's treatment of his other precursors in *Doctor Zhivago*. Even my brief references to Blok, Chekhov, and Merezhkovskii do not do justice to the wealth of intertextual parallels, transformations, and shifts uncovered by many Pasternak scholars over the last fifty years.[48] In fact, Pasternak could have said about his own magnum opus what Nabokov said about *The Gift*: "Its heroine is not Zina [Lara in Pasternak's case], but Russian literature." I simply point to some general tendencies in Pasternak's treatment of the works of his immediate predecessors.

The Poet Is Dead. Long Live the Poet!

As I have demonstrated, in *Doctor Zhivago* Pasternak painstakingly translates the prerevolutionary esoteric legacy by reconstructing the initial context, restoring missing links, and filling in gaps. However, the names of Blok, Kustodiev, Merezhkovskii, Chekhov, and other cultural figures of the period are not explicitly mentioned at the moment of such translation. Pasternak's method of transposition was different from Fedorovian literal resurrection: consequently, he did not resurrect Blok's protagonists or Blok himself to make them participate in modern life. As Yurii explains to the dying Anna Ivanovna: "Resurrection—In the crude form in which it is preached for the consolation of the weak, the idea doesn't appeal to me. I have always understood Christ's words about the living and the dead in a different sense" (70).

Furthermore, by not writing his article on Blok in 1946 (although he had the material for it), Pasternak in effect declined the role of official interpreter of his writings for the Soviet reader, that is, he refused to function as a comprador. Nor did he allow his character Yurii Zhivago to become one. The problem of refusing or accepting an official stance assumed crucial proportions for Yurii when he was employed by his half-brother Evgraf, a representative of the Soviet system, to write poetry in more comfortable surroundings. Zhivago not only accepts this invitation but even prepares himself for work in a government institution.

Further episodes in the novel, which show Zhivago living as a recluse so that nothing should distract him from writing good poetry, are in fact highly reminiscent of similar passages in a novel by Pasternak's close friend, Vsevolod Ivanov, *Taking Berlin* (*Pri vziatii Berlina*, 1945). Ivanov's protagonist, Viktor Mikheev, is a painter who like Zhivago at some stage finds himself in love with two women at once. In 1942 he sees Stalin at a Moscow industrial plant, and three years later General Bursakov asks him to paint a portrait of Stalin in a panoramic setting to boost the morale of the workers. Like Evgraf, General Bursakov insists on Mikheev's leaving his home and moving into a specially prepared big room where he would sleep and work without interruption for the next few weeks. Mikheev is provided with all necessities, including imported coffee. Mikheev goes through all the agony and rapture of artistic creativity and finally manages to produce a portrait that brings him recognition as one of the most talented painters of his time.[49]

Significantly, Pasternak describes Zhivago's apartment, which he receives from Evgraf for an indefinite period, as a "painter's studio," while his notebooks are compared to "unfinished pictures" (435). Recall that in his poetry Zhivago wanted to focus on postrevolutionary Moscow. Had he succeeded, Zhivago's poems might have been similar to Bely's later writings, in which (in Pasternak's view of 1952) he desperately tried to pour his old wine into new bottles. However, Yurii himself soon perished and no such poems were found among his papers—a fact emphasized by the narrator.[50]

Zhivago's death after a heart attack in a streetcar in August 1929 has been interpreted and reinterpreted by many scholars. It is usually assumed that this date is meant to evoke the wave of political and cultural repression that began in 1928 marking the end of independent art and literature in Russia.[51] This, however, does not explain Pasternak's choice of month and the streetcar setting. Although there is no conclusive evidence of a connection, it is worth noting that on August 13, 1926, Andrei Bely was violently struck by a streetcar while returning home from the publishing house Circle (Krug). Bely, who had always felt that August was his unlucky month, was extremely shaken both emotionally and physically and attributed his miraculous escape from death to his instinctive leap to avoid the wheels of the vehicle. Bely was in fact notoriously preoccupied with the nature of the subconscious and used to analyze such situations in great detail, recounting them to members of his inner circle. It is quite likely that Pasternak heard about this episode either from Bely himself or from his wife, Klavdiia Bugaeva, who meticulously recorded those events in her memoirs.[52] Thus, had Bely died in 1926, he would have not written those later novels and memoirs that were particularly criticized by Pasternak when writing *Doctor Zhivago*.

In curtailing Zhivago's life, Pasternak asserted the freedom of a narrator and author, exercising powers that in real life are controlled by fate.[53] Here it is useful to recall Pasternak's letter to Mark Grigor'evich Vatagin written on December 15, 1955, a few days after *Doctor Zhivago* was completed. In it Pasternak talks about the mysterious divine force whose function it is to "restrict" the otherwise destructive freedom of the artist:

> Even in the case of totally immortal divine texts, such as, for example, those of Pushkin, the crucial role is played by the act of selection that confirms a particular line or page among hundreds of others. This selection is not made by the author's taste or genius but by a secret transcendental force, which is never known from the beginning and is always recognized only belatedly—a force whose apparent relentlessness in confining the author's arbitrariness prevents him or her from getting entangled in the limitless freedom of his options.
>
> In some cases this ability to choose is a tragic gift and the manifestation of a melancholy agency that subsequently materializes in an early suicide; in other cases it is a sign of prescience that later reveals itself in a posthumous victory, sometimes only a hundred years later, as it happened in the case of Stendhal.[54]

The prosaic part of the novel ends with Gordon and Dudorov deeply immersed in a rereading of Yurii's poetry in the 1950s. Following this, the final chapter consists exclusively of Yurii's poetry. Although it was not possible to preserve all of Zhivago's verse, what remains of it his friends "almost know by heart" (463). Zhivago's poems that "survive" the state of flux are those written, of course, by Pasternak himself. In other words, Pasternak unselfishly bestowed on his character, who was active in the late 1910s and 1920s, his best poems, written between 1944 and 1955, at a time when Pasternak struggled to achieve the utmost clarity and simplicity in his writings.[55] No wonder that Zhivago's poems survived so well and did not lose their appeal for Gordon and Dudorov thirty years later.

Braving the Thaw

ANNA AKHMATOVA IN THE 1950s AND THE 1960s

> We're living at a strange time that reminds me of a thaw. The air itself is full of some unhealthy relaxation and pliability. Everything is melting. . . . What used to be virginal and white, like snow, has turned into a dirty slush. Rivers and lakes are covered with thin, treacherous ice on which one is afraid to tread. And the muddy spring streams are flowing noisily from the most suspicious sources.
>
> —Dmitrii Merezhkovskii, "O prichinakh upadka i o novykh techeniiakh sovremennoi russkoi literatury," 1892

In June 1960, Akhmatova learned of Pasternak's death while she was recovering from a heart attack at the hospital. She was a few months older than Pasternak and was deeply affected by his death. Apparently, Joseph Brodsky saw Akhmatova as significantly older than that. He mentions their age difference and Pasternak's short stature (Akhmatova was taller) as decisive factors in making Akhmatova decline Pasternak's repeated proposals to marry him in the 1930s.[1] Brodsky was not alone in his view of a generational difference. In 1935, a Soviet critic, Mikhail Levidov, rejoiced over the poetic victory of the new postrevolutionary poets, such as Pasternak, over prerevolutionary poets such as Akhmatova:

But the new people, born during the course of the revolution, also rushed headlong into the poetic battle. They armed themselves not only with political weapons but also, figuratively speaking, with Blok, Briusov, and even Gumilev. Maiakovskii, Pasternak, Aseeev, and Bagritskii, followed by Sel'vinskii, Svetlov, and Tikhonov, polemicized with Blok, Sologub, Annenskii, and Akhmatova and, on occasion, even defeated them [preodolevali ikh] not only thanks to their being people of the revolution but also because, in some instances, they proved to be superior masters of poetry.[2]

Levidov was wrong. Akhmatova outlived Pasternak by nearly six years and received the title of Russia's preeminent living poet. As Gleb Struve put it in 1965, "There can be no doubt that, since the death of Boris Pasternak, Anna Akhmatova is the greatest living Russian poet."[3] In a sense, Akhmatova's fate can be compared to that of "old, very old" Mademoiselle Fleury, who comes to Moscow to obtain permission to return to France on the day of Zhivago's death. Yurii sees her out of his tram window. "She walked on, overtaking the tram for the tenth time, and quite unaware that she had overtaken Zhivago and survived him."[4] Roman Jakobson remarked in 1931, "The relationships between the biographies of a generation and the march of history are curious. Suddenly history finds use of Beethoven's deafness and Cézanne's astigmatism. . . . History mobilizes the youthful ardor of some generations and the tempered maturity or old wisdom of others."[5] Akhmatova clearly belonged to the latter.

The last decade of Akhmatova's life coincided roughly with the Khrushchev Thaw. During that period her position in the cultural hierarchy changed from that of a famous persona non grata to that of a Soviet and international celebrity. Her poems were no longer circulated only among a group of devoted friends and admirers but also reached a wider audience through Soviet periodicals and publishers that were engaged in preparing her collected works. Akhmatova received international awards and was allowed to travel to receive them. She was blessed with the friendship of young poets in Leningrad and

Moscow who sought her guidance and worshiped her. Even though Akhmatova's main project, *Poem Without a Hero*, which took her more than twenty years to finish, had been smuggled out of the country and published abroad, it also received a glowing review in the *Moskva* literary journal in May 1964. The review, written by Kornei Chukovskii, granted Akhmatova the privilege of looking back at the prerevolutionary culture not only with anger, but also with love and nostalgia.[6] In her self-promoting article about the *Poem* in 1963, Akhmatova appreciatively credited time for being on her side:

> Time was on the side of *Poem Without a Hero*. Over the past twenty years, an amazing thing has happened, that is, we are witnessing an almost complete renaissance of the 1910s. This strange process isn't over yet. Post-Stalin youth and foreign Slavic scholars are as fascinated as ever with the prerevolutionary period.... Almost nobody has been forgotten; almost everyone has been remembered. I say all this in connection with my poem because, while remaining a historical poem, it is very close to the present-day reader, whose secret wish is to wander about the Petersburg of 1913 and to get to know personally all those whom he or she loves so much (or doesn't love).[7]

However, despite her growing international fame, in the 1960s Akhmatova was still beset by uncertainties and anxieties similar to those she experienced in the 1920s and 1930s, when she was marginalized by the authorities. Traditionally, the writers of the so-called Silver Age who managed to survive the revolution have been seen as "living links" between tragically disjointed segments of Russian culture, such as the culture of Soviet Russia and that of "Russia abroad," or the cultures of the periods immediately before and after the revolution.[8] The real-life experiences of writers, such as Akhmatova (and to a certain extent, Nabokov), were by far more problematic and even tragic. "So many people came to visit her [in the 1960s]," Natalia Roskina recalled, "young poets, elderly ladies, and all kinds of foreigners." During these meetings Akhmatova:

liked to talk about herself, or more precisely, about what was being written about her in the foreign press. She was displeased with everything that was published about her and Gumilev and demanded that the visitors set about rebutting this information and publishing her version of the facts. Several of the foreign Slavonic specialists I knew complained to me of this. They couldn't even understand what she wanted of them: they didn't think the information she objected to deserved to be rebutted.[9]

In frustration, Akhmatova compiled lists of people whom she declared untrustworthy, making brief annotations, such as: "Those who should be warned against: (1) Makovskii (eighty-five years old, bad inner circle [*durnoe okruzhenie*]) . . . (3) A. A. Gumileva (my brother's widow, with whom [Nikolai Gumilev] had never had a relationship). She didn't know anything. Mixes everything up. I never exchanged ten words with her. (4) Strakhovskii—nothing but an impostor. (5) G. Ivanov must be condemned as someone who had slandered the whole epoch, all the 'Silver Age,' an ignorant, idle hooligan."[10] Did she believe that all those people and their recollections (mostly benevolent) were indeed all that ruinous to her reputation as one of Russia's greatest poets? Could she possibly imagine herself powerful enough to reverse or stop that flow of information?

Comparing Akhmatova's comments with the well-known memoirs of Russian emigres such as Sergei Makovskii, Georgii Ivanov, and Irina Odoevtseva, whose works became available during the Thaw and whose versions of their shared past Akhmatova found particularly distasteful, sheds little light on either. "The maturity of the late works of important artists is not like the ripeness of fruit," Theodor Adorno reminds us in his famous observations on Beethoven's "late style." "As a rule, these works are not well rounded, but wrinkled, even fissured. They are apt to lack sweetness, fending off with prickly tartness those interested merely in sampling them."[11] Likewise, page after page of Akhmatova's famous *Notebooks* (*Zapisnye knizhki*, 1958–1966) is covered with unfair accusations, rebukes, and name-calling. Certain passages, repeated verbatim, travel from one notebook to another. Some of those statements have been skillfully analyzed by Alexander Zholkovsky, who has exposed Akhmatova's "narrative, directorial, and histrionic skills," which helped her to conceal her "strong" and "manipulative" personality under the mask of a "fragile" and "ostensibly victimized" persona, as "obverse Stalinism."[12]

To say that Akhmatova was a petty dictator whose Stalinist modus operandi had become obsolete under Khrushchev would, therefore, add little to existing Akhmatova scholarship. Whereas Zholkovsky sees Akhmatova's life and works as a uniform whole and as a "sustained example of self-preservation that is grounded in historical circumstances,"[13] I view the last decade of Akhmatova's life as a distinct stage in her personal and poetic development that called for another reinvention of her Self in accordance with the new cultural and political developments. In contrast to some of her celebrated contemporaries, such as the writer Il'ia Ehrenburg, who thrived during the Thaw, Akhmatova fell victim to its liberating processes. The new angst accounted for her poor health (a succession of heart attacks) and increasing anxiety that manifested itself in repeated assaults on real and imaginary opponents and in her damning remarks about any other interpretation of the pre-revolutionary period except, perhaps, for that in Nikolai Berdiaev's autobiographical *Self-exploration (Samopoznanie,* 1940–1948).[14]

The Thaw, with its "unhealthy relaxation and pliability"—to borrow Merezhkovskii's apt definition from the 1890s—was a torturous time for Akhmatova, often leaving her at a loss for words, as when she encountered the budding Slavophile Stanislav Kuniaev, who visited her in the early 1960s with another young poet, Anatolii Peredreev. Kuniaev came to see Akhmatova "on business." He brought her the galley proofs of her selection of poems which she read and signed in his presence. Although Kuniaev is today one of Akhmatova's staunchest admirers and her portrait graces the cover of his memoirs, *Provoking Fire (Vyzyvaiu ogon' na sebia,* 2001), he does not spare his readers the ugly details of the Moscow communal apartment Akhmatova lived in at the time.[15] The apartment and the dirty staircase smelled of fish and cat urine. He describes Akhmatova herself as a gray-haired overweight woman, sitting by a never-washed window. The room and the corridor were cluttered with old furniture. Whether Kuniaev was aware of it or not, his description of his visit to Akhmatova reads like an updated version of Lidiia Chukovskaia's description of her first visit to Akhmatova that opens the first volume of her *Notes*.

Being half-drunk, Kunaiev's guest Peredreev immediately went off to sleep in a squeaky armchair. When he regained consciousness, he asked Akhmatova to read them something that she herself liked most. The terrified Kuniaev expected Akhmatova to show them the door. Instead, she headed in silence for an old record player and turned it on. All three listened to Akhmatova's recording of her "I Heard a Voice Call Consolingly" ("Mne golos byl. On zval uteshno"). While Kuniaev burned with embarrassment, though savoring the moment, Peredreev went back to sleep. Finally, Kuniaev and Peredreev found themselves outside, breathing "the fresh air of the Garden Ring Road." As it turned out, Peredreev had joined Kuniaev out of curiosity and, in fact, "preferred to read the poetry of Zabolotskii and Khodasevich, and, occasionally, even of Mandelstam." Although Kuniaev felt in the end that his revered poet had taught them a lesson, Akhmatova most likely had felt uncomfortable; to the best of my knowledge, apart from Kuniaev's testimony, there are no other references to this episode either in Akhmatova's records or in the accounts of her various memoirists. It appears that this was not one of those amusing stories she wanted to have preserved for posterity.[16]

In her most charitable version of memoirs about Akhmatova, Nadezhda Mandelstam suggests that Akhmatova, always anxious to produce a lasting impression on her visitors and potential memoirists, became vain in her old age and that it was her vanity that ultimately got in the way of her writing:

> Once she read in someone's memoirs (a woman's, of course) published abroad that she was not pretty and that Gumilev did not love her. "Nadia," she said to me, "explain to me why I should be pretty. Was

Walter Scott handsome? Or Dostoevskii? Who would even think about asking such a thing?" I thought she would forget about these memoirs, but nothing of the sort. From that day on she began to collect photographs. All her friends brought her pictures and she collected those where she looked pretty and pasted them in an album. She collected heaps of pictures, so many it was impossible to count them all. . . . But she did not find time to write down poetry. Large numbers of poems remained not written down.[17]

How should we interpret Nadezhda Mandelstam's self-righteous observation? One thing is certain: Nadezhda Mandelstam firmly believed that in the 1960s Akhmatova should not have wasted her time on anything else but her poetry. This is not necessarily how writers live and work. In fact, Akhamtova's self-recorded obsessive accusations of others and the sudden tantrums that even her most tolerant and supportive friends found difficult to explain, point to extreme stress and even exhaustion.[18]

Unlike some other poets, Akhmatova lived a long, productive life. She did so because she knew how to pace herself. In his remarkable study, *Art and Artist* (1932), the psychoanalyst Otto Rank reveals that as much as an artist needs to "flee from life into creation," he is equally driven by a self-preservation instinct that forces him to resist a "complete surrender to his work":

> There will be of course special modes of escape for each artist or artist type. But I think that certain ways are universally accessible, of which I will mention a few that are typical. One means of salvation from this total absorption in creation is, as in ordinary life, the division of attention among two or more simultaneous activities; and it is interesting in this connection to note that work on the second activity is begun during work on the first just at the moment when the latter threatens to become all-absorbing. The second work is often an antithesis in style and character to the first, though it may be a continuation at another level. This can, of course, only happen with artists who have various interests and capacities; thus Goethe indulged his scientific, and

Schiller his philosophical, studies at periods apparently of weakness in poetic creativity, but really, according to our view, of danger to the poet when he had to find respite from that creativity. If a second sphere of interest of this sort—which is frequently a second form of artistic achievement—is lacking, periods of disappointment, depression, and even illness are likely to occur, which are then not so much a consequence of exhaustion as a flight from it.[19]

How do Rank's commonsensical observations apply to Akhmatova? In the most direct way. I have discussed Akhmatova's extended period of poetic silence (1923–1935), during which she did "divide her attention among two or more simultaneous activities," in Rank's words, "indulging" her studies of Pushkin or undertaking research for her male companions. She took day-long dictations from her second husband, Vladimir Shileiko, and later translated from the French for her third husband, Nikolai Punin, to help him prepare for his lectures. Knowing how independent and willful Akhmatova was, it is hard to imagine that she did not perform those chores of her own free will. According to her friend, Salomeia Andronikova, Akhmatova's willpower alone was enough to make a character (even a historical character) do whatever she pleased: "[a minor poet, Vsevolod] Kniazev was in love with [an actress, Olga] Sudeikina. Akhmatova writes that he committed suicide by shooting himself because of her. . . . I do not attach any factual significance to that: it didn't happen the way she describes it. If [Akhmatova] wants him to, [Kniazev] will shoot anybody."[20] As far as her Pushkin studies are concerned, Akhmatova definitely reveled in them. Likewise, Pasternak, who lived to be seventy, did plant potatoes and did work on his translations while writing *Doctor Zhivago*.[21] During the Thaw, Akhmatova had no other choice but to change her work routine.

Like many intellectuals at the time, Akhmatova became actively involved in revisiting her past. For some writers, such as Il'ia Ehrenburg, this process meant readjustment of the past to the needs of the present.[22] For Akhmatova, this process was more burdensome, since she had to create both a life story to fit her creative output and a creative output that would fit her newly reconstituted life story. Her inexplicable periods of silence that had suddenly become public knowledge through the works of various commentators had to be addressed and accounted for. To begin with, Akhmatova did what she always did: first she rearranged some of her poems by backdating them to explain those gaping holes that had to be filled in.[23] In a sense, this practice (common for many poets and even painters like Kazimir Malevich) of faking chronology, of adding and deleting dedications and epigraphs, is similar to that of the Soviet Stalinist and post-Stalinist historians when they eliminated certain politicians and cultural figures from their historical narratives and readjusted them to fit the currently acceptable ideologized version of bygone eras. With poets such creative appropriation of the past is ultimately more dangerous, since they have to live the life they have devised for themselves.

Her first surviving notebooks of the 1950s bear witness to how much Akhmatova was driven by the need to provide a plausible explanation of her "meager" output in the 1930s. The solution was found. In the spirit of the 1950s, Akhmatova claimed that she had succeeded in recovering some of her poems she considered lost and forgotten. One such forgotten piece was her "Seventh Elegy," in which Akhmatova unequivocally attributed her periods of silence to the political pressure and mass executions of the time.[24] Due to its inner contradictions, the "Seventh Elegy," which was meant to testify to Akhmatova's inability to speak and at the same time tell the story of her heroic resistance, was never finished.

The main victim of Akhmatova's self-imposed coercion and restructuring was *Poem Without a Hero*. She endeavored within one poem not only to overcome once and for all the influence of her former mentors and poetic rivals, which would have been expected, but also to condemn Stalinism. This must have been a nightmarish undertaking, for as Nadezhda Mandelstam testifies, "Akhmatova could never stop worrying about her poem. She thought that the [existence of the] poem was justified only if it were far better than anything else."[25] As time went by, the body of the poem continued to expand in response to the vast influx of poetic and historical material that it had to process. Such all-inclusiveness and omnivorousness, however, did not please most of Akhmatova's readers. In her entry for November 19, 1960, Lidiia Chukovskaia conveyed her frustration with Akhmatova's attempts to combine the prerevolutionary cultural scene with the Stalinist purges of the 1930s and their aftermath:

> The new times we have eventually lived to witness create new abysses in the depths of the *Poem*. It would seem, however, that this current newness is new to others but not to Akhmatova. . . . Why is she so long-winded and verbose, using the genitive case zillions of times, when there exists the short, clear, old Russian word *zastenok* [torture chamber]? Yes, the torture chamber has always been a concrete reality, but it is only in the last few years that the torture-chamber theme has been a burning issue in the *Poem*. Not her poetry, just the *Poem*.[26]

Chukovskaia wasn't impressed by Akhmatova's attempts at writing her own biography, either. "A strange work, a mixture of facts from the dictionary of biographies and true 'poet's prose,'" she noted in March 1960. "The choice of facts about herself is totally arbitrary: they don't express any central idea either about [Akhmatova's] creative or personal development. . . . Gumilev only gets mentioned in a subordinate clause, when she talks about their summer trips to her mother-in-law's estate." As usual, Chukovskaia hid her negative impressions from Akhmatova: "I had mixed feelings about all this, so I reserved my judgment."[27]

Chukovskaia's criticism aside, Akhmatova was the first to verbalize the link between two seemingly disconnected phenomena—the Silver Age and the Soviet age. She defined historical retribution in the Russian context: the irresponsible, hedonistic behavior of a small group of Russian intellectuals on the brink of WWI, according to Akhmatova, laid the groundwork not only for the subsequent Bolshevik Revolution but also for Stalinist terror. The enormity of Akhmatova's enterprise was daunting even for Akhmatova, hence her numerous complaints in her *Notebooks* about the viselike grip the *Poem* had on her life. She kept trying to break that grip. Her complaints were interpreted as coquetry or as rather ineffectual attempts to justify her never-ending work on her "poem-without-a hero-project." Those complaints should be taken in their literal sense. The fact that the *Poem* exists not only in several different versions but also in several genres (as a long poem, a libretto, a work of drama, as well as an extensive commentary on life meant to become the closing chapter in Akhmatova's biography) reveals Akhmatova's urge to compartmentalize her work. By channeling her energies into different activities, she successfully resisted being consumed by any one of them entirely.

Apart from restoring her energy, Akhmatova also used her periods of silence to illustrate the measure of her unhappiness with this or that by then abandoned companion. It is clear from Chukovskaia's records that she was duly impressed when Akhmatova revealed to her that she had been silent for thirteen years while living with Punin. In Chukovskaia's eyes, that was reason enough to stop living with Punin. While this was a plausible explanation for the periods of silence during the Stalin years, it became increasingly inadmissible during the Thaw.[28] While in the late 1920s and the 1930s Akhmatova could have been satisfied with the role of Gumilev's widow and biographer, Punin's wife, and Lev Gumilev's mother, in the 1950s and particularly in the 1960s she did not have to live in anybody's shadow anymore. But she was expected to have had an exemplary past, one worthy of a famous poet who shared all misfortunes with her people by describing them on a daily basis in her poetry.

During periods of liberal reforms, the privileged autobiographical (and biographical) genre becomes the apologia of a misunderstood public figure. Despite Akhmatova's repeated statements to the contrary, she was actually lucky to feature prominently in the memoirs of her former compatriots. For example, the allegedly vicious campaign against her by Georgii Ivanov in the late 1920s, echoed by Sergei Makovskii in the 1950s and the 1960s, gave her an opportunity to declare herself a victim of intentional distortions. It is quite incredible how few of Akhmatova's confidants had actually read Ivanov's memoirs, *Petersburg Winters* (*Peterburgskie zimy*, 1928, 1952) while she was alive and even after her death. Almost every memoirist writing about Akhmatova regurgitates the same old story of Georgii Ivanov's treacherous and despicable behavior toward both Gimilev and Akhmatova.[29] The reason Akhmatova's listeners and readers retained such a negative image of Ivanov was the context in which she discussed his name. She compared an episode in Ivanov's memoirs in which he described Akhmatova reading her poetry in public in the early 1920s (a story that Ivanov subsequently deleted from the 1952 edition of *Petersburg Winters*) to the last chapter of *The Trial* (1914), in which Kafka depicts the senseless and brutal murder of his protagonist.[30] Akhmatova's evocation of this particular novel was carefully thought out. *The Trial* was not only widely popular in the 1950s but was also read as a remarkable prophesy of the Holocaust in Europe and the Stalinist purges in Russia. The fact that Kafka considered *The Trial* unfinished (the trial was meant to continue indefinitely) and wanted his novel to be destroyed along with his other unfinished work (but was nevertheless preserved for posterity by Max Brod) gave the book an aura of martyrdom. Like *The Trial* and its author, who died prematurely of tuberculosis (a disease Akhmatova was familiar with), Akhmatova was also a victim par excellence. While the Stalinist executions stopped with Stalin's death, Akhmatova's ordeal was far from being over as long as her emigre contemporaries continued to distort the story of her life and vandalize her poetic legacy.

Akhmatova was not the only poet who was unusually anxious about how she and her creativity were perceived by readers during the Thaw. Vladimir Orlov's folders in RGALI, The Russian State Archive of Literature and Art, contain in-house reviews of various collections of poetry that he, as the editor-in-chief of the famous series *Biblioteka poeta* (*Poet's Library*), solicited in the 1960s from his esteemed contemporaries, such as the poets Aleksandr Tvardovskii (1910–1971) and Nikolai Tikhonov (1896–1979) and the literary scholar Viktor Zhirmunskii (1891–1971).[31] In his review of Mandelstam's *Selected Poems* (*Stikhotvoreniia/Izbrannye*) of January 13, 1961, Tvardovskii remarked,

"It is very unfortunate that poets like O. Mandelstam, M. Tsvetaeva, N. Gumilev, and B. Pasternak haven't been published in our country for a long time; it is especially unfortunate for young poets, who often have a very vague idea of what real poetry is all about." In his review of Marina Tsvetaeva's *Selected Poems* (*Izbrannoe*) of May 5, 1961, he qualified his call for publication of such poets as Mandelstam and Tsvetaeva by elaborating that such publications "will . . . reveal one of the sources of the 'innovations' attributed to the likes of [Andrei] Voznesenskii and [Yevgenii] Yevtushenko." In the absence of such publications, poets like Voznesenskii and Yevtushenko had "a beguiling influence on simpletons." Change this situation and "it will become obvious that what those poets flaunt today has existed for a long time and was already better than what they have to offer now the first time it was brought into being," Tvardovskii concluded. In another review of Tsvetaeva's *Selected Poems*, a Soviet critic, A. N. Makarov, echoed Tvardovskii's anxieties and accused "young poets, especially female poets ('the robbers of the dead')," of "robbing Tsvetaeva in a most unscrupulous way, by passing off something that has long existed as their own innovations. It is, therefore, absolutely necessary to introduce into literary circulation not just her name but also her poetry in order to set the stage for criticism of such pseudoinnovations," Makarov persisted.

Four years later, Viktor Zhirmunskii concluded his review of Tsvetaeva's *Selected Poems* (August 9, 1965) with the following passage:

> I would like to remind the editorial board, yet again, of the necessity of publishing, as soon as possible, the poems by O. Mandelstam, N. Zabolotskii, and A. Bely, which are now ready to go to press. The Soviet reader and, in particular, the Soviet writer, should at last be given an opportunity to familiarize themselves with the works of these outstanding Russian poets of the recent past, published as prestigious editions with accompanying solid historico-critical commentaries. It is high time we dismantled the monopoly of Americans on the publication and study of these poets, allegedly "forbidden" in our country, thereby stopping our ill-wishers from using that monopoly to earn

political mileage. It is the duty of the *Poet's Library* editorial office to follow A. M. Gorky's instructions and do all in its power to change the current state of affairs.

Although it is highly unlikely that Zhirmunskii himself feared any American monopoly on great Russian poets, his discourse was clearly meant to strike a chord in the hearts of distinguished Soviet poets, literary administrators, and cultural custodians.

Apart from the manifest anxiety with regard to younger writers and the uncritical reading public, these reviews from the 1960s also reveal how little even the privileged members of the literary community knew about the personal lives of many pre- and postrevolutionary poets and writers. In his review of Tsvetaeva's *Selected Poems* (August 11, 1965), Nikolai Tikhonov expressed his astonishment that Tsvetaeva had died in the town of Yelabuga (and not in Chistopol', as he had thought) in complete solitude. "Is this what really happened?" He urged Orlov "to clarify" (*proiasnit'*) the circumstances of her husband's death, specify the whereabouts of her daughter at the time of her suicide, and tell more about Tsvetaeva's mysterious end. "Let's assume that everything happened the way [Orlov] says it did: in Yelabuga, with no one near her, and the whereabouts of her grave unknown. But one could use some other words to describe all this. That's what I think; maybe I am wrong. But I had to share my concerns, since I have them," Tikhonov explained.[32] At a time when information about writers' personal lives was still very scarce, while literary scholars were eager to present their accounts and interpretations of them, it was only natural that in the 1960s Akhmatova would become adamant about elucidating her life for posterity. Akhmatova lived to witness the deaths and, more important, the posthumous fame of all her distinguished contemporaries, but she was hard put to envision her own legacy. Anxiety about how she would be evaluated in the future may account for her persistent attempts to write her own biography. Not surprisingly, the pomposity and solemnity of some of the remaining excerpts is reminiscent of the tone of obituaries.

In *The Words (Les mots)*, which Akhmatova may have read since it was published in 1964, Jean-Paul Sartre not only exposed all the pitfalls and deficiencies of autobiographical writing but also drew attention to its inherently collaborative nature. The narrator, a little boy, contemplates fame and thinks about ways of informing posterity about his talent before it reveals itself:

> I concocted double-edged remarks, which I let fall in public. Anne Marie would find me at my desk, scribbling away. She would say: "It's so dark! My little darling is ruining his eyes." It was an opportunity to reply in innocence: "I could write even in the dark." She would laugh, would call me her little silly, would put on the light; the trick was done; we were both unaware that I had just informed the year 3,000 of my future infirmity. Yes, toward the end of my life, more blind than Beethoven was deaf, I would work gropingly on my last book. People would say with disappointment: "But it's illegible!" There would be even talk of throwing it into the garbage. Finally, the Aurillac Municipal Library would ask for it out of pure piety. It would lie there for a hundred years, forgotten. And then, one day, out of love for me, young scholars would try to decipher it; their entire lifetime would not be enough to restore what would, of course, be my masterpiece.[33]

In a similar way, Akhmatova revealed to her future biographer, Amanda Height (1941–1989), a very young woman eager to learn and write about Akhmatova, that she had started to write poetry as a result of her mysterious sickness at the age of eleven when she suddenly lost her hearing for a while and started to hear inner voices instead.[34] It is not clear whether this revelation was made in order to convey the sense of her singularity or to account for her progressive deafness.[35] In any case, in her efforts to rewrite her life into a story of national importance, Akhmatova faced a more serious dilemma. If her poetry were to depict the Stalinist horrors, she could either cast herself in the role of their witness and survivor or, conversely, in the role of a victim or casualty who had not survived them—but dead people did not write poetry or fiction. The desire to achieve both statuses at the same time was typical of Akhmatova. For example, she always wanted to be seen as a link between the prerevolutionary and postrevolutionary cultures, yet at the same time she wanted to be firmly in the vanguard. She also wanted to cast Gumilev as an influential poet, yet she denied him any influence on her own poetic development. The consequent psychological bifurcation may well explain her general state of anguish and, by way of example, on a subconscious level her strange request of Chukovskaia to tell Amanda Height about the Stalinist terror while she herself took a nap.

This happened in May 1964, when Akhmatova invited Chukovskaia to join her in another of her meetings with Height. When Height arrived on the scene, to Chukovskaia's surprise, Akhmatova instructed Chukovskaia to tell Height about the Stalinist terror. Akhmatova did not leave the room, however. Nor did she appear to be listening or taking part in the discussion. She simply lay down on her bed and went to sleep. Chukovskaia listened to her even breathing and embarked on telling Height what later formed the bulk of the first volume of her *Notes (Zapiski ob Anne Akhmatovoi)*. Then Akhmatova woke up and started making jokes about her babysitting for the Smirnov family in the late 1930s. I believe that this piece of theatrics was inspired by Akhmatova's favorite cemetery scene in Pushkin's *The Stone Guest (Kamennyi gost', 1830)*. Akhmatova's fascination with this particular *Little Tragedy* is well known.[36] In her essay "Pushkin's *Stone Guest*" ("*Kamennyi gost'* Pushkina," 1947, 1958), Akhmatova interpreted *The Stone Guest* as a projection of Pushkin's thoughts about his future marriage to Natalia Nikolaevna. "Poor thing! She is so young, so innocent, but he is such a frivolous, such an immoral man," Pushkin wrote about himself in the third person on May 13, 1830.[37] Akhmatova believed that Pushkin identified himself both with Don Juan and the Commander, making them the embodiments of the two distinct but related periods in his life—his carefree sinful youth and his more mature self. At the cemetery, the Commander's monument witnesses in silence Don

Juan's seduction of his widow, Donna Anna. As Akhmatova convincingly demonstrates, Pushkin's Commander, unlike any other Commander from the Don Juan tradition, was simultaneously a lucky husband, a victim, and a symbol of retribution, which may explain why Akhmatova identified herself most clearly with the statue rather than with Don Juan, although—as Akhmatova points out—he was a poet. I believe that the monument that Akhmatova famously erects to herself in the concluding portion of *Requiem* may stem not from her unbecoming vanity (as some critics believe) but from the same insatiate desire to perform simultaneously two mutually exclusive roles, those of a victim and a witness.

Her very own cemetery scene, which Akhmatova staged for Height's benefit, was probably the only instance when Akhmatova succeeded in fulfilling several functions at the same time—she is a witness (Chukovskaia's story revolves around her *Requiem*), she is a victim (which is clearly marked by the fact that she is asleep/dead—a transformation she failed to achieve in her writing, even when she turned to third-person narratives about herself), she is the author of all stories told in the room (the story of Akhmatova's life, coauthored by Chukovskaia); in addition, she is the author and director of the play in which she has the leading part without saying a word, and she is the censor (Chukovskaia was not quite sure whether she was telling what Akhmatova wanted her to tell and whether Akhmatova was really asleep).[38] This performance clearly had a therapeutic effect on Akhmatova, since she woke up full of energy and started telling jokes. In fact, Akhmatova's stone guests (*Requiem* and the above scene, as recorded by Chukovskaia) reverse the established paradigm—instead of bringing death to the living, they bring life to the dead. In *The Stone Guest,* as Akhmatova points out, Pushkin decisively resisted moralizing. In her stone guest scene, Akhmatova was seemingly good-humored as well. Chukovskaia, however, summed up her entry by issuing a warning to Height on the importance of writing down Akhmatova's every word correctly: "Otherwise, every Tom, Dick, and Harry will make it their job to churn out memoirs, and torrents of lies will gush forth, unimpeded, from under their pens—in response, no doubt, to the perceived 'exigencies of the moment.'"[39] Such concluding remarks were only to be expected after the emblematic séance of transference.

By the mid-1960s, Akhmatova apparently succeeded in disseminating an idealized version of herself, that is, as a poet who never stops writing new poetry, even if it means one line at a time. "I did not stop writing verse," Akhmatova ended her introduction to the 1961 edition of her collected works. "For me poetry is a link with time, with the new life of my people. When I was writing, I lived under the same rhythm that sounded during the heroic past of my country. I am happy to have lived during those years and to have been witness to such incomparable events."[40] Various periodicals were eager to publish her poems. Whereas in the early 1950s, the editors were prepared to publish her old work and were amazed when she gave them something from her most recent poems, by the mid-1960s this situation became the norm.

The torture of turning out poem after poem to sustain this image of a perpetually productive poet must have been excruciating. In her diary entry for July 19, 1965, one month after her long-awaited trip to England and France, Akhmatova confessed that she felt "happiest" in 1956 when she "was laid up with some interminable and rather malignant flu," which gave her an excuse for not going to Moscow. The deep-seated source of her happiness, as it turns out, was her knowledge that not one line of her poetry was ever going to be published. "How comfortably and freely that certainty lived in my consciousness without causing me the slightest distress!"

> How easily and freely I told the three guys from [the journal] *Literaturnaia zhizn'* who came to pick up my poems, "You won't print them anyway." That's [the kind of] life worthy of a decent person! But now . . . That time I gave them the "Summer Sonnet," which had just been written, and something else. So it'll soon be ten years since they began to publish me again. It's so confining *[Nu i puty zhe eto]*.[41]

A few months later, in response to an offer to start work on a new edition of her collected works, Akhmatova admitted that she wanted to "take a rest from her poems" and "even to forget them." She explained,

> Khrenkov asks me to select some poems to be published by Lenizdat. How I hate being bothered with them, how I want to take a rest from them or even forget them! The job means thinking again along the lines of "this isn't allowed," "that is allowed," and "better this than that." How draining these thoughts are! How harmful it is to be one's own critic, censor, and executioner....
>
> All of this already puts me in mind of Moscow, Nina, my friends and enemies, translations, night taxis, elevators, and the never-ending "akhmatovka."[42]

When later, at the hospital, she analyzed what might have caused her fourth heart attack, she concluded that it resulted from her work on her last edition of her collected works, *The Flight of Time (Beg vremeni)*.[43] Half a year earlier, upon her return from Oxford, Akhmatova confessed to Chukovskaia that she had more or less decided to give up her struggle against various unauthorized versions of her life:

> "I was very tired in Oxford. I spent days correcting people's dissertations.... You bet, over there, everyone is writing a dissertation about Mandelstam, Gumilev, and myself. They make a royal mess of things and write a pack of lies, and it's I who have to make corrections."
>
> I said, "You were lucky to be given such an opportunity."
>
> "No. Lidiia Korneevna, I realized that all those writings are hopeless. None of them can be corrected. The vicious lies propagated by Nevedomskaia, Anna Andreevna Gumileva, and Makovskii are treated as primary reliable sources and find their way into serious research. I have no time to refute anything. I have no energy for that."[44]

Shortly before her death, Akhmatova read Gleb Struve's article about herself. The article infuriated her and she poured her rage into her *Notebooks*. In his article, Struve recalled the tragic deaths of Pushkin, Lermontov, Gumilev, and Blok. These last two, Struve explained, died "in Akhmatova's own time." But Akhmatova was spared their tragic fate. Her fate was like that of Afanasii Fet (1820–1892) who "lived to an old age and . . . experienced something like a 'second rebirth.'" According to Struve, Fet's "collection *Vechernie ogni*, published between 1883 and 1891, was a miraculous testimony to such a poetic rebirth." Consequently, "all the admirers of [Akhmatova's] poetry must rejoice at the thought that, at the age of seventy-six, she is in full possession of her poetic gift and, judging by her recent work, holds out a promise of new and remarkable achievements."[45]

Apparently, Akhmatova did not plan to fulfill Struve's expectations. (Or had she already fulfilled them in 1912 by turning Fet's *Vechernie ogni* into her very own *Vecher*?) All she wanted to do was to return home and reimmerse herself in ordinary life, which even included working on translations, generally believed to stand in the way of her poetry. She wrote in her diary: "If only I could get good translations and also write prose in which one thing follows from another and the reader starts breathing so much more easily. . . . But I'd like to get back home; I wish I had more strength. I'd like to have a simple life at home. As for prose, I practically hear it."[46] For her future biographer, Mikhail Ardov (b. 1937), she recorded a line she wanted him to develop in his memoirs: "We, Akhmatova's contemporaries, see her in a more prosaic light (or: we do not expect too much from her) [*Dlia Mishi:* . . . *My, sootechestvenniki Akhmatovoi, vidim ee gorazdo proshche*]."[47]

The Silver Age in the 1960s and in the 1970s

Akhmatova's *Poem Without a Hero* was one of the last attempts by writers born of the prerevolutionary tradition to overcome this tradition from within by eating their own flesh, so to speak. Any subsequent attempts at assimilation and internalization of the prerevolutionary cultural legacy were undertaken by people for whom this period meant not life, but literary history.

The complex structure and texture of Akhmatova's *Poem Without a Hero* provoked a number of first-rate scholarly analyses. "Akhmatova and Kuzmin" by Roman Timenchik, Vladimir Toporov, and Tatiana

Tsivian is one of them.[48] What rapidly turned this analysis into a classic was not so much its numerous insights into the creativity of both poets, but that it was a detailed reconstruction of the social, historical, and particularly cultural background of the 1910s, which was pertinent to the appreciation of the literary works in question (Akhmatova's *Poem Without a Hero* and Kuzmin's *The Trout Breaking through the Ice*). The authors of this and other similar studies belonged to a new generation of Soviet scholars and writers for whom the multifaceted Silver Age was a welcome relief from the gray monotony of socialist realism. For these young people, the Silver Age was like a newly found exotic oasis, lit up by every hue of the World of Art Movement and populated exclusively by free-spirited artists. These "products" of Khrushchev's Thaw were bound to find kindred spirits in the habitues of the Stray Dog (Brodiachaia sobaka) cabaret, whose adventurous lives and deeds they were determined to study and emulate.

In the 1960s and the 1970s, the Silver Age to a certain extent lost its definite geographical outlines. Thus, in *Ada* (1969) Nabokov stopped looking back nostalgically at Russian estates lost in the 1917 revolution and instead moved his typically Silver Age Ardis and its inhabitants to America. A similar intention was already present in *Pnin* (1957) in its mocking description of "The Pines," a North American villa that every other summer generously opened its doors to "liberals and intellectuals who had left Russia around 1920."[49] In the same novel Nabokov has a mediocre poet, Liza—an overt parody of Akhmatova and her acolytes—first move to Europe and then to North America, where he puts her and her spouse in charge of psychoanalytic studies.

Thanks to officially sanctioned memoirs and particularly to smuggled or samizdat copies of Pasternak's *Doctor Zhivago*, and Nabokov's novels together with photocopied or handwritten copies of some prerevolutionary editions, the Silver Age acquired in the eyes of Soviet intellectuals strong associations with political and artistic freedom and democracy. This can be seen in numerous allusions to Bely's *Petersburg* in Vasilii Aksenov's seminal work *The Burn* (*Ozhog*, 1969–1975), in which he describes the strivings of his generation for moral freedom and spiritual perfection, or in Venedikt Erofeev's short story "Vasilii Rozanov through the Eyes of an Eccentric" ("Vasilii Rozanov glazami ekstsentrika," 1978). In the latter, according to one critic, "the author represented the momentous meeting of Russian independent culture of the sixties and seventies with the 'Silver Age' as the only 'hope' for a contemporary intellectual who was planning to do away with himself, disillusioned as he was with the truisms of rationalism. The unforeseen but long-awaited contact with Vasilii Rozanov's dizzying paradoxes put everything in its place."[50]

"The long-awaited contact" with the cultural past, as well as how this past could be assimilated and internalized, became one of the major themes of Andrei Bitov's *Pushkin House* (*Pushkinskii dom*, 1965–1970), the story of the Odoevtsev family in the late 1950s and early 1960s. Significantly, all the men in this family are professional students of literature. One day, the stilted atmosphere in this family is suddenly perturbed by a number of seemingly disconnected but actually related events. When "Uncle" Dickens ("Uncle" Mitya, the mysterious neighbor of the Odoevtsev family) returns home from his place of imprisonment where he had been periodically incarcerated over the last twenty years, the protagonist Lyova and his parents excitedly rejoice over his liberation. It should not take long for the reader to identify Uncle Dickens with the Silver Age; even his personal belongings suggest this analogy. It turns out that the best, the most exquisite things that the Odoevtsevs possessed—"a mirror, oval, in a frame of gilt-and-black grapevines; a table lamp with two little carved Negro cupids (they were augurs); and a long polished mahogany chest"—were in fact not theirs, but were given to them on loan by Uncle Dickens.[51] The word "silver" is also mentioned frequently enough in the description of the Uncle's appearance to alert the "quick-witted" reader:

> He was uncommonly skinny and swarthy; his last little silver threads were so painstakingly parted (Lyova subsequently spotted a special silver brush for this purpose at Uncle Dickens's apartment). ... Absolutely everything associated with Uncle Mitya underwent

an unexpected regeneration for Lyova. Even what belonged to all men—for example, history, the instant he substituted Uncle Mitya in it—would take on an extraordinary optical effect: Lyova would begin to see it as though it had really happened. As though nothing around Uncle Dickens grew dim—he was like silver coin dropped into the water of time . . . Grandma used to propagandize on the benefit of silver water, Lyova remembered. . . . And Lyova would swallow his saliva, tasting in his mouth the metal of authenticity.[52]

Despite his many years of imprisonment and his considerable age—Uncle Dickens was an officer in the tsarist army—he is extremely elegant and attractive, making young Lyova feel clumsy and boorish:

> Everything about him was attractive: the fastidiousness, the coldness, the harshness . . . the thuggish aristocracy. And the blue print stripe dangling on the dried-up body like a smock—an outdated prewar suit that must have lain in the trunk all these years folded in four, like a letter, and those four crosswise creases were mostly all the crease it had left—so elegant was that suit, he thought, it would come into style only in a future season (Lyova's English suit was tailored to a cow, for cows).[53]

The Uncle's unexpected return has a healthy effect on the Odoevtsev family. Lyova's estranged parents are reunited and gaze lovingly at each other, they "fawn on the old man; his foul language so *forbidden* in the family, seemed to caress their ears. Their faces were smoothed, clear, almost as in the wedding picture, the way faces seem to become at the first possibility of love. . . . That possibility was youth. . . . The air in the apartment shifted again, as though there were a certain piled-up little room, which they had *always remembered* but *forgotten*, and it had been shoveled out."[54] Lyova is equally obsessed with the Uncle, to the extent of cherishing a dream that the latter was his real father, and spends his time studying pictures taken in the Uncle's youth.

With the Uncle's release from imprisonment, everything that

was previously forbidden or forgotten—these words are almost interchangeable in *Pushkin House*—starts gradually filtering back, filling in the gaping holes in people's memories and even in Lyova's upbringing. Lyova is particularly mesmerized by the Uncle's living quarters,

> [which had] to be sneaked into by children despite a ban. A book *forbidden in childhood*—that's exactly what Uncle Dickens's tiny apartment was like. . . . Lyova loved to be left there for a moment by himself, on a settee created for uncomfortable sitting, to leaf through a monograph sweet and small as a childish sin, about Beardsley, let's say, but also to examine the *forbidden little room* he had *missed out as a child*. And the books that he borrowed and returned to Uncle Dickens (which served as the occasion for his visits) were also a *filling in* of his childhood: *Aphrodite*, *L'Atlantide*, *The Green Hat*. When could he have read them, except under the bedcovers by flashlight?[55]

For quite a while the Uncle plays an important role in Lyova's maturing by contributing inadvertently to the formation of his literary tastes and the personal attachments in his life. He is the only one to whom Lyova can turn for money in order to keep up a rather costly relationship with the love of his life, the dazzling Faina.

Despite the Uncle's undeniable virtues, such as the reportedly untarnished quality of his silver-rich personality, his portrait is far from being solely complimentary. He often swears foully and jabs "his tiny fist into the janitor's ribs" while the latter is helping him to carry his chest.[56] As one finds out, he can be obnoxious, capricious, and difficult to deal with. His pronouncements, however eye-opening they may sound to the Odoevtsevs, have no practical implications: "It wasn't that Uncle Mitya said anything in particular. What made him attractive when he got drunk was his increasing definitiveness and soberness toward the world. 'Shit'—that was the sum of it; yet when Uncle Mitya summed it up that way, the sun practically came out."[57] The powerlessness of the attractive Uncle is emphasized by his toothlessness; the narrator repeatedly draws the reader's attention to his barren mouth. After the Uncle's death, the Odoevtsevs are introduced to his sister who puzzles them with her short fat fingers, ungracefulness, and almost hyperbolic greediness. As far as the Uncle's literary legacy is concerned, Lyova is equally stunned by the naiveté and bad quality of the Uncle's poetry and of the works of prose that were handed over to him by his mother for a professional evaluation.

If it is correct to identify Uncle Dickens with the Silver Age, then we might say that in *Pushkin House* Bitov not only testifies to the ways in which the legacy of the Silver Age was assimilated in the 1960s and in the 1970s, but also offers a certain antidote against the spreading infatuation with it, which was hailed by many as a panacea for many social and cultural diseases. In doing so, Bitov continued Akhmatova's tradition. However attractive the idea of finding a father in the easily lovable Uncle Dickens might have seemed to Lyova to begin with, by the end of the novel it becomes clear that as the curator of the Pushkin House—the epitome of Russian literature in general—he also has to come to grips with his own father, his grandfather, Faina, a betrayed Jewish colleague, and his Dostoevskian double Mitishat'ev, to name but a few. Uncle Dickens is not abandoned or dethroned by the end of the book: on the contrary, we are told that he can be resurrected in the future with the help of some literary device if we ever have further need of him. For the moment, he is simply history, literary history.

8

The Apocalypse Revisited

VIKTOR EROFEEV'S *RUSSIAN BEAUTY*

> It's nice, when you go away or die, to leave behind a clean space.
>
> —A. Terts, *Random Thoughts*

In the 1980s, the cultural legacy of the Silver Age was further reexamined by the so-called *alternative prose* writers. For example, Sasha Sokolov (b. 1943) in *Palisandria* (1985) debunked a highly popular belief that the Silver Age continued after the revolution in Russian emigre circles. When the main character, Palisandr Dal'berg, is sent abroad by the Soviet leader Yurii Andropov to establish links with old Russian emigrants, he finds himself in an assisted living facility for senile men and women. It does not take him too long to discover that the only thing that ties all these people to the Silver Age cultural tradition is perverted sex, which they maintain in memory of the prerevolutionary decadent lifestyle. As it turns out, the old emigres cannot give anything new to Palisandr. On the contrary, his androgynous nature is heavily abused by them and livens up their otherwise dull existence. Sokolov shows that the contact between the two cultures is unnecessary and virtually impossible on any meaningful level. At best it is approximated when Palisandr, a keen collector of graveyards, is appointed by the new Soviet government as the "manager of the Russian Cemetery Diaspora" *(komendant Rossiiskogo Kladbishchenskogo Zarubezh'ia)*, which gives him the opportunity to transport his vast collection back to the Soviet Union.

Speaking of the cultural and literary sources of Russian alternative prose, Viktor Erofeev (b. 1947) acknowledges that it "has learnt from a strange mixture of teachers."[1] The incomplete list of sources includes the Marquis de Sade, decadents, surrealists, mystics, pop artists, and Nabokov.[2] For Erofeev, a renowned representative of the alternative prose school and one of Russia's leading literary critics, "learning" results from very careful study, almost X-ray examination and scrutiny. His collected works include scholarly articles on Rozanov, Shestov, Dostoevskii, Nabokov, Sologub, Bely, and Chekhov. Erofeev does not lose sight of Western European and American cultural traditions. The list of the non-Russian cultural figures that have attracted his attention over the last twenty-five years is equally impressive. Apart from this, he wrote introductory articles to the selected works of Shestov, Rozanov, Nabokov, *The Penguin Book of New Russian Writing,* and a collection of stories by twenty-first-century Russian writers entitled *Time to Give Birth* (*Vremia rozhat'*, 2001). He was the second Russian writer after Nabokov to be invited by the *New Yorker* to contribute his memoirs about his privileged Soviet childhood, as well as stories and essays.

Erofeev's apparent narrow focus in the 1980s and in the 1990s on representatives of the Russian Silver Age, and its immediate successors like Nabokov, cannot be fortuitous. Brezhnev's Russia of the 1970s and early 1980s (when alternative prose was in a state of gestation), followed by a period of democratic reforms and cultural revitalization in the late 1980s and early 1990s, had much in common with a similar period of stagnation in Russia in the 1880s that gave way to a cultural renaissance. Whether a believer in "eternal recurrence" or not, Erofeev drew explicit parallels between Russia's new alternative prose and its silver-haired ancestors.[3] His celebrated articles "A Funeral Feast for Soviet Literature" (1989) and "Russia's *Fleur du Mal*" (1993), in which he presents a retrospective view of Russian literary tradition and provides a theoretical background for the emergence of alternative prose, sound very much like the apology for decadence and symbolism voiced by Dmitrii Merezhkovskii in 1893 in "On the Reasons for the Decline and New Trends in Contemporary Russian Literature."

Erofeev proves himself to be a quick learner. Like his beloved Vasilii Rozanov (1856–1919), he "pricks up his ears" *(vslushivaetsia)* and "peers tirelessly" *(vsmatrivaetsia)* at the most ordinary things.[4] The results of such scrutiny well surpass those of Rozanov. Where Rozanov sees only a phallus ("the pine-tree, silver fir, spruce tree, particularly, particularly the cone of the spruce tree, 'the sight of a tree,' the sky dome—everything is phalluslike"), Erofeev observes "with the meticulousness of a naturalist [that the cone of] the regal spruce tree looks more like a little brown sausage of dog shit."[5] From Nabokov via Gogol Erofeev's narrator inherits a sensitive nose which allows him to detect not only "a sharp stink of the man's mouth" and "the discreet scent of a poor aging woman" but also a variety of smells that are exuded by male and female genitalia.[6] If Nabokovian characters produce a farting noise mostly with their lips *("Ardalion puknul gubami")*, then Erofeev's characters do it not only less delicately and discreetly but considerably more often.[7] For an epigraph to a story about a man admiring graffiti in the men's washroom, Erofeev shamelessly pulls a line—"leaning against a doorpost" *("prislonias' k dvernomu kosiaku")*—out of Pasternak's poem "Hamlet" from *Doctor Zhivago*.[8] Moreover, he manages to outscore even the seemingly unsurpassable Chekhov. Erofeev's characters religiously eat the notorious Chekhovian watermelon not only "*after that*" (a sadomasochistic gang rape orchestrated by the protagonist of *The Last Judgment* for the "benefit" of his sweetheart of ten years), but also "*before that*" (a sacrificial rape in *Russian Beauty*).

Alternative prose is omnivorous; it swallows and quickly digests both refined and unrefined food. The results of this digestion are more shocking than aesthetically pleasing. After many years of enforced abstinence and strict diet, the alternative prose writers are particularly fond of chewing on sacred cows, whether objects of national pride or of traditional reverence. The new Russian literature, in Erofeev's words,

> has called everything into question: love, children, faith, the church, culture, beauty, nobility of character, motherhood, and even the wisdom of the common people, thereby destroying those populist illusions in which the intelligentsia kept believing through all the years of Soviet power.... [*Alternative prose*] is a joint reaction to the wild Russian reality and the excessive moralism of Russian culture.[9]

In this chapter I will show how Erofeev called into question the Russian tradition of messianic and eschatological writing and presented his inimitable version of the Apocalypse in his first novel, *Russian Beauty* (*Russkaia krasavitsa*, 1982, 1990). Erofeev's constant highlighting of sexuality and gender-related issues in *Russian Beauty* stems not merely from a desire to shock his readers but primarily from the subversive and revisionist approach that he adopted toward the legacy of his predecessors.

As scholarly interest in Erofeev continues to build, Oleg Dark and Robert Porter trace the various ascribed and unascribed literary allusions and quotations that one encounters in *Russian Beauty*.[10] Their work shows how Erofeev slaughtered not one but many sacred cows in his novel. However, in addition to fragments of various literary texts, something much more pervasive is addressed and appropriated in *Russian Beauty*—what Linda Hutcheon calls "the target text."[11] This "target text," I believe, is the book of Revelation, more specifically its reinterpretation within the cultural context of the Russian Silver Age.

Without doubt one of the most prominent sources in Russian literature, the book of Revelation acquired the status of an all-permeating artistic structure during the quarter of a century before the Bolshevik Revolution.[12] Many a Russian intellectual welcomed the vision of Apocalypse, while striving to usher in its more tangible version, the socialist revolution. The preceding dark period of reaction and all-encompassing lethargy provided fertile soil for nursing and nurturing ideas about how to foster the spiritual rebirth of humanity. During the subsequent period of cultural vitality, however, intellectuals got weary of waiting for the event; the change had to be instantaneous—as in the Apocalypse. The apocalyptic theme played an important role in writers as diverse as Vladimir Solov'ev, Berdiaev, Fedorov, Merezhkovskii, Shestov, Bely, and Blok—to name but a few—till it reached its culmination in Rozanov's *The Apocalypse of Our Time* (*Apokalipsis nashevogo vremeni*, 1918), written simultaneously with the unfolding of postrevolutionary events.[13] These, in Rozanov's words, turned the mock apocalypse—as used to be the case—into "events truly apocalyptic in nature."[14]

The origin of Erofeev's apocalyptic moods at the time of writing *Russian Beauty* can be found in his personal life. The early 1980s were a tough and disappointing period for Erofeev: his joint venture, a literary miscellany entitled *Metropolis* (*MetrOpol'*), the cradle of the alternative prose, was closed by Soviet officials, and Erofeev's membership in the Writers' Union was suspended for an indefinite period. Many of his friends were sacked, some choosing to leave the country. *Russian Beauty*, written immediately after the fiasco, provides numerous allusions to these events. For example, the protagonist's parting with her beloved Ksiusha, who is not allowed to reenter Russia, is reminiscent of Erofeev's parting with his close friend, the writer Vasilii Aksenov (b. 1932), who left Russia shortly after the fiasco with *Metropolis* in 1980. Ira's persecution by the authorities after arranging for the publication of her pictures in *Playboy* magazine is a parody of a similar campaign against the contributors to *Metropolis*, who prudently sent extra copies of their magazine to the American publisher. According to Erofeev, there were even rumors spread by the authorities that he and Aksenov (like the fictional Ira and Ksiusha) were involved in a homosexual relationship, using their partnership in *Metropolis* as a disguise. The support of six fictional American beauties for Ira parallels the actual support of American writers (Updike, Vonnegut, Albee, Miller, and Styron) for contributors to *Metropolis*.[15]

Erofeev and his friends were forced to go through various trials and tribulations. The behavior of fellow writers who went out of their way to demonstrate their loyalty to the existing regime was particularly shocking and disappointing. As Erofeev remarked later, Russian alternative prose was purged by the Soviet establishment. This, according to Erofeev, was reminiscent of the Silver Age culture being "aborted" by the establishment some sixty years earlier.[16] It would seem therefore that, like his Silver Age predecessors, Erofeev had every reason to bring the Apocalypse to his country for the edification of its citizens. His identification with and appropriation of the Silver Age's discourse on the ways of improving human nature was only to be expected. Erofeev, however, chose not to follow in the wake of his forerunners.

Russian Beauty is recounted by a first-person narrator, Irina (Ira) Tarakanova, an object of many men's sexual desires, which in most cases she is willing to satisfy. One day she meets a distinguished writer, Vladimir Sergeevich, considerably older than she, and rapidly falls in love with him. Two years later, Vladimir Sergeevich dies in Ira's presence as a result of sexual intercourse. Ira is left to answer various uneasy questions from the media and Soviet authorities, not to mention having to face the hatred of Vladimir's widow and the betrayal of her friends and colleagues. Heartbroken, Ira decides to save the nation by sacrificing herself at the grounds of the historically famous battlefield, presumably Kulikovo. However, instead of turning into a martyr, she is visited by the ghost of her late lover and mysteriously conceives a child by him. Disturbed and frightened, Ira lives in seclusion and resolves to write about what has happened to her.

Unlike many postmodern narrators, who are engaged in confusing the reader, Ira places great importance on the question of verisimilitude: on the one hand, she longs for a scientific explanation of her supernatural experiences, and on the other, she fears ending up in a madhouse as the result of her writing. Thus, she proceeds with her revelation, which she models "unwittingly" on a text that is quintessentially authentic, namely, the Bible. Like the Gospel according to Luke, Ira's story starts with the Annunciation.[17] Not unlike the angel

Gabriel, the cunning gynecologist Stanislav Al'bertovich tells Ira about her extraordinary pregnancy and declares it to be a miracle. However, the fetus suddenly starts to rot, and by the end of the story Ira commits suicide two-thirds of the way through her pregnancy, providing apocalyptic allusions to the book of Revelation. Erofeev boldly superimposes the book of Revelation upon the Gospels and presents an intricate collage of the two.[18] As a result, we have an immaculate conception, but the expectant mother turns out to be the "grandmother of Russian abortion," as Ira is often cursed by others; furthermore, her child instead of being an expected savior turns, in Ira's own words, into "a monster . . . like Hitler or some such monsters."[19]

Erofeev's version of the Apocalypse, apart from being informed by the works of Russian intellectuals (to be discussed below), rests on the multiple semantics of the word *konets* (the end) and its derivatives. The word *konets,* which is used in apocalyptic writings to mean the end of the world *(konets sveta),* has several connotations. In addition to the general meaning of an ending, and more specifically death, in colloquial Russian the word *konets* is often used to denote a phallus.[20] By analogy, the verbs of a similar root *(konchat'* and *konchit')* mean not only to end something or to kill someone, but also to reach sexual orgasm. Because of such complex semantics, the phallus performs a great variety of functions in *Russian Beauty*. For example, Vladimir Sergeevich gets out of a scandalous situation with the help of his reproductive organ: "Then, growing bolder, Vladimir Sergeevich told me how the incidents with the oranges had ended, how he'd put out that bonfire by pissing on it, and everything had turned out very nicely, all had ended well" (111).

Many of the pornographic scenes in Ira's narrative evolve from its intimate links with the book of Revelation. Regarding Vladimir Sergeevich's orgiastic death, the words *konchit'* (to come) and *konchit'sia* (to die) are bound by a cause-and-effect relationship:

> Let him enjoy everything to the full, and he came *[konchal]* gratefully.
> . . . "It was horrible: he died *[konchilsia]* before my very eyes, not to put

it more crudely"; . . . he looks at me with an unloving gaze and doesn't answer. He doesn't utter any last words after coming *[konchil]*, and he came *[konchil]* like a young man—powerfully and hotly—only he overstrained himself, and everything in him finally burst *[okonchatel'no lopnulo]*. I look—his eyes are growing muddy, like a sparrow's, which means finis, you know. (74, 121)

Moreover, as we find out, the approaching "end of a great people" (*konets velikogo naroda,* that is, the Russians) can be easily averted only if Ira offers her services to "Russia's greatest foe" (219), presumably, the devil. Thus, when Ira agrees to save the nation, her death should come as the result of her being impaled on the phallus of the "voluptuous" rapist *(na konets natianut')* (257). Ira offers her body as an arena for the unraveling of the apocalyptic events, and she hopes that the ultimate destruction will take place not throughout the whole of the Soviet Union but only inside her own body. She rationalizes her decision:

"But won't this, Irina Vladimirovna, be terrorism? Won't it be ecologically harmful?" "No," I say, "it won't harm anything, and no human blood will be spilled." "So what will be spilled?" "Everyone knows what: the semen, stinking like pus, of Russia's great foe, the voluptuous flesh-devouring demon, usurper, and autocrat. And once it is spilled, he will rapidly droop, grow wrinkled and weak, and then justice will prevail, the sorcery's endless spell will be broken *[zakonchitsia vekovechnoe koldovstvo]*, because the only explanation for all this is witchcraft." (217–18)

Ira's Christlike gesture fails to save the world, however. She returns home absolutely exhausted and falls sick. The fact that such a truly Christian idea as improving the world through voluntary sacrifice and martyrdom is shown to be barren might be viewed as an allusion to the so-called crisis of traditional Christianity, which was much talked of in Russia at the turn of the twentieth century and was reflected in many works of the period. Their authors sought new and more radical solutions to the improvement of mankind, involving, apart from social change, drastic changes in human anatomy and physiology such as castration, sexual abstinence, cultivation of androgyny, resurrection of the dead, and vegetarianism.[21] Rozanov's *The Apocalypse of Our Time* is particularly noteworthy in this respect. In this work Rozanov speaks openly about the impotence of Christianity and interprets the book of Revelation as an appeal to and the only means to reshape a dying tradition.[22]

Therefore, it is only to be expected that instead of the semen of "Russia's great foe," Ira's body receives the new revelation. This happens when she returns from the battlefield and is visited by the ghost of her lover, who forces her into lovemaking. That night Vladimir Sergeevich not only seduces her but requests her to start writing a new revelation in order to save the dying culture: "He said that culture has been emasculated on all sides, that only a new revelation is capable of bringing it back to life" (295).

In fact, Ira's encounter with Vladimir Sergeevich has all the necessary ingredients for an apocalyptic plot device, for, in the words of Collins: "'Apocalypse' is a genre of revelatory literature with a narrative framework, in which a revelation is mediated by an otherworldly being to a human recipient, disclosing a transcendent reality."[23] The seer, however, should be "a member of the elect deeply troubled by the affairs of his church in this world."[24] Then, why is Ira worthy of a revelation? The idea that a woman with abnormal sexual desires should be endowed with more religious zeal than anybody else most likely echoes certain statements from Rozanov's *People of the Moonlight* (*Liudi lunnogo sveta*, 1912).[25] In this work, Rozanov recounts a story of a woman who "poisoned" the life of her husband, children, and even grandchildren by her inability to control her sexual desire. Apart from her remarkable sexual appetite, this woman leads an exemplary life: she is a hard worker, is extremely patient and benevolent, and in every other way is a really decent human being, a true Christian. Rozanov does not conceal his admiration for women of this kind. This and many other analogous situations allow him to conclude that such women often combine powerful sexual desires with religious ardor and devote their lives to various heroic deeds. Such women are truly remarkable: their state of delirium is informed either by erotic or religious visions, and even if they use foul language, it is steeped in religious mysticism. Such conclusions allow Rozanov once again to revel in his favorite speculations that sex and "the really true religion" originate from the same root.[26]

Ira's sexual intercourse with Vladimir Sergeevich (which Ira experiences in a state of delirium because of her sickness) is in fact modeled after chapter 10 of the book of Revelation in which Saint John the Divine describes how he "ate" the book:

> 9. And I went unto the angel, and said unto him, Give me the little book. And he said unto me, Take *it*, and eat it up; and it shall make thy belly bitter, but it shall be in thy mouth sweet as honey.
>
> 10. And I took the little book out of the angel's hand, and ate it up; and it was in my mouth sweet as honey: and as soon as I had eaten it, my belly was bitter.
>
> 11. And he said unto me, Thou must prophesy again before many peoples, and nations, and tongues, and kings.

Recall that when Vladimir Sergeevich makes love to Ira, she is consumed with pleasure that she never experienced before: "First he occupied me with intellectual conversations about God, and then, blowing his cover, got down to business. . . . Aah! More, oh, more, Leonardik! Oh, yes, yes... how sweet! A-a-ah! a-a-ah . . . how delicious! My dear . . . ooh! a-a-ah! God! Ooh, a-a-a-a-ah!" (291). Soon this sweet taste of lovemaking gives way to "the unmistakable aftertaste, the earliest herald of alarm . . . [accompanied by] a nagging pain down below," which tells Ira that she is pregnant (3). The above-mentioned intertextual parallels suggest that, like Saint John, Ira also carries the little book in her belly. The idea that a sexual organ can function as a writing instrument is observed by Ira when she compares the phallus of one of her lovers to "a sharpened pencil."[27] In Ira's case, the Word is literally made flesh, and this flesh immediately starts to rot, with the smell of this rotten flesh replacing Ira's famous smell of bergamot.

To understand what went wrong with Ira's child, we should look at its parents. The father of Ira's baby is an eminent writer who is wooed by the authorities. And he is not the only one. Prominent men of letters (dead and alive), striving underground writers, and official Soviet journalists abound in *Russian Beauty*. The problems of what to write and how to write are at the core of the motivations and ambitions of many characters. Before his death, Vladimir Sergeevich compares himself to Fedor Tiutchev (1803–1873), a renowned poet and a precursor of the Russian symbolists, and declares to Ira his decision to devote himself solely to writing an autobiographical novel. In his novel he was going to portray the aging colonel who, after learning about the infidelities of his young lover, "shoots her himself with his smoking revolver." He describes the scene for Ira: "He stands above her, his legs apart, with a smoking revolver; nearby are the burning remains of a supply train, and in the sky delicate fighter planes fly west: a mixture of Tiutchev and the shockheaded colonel, he then departs to take Warsaw, or Prague, or Copenhagen" (117). The fact that the novel was going to be written "against the background of earth-shattering events" (116), together with his predilection for burning trains and fighter planes, indicates that Vladimir Sergeevich was thinking about writing his own version of the Apocalypse. The pun of Vladimir Sergeevich's identifying himself (and his character) with Tiutchev lies not only in the obvious parallels between his affair with Ira and Tiutchev's relationship with Elena Denis'eva. The fact that in this novel the colonel actually murders his lover seems to be a crude materialization of Tiutchev's famous line, "Oh, how murderously we love" *(O, kak ubiistvenno my liubim)*, which was meant to be taken metaphorically.

Ira's relationship with Vladimir Sergeevich is informed not only by personal events (like those of Tiutchev's relationship with Denis'eva), but by more general discourses—pertinent to the apocalyptic moods that pervaded late imperial Russia—on subjects such as love, sex, death, and resurrection. Thus, Vladimir Sergeevich's appeal to write a new revelation and Ira's subsequent pregnancy parodies the cherished dream of Nikolai Berdiaev (1874–1948) about the "immanent" Apocalypse and the third revelation that was going to save the world. It is noteworthy that Berdiaev expected this new revelation to come not from heaven but from within a human being of his own free will: "The immanent Apocalypse presumes creative activity of the man himself, his own revelation. . . . One should not expect the third testament to come from above. . . . Only within one's own depth and of one's own free will can the man uncover the third testament. The testament of the spirit."[28]

Ira's lover is also spiritually indebted to yet another thinker whose first name and patronymic—Vladimir Sergeevich—are identical to his own. This is Vladimir Sergeevich Solov'ev (1853–1900), one of the most influential late nineteenth-century Russian philosophers. The Solov'evian connection throws light on Vladimir Sergeevich's sudden death. In his seminal work *The Meaning of Love* (*Smysl liubvi*, 1892–1894), Solov'ev condemns promiscuity as well as any type of relationship between men and women that might result in procreation, being in favor of pure (unconsummated) love. This might explain both Vladimir Sergeevich's inability for a long time to consummate his relationship with Ira and his sudden death immediately after making love to her. As many of his fin-de-siècle predecessors did or as they wished to do, Vladimir Sergeevich dies by the hand of his lover, screaming and "roll[ing] around at [her] feet" while she whips him with his leather belt (118). His countenance is compared to that of a dying sparrow ("his eyes are growing muddy, like a sparrow's"), which can be read as a reference to Solov'ev's name derived from a bird.[29] Ira's unfading beauty, her bisexuality, together with her patronymic, Vladimirovna, might be seen as a reflection on Solov'ev's vision of perfect human beings of the future, whom he expected to be androgynous.

A man who shunned women in real life, Solov'ev received subsequent recognition in artistic and literary circles for his cult of the Eternal Feminine, which was expected to save the world.[30] The mysterious Eternal Feminine was more of an abstract philosophical category than anything connected with actual women. Nevertheless, Solov'ev's ideas inspired many of his followers, Blok and Bely among them, to search for possible incarnations of the Eternal Feminine among their female contemporaries. As Blok's poem "The Stranger" ("Neznakomka," 1906) attests, the boundary between a prostitute and the national savior eventually became considerably blurred. Thus, Ira, an avid reader of Blok's poetry and the "unearthly bride" of Vladimir Sergeevich (109, 119), might be seen as a Soviet incarnation of the Solov'evian-cum-Blokian feminine ideal. (In fact, Ira's last name, Tarakanova, contains a hidden reference to Blok, because Blok and Liubov' Dmitrievna were married in the church of the village Tarakanovo in 1903.) Moreover, by the end of his life Solov'ev identified his Eternal Feminine with "woman clothed in the sun," an image that comes from the book of Revelation.[31] According to Solov'ev, this woman (not unlike Erofeev's Ira) was expected to "reveal the truth [and] give birth to the word . . . in the end the eternal beauty [was going to] be fertile, and from her [was going to] emerge the world's salvation."[32]

Another thinker whose works informed Ira's relationship with her lover is Nikolai Fedorov (1829–1903). Fedorov did not rely on the Apocalypse alone in bringing universal salvation closer, so he supplemented it with his *Philosophy of the Common Task* (*Filosofiia obshchego dela*, 1906–1913), which propagated the all-inclusive resurrection of the dead "fathers." The words "resurrection" and "raising from the dead" abound in *Russian Beauty*.[33] Here, however, they are used by Ira as euphemisms for erection. Thus, she refers to the long-term process of arousing Vladimir Sergeevich as the resurrection of the biblical Lazarus, with Lazarus standing only for the phallus: "Ksyusha asks: have I raised his Lazarus? Well, I'm not going to boast, but I resurrected it, although the situation was tricky, he was not promising" (74). Ira's choice of words is not accidental. As is often the case with Erofeev, what looks to be only a risqué episode on the surface, has in fact a complex multilayered structure underneath.[34] For, according to Fedorov, the resurrection of Lazarus was the most important deed performed by Christ. "Restoring him to life, Christ proved an ordinary mortal to be resurrected even in an advanced state of decay and demonstrated the capacity of the human body for reversing the process of disintegration."[35]

Like a true Fedorovian, Ira combines the process of resurrection with moral improvement: "I had encouraged him to shout wildly: Shout for all you are worth, I would urge him. Spew all that grandeur out of you, and Lazarus will come alive, and he did come alive, and now, I see, he is coming to life slowly, slyly, a muddy drop of jism is quivering on the naughty fucker!"[36] Ira follows Fedorov's teaching reasonably closely, except for one point.[37] According to Fedorov, "One component of the human body that will not be needed after the abolition of death, and so will not be reconstructed at the time of resurrecting, is the sexual-reproductive system."[38]

Vladimir Sergeevich's nickname—Leonardik—which stands for "Leonardo da Vinci, formerly an Italian artist," as Ira refers to him in her final letter (323), endows his personality with the traits of an outstanding Renaissance man. In Russian culture the image of Leonardo was formed under the influence of a powerful portrait of Leonardo da Vinci, created by Dmitrii Merezhkovskii in his novel *The Romance of Leonardo da Vinci* (1901). From Leonardo, Leonardik inherits his omnivorousness and unscrupulousness. Merezhkovskii's Leonardo is equally friendly with worthy and unworthy people. With the same enthusiasm he devises projects and prepares blueprints for a new environmentally clean two-story city, a brothel, a flying machine, and a gigantic canal. He interrupts his work on the head of Mary, the mother of Christ, in order to draw a sketch of two crudely deformed persons. Vladimir Sergeevich's cherished dream of having sex with the Siamese twins can be traced to Leonardo's astounding passion for new experiences and experiments. Although there is no evidence of Leonardo's sexual involvement with women, his disciple believes that his master would definitely have had intercourse at least once, if only out of sheer curiosity.

Leonardo's treatment of Mona Lisa—the love of his life—is equally instructive. Instead of addressing problems of a real woman who happens to be in love with him, Leonardo chooses to immortalize her in his painting. The living woman is interesting to him only as an object for his art. Day after day he slowly transfers her features to the canvas. The portrait comes to life, while the real woman dies.[39] Leonardo's treatment of Mona Lisa serves as a model to follow for Leonardik when he resolves to part with Ira and immortalize her in his future writings: "Well, okay, have it your way, we'll never see each other again, but I will portray you and will suffer as if you had died" (117). Only Erofeev's Leonardik is much too human. He begs Ira for a farewell lovemaking and his ailing heart fails him.

It is possible to squeeze out yet another association between these two characters. Leonardik's preference for operating from his dacha, the wife, Zinaida, who persecutes her young rival, even preventing her from taking an "active" part in his funeral—all of this points to Vladimir's other prototype, namely, Boris *Leonidovich* Pasternak, whose fondness for his country house in Peredelkino and his affair with Olga Ivinskaia became legendary.[40] Such a nickname—Leonardik—also brings to mind the literary activity of Vladimir's immediate contemporary, namely Leonid Brezhnev (1906–1982), who at the end of his life shared his war and postwar experiences in a series of ghost-written books such as *The Little Land (Malaia zemlia,* 1975), *Virgin Soil (Tselina,* 1977), and *Revival (Vozrozhdenie,* 1978). In his books Brezhnev presented an eyewitness account of the crucial events in the life of the Soviet people that can be read apocalyptically.[41] It was also common knowledge that Brezhnev's books were ghost-written. In Russian *vozrozhdenie* means both revival and the Renaissance. This is why Ira insists on calling her lover a "Renaissance artist" *(khudozhnik Vozrozhdeniia)*: he is a peculiar crossbreed between an artist who inherited the cultural vitality of the Silver Age and a corrupt communist, between a philosopher who admires the Renaissance and an author of mediocre books. Erofeev employs an unreliable *skaz*-narrator (who is "uneducated," always conveniently drunk and confused), which makes possible and justifies the existence of such cultural crossbreeds in the fictional world of *Russian Beauty.* Ira's joke on the eve of her mock sacrifice can serve as an illustration of its basic principles: "Do you know . . . why Vasilii Ivanovich [Chapaev] wanted to cross a watermelon with a cockroach? So that when you cut it, all the seeds will scurry away" (244).

The joke is especially poignant if one remembers that Ira's last name is Tarakanova (which literally means "of the cockroaches").

Such peculiar crossbreeding allows Erofeev to put his "silver-rich" amalgam (Tiutchev-Merezhkovskii-Solov'ev-Berdiaev-Fedorov-Pasternak) within a certain time frame. Not only did Vladimir Sergeevich absorb the features of cultural figures of the Silver Age, he is also a peculiar crossbreed between *Vladimir* Nabokov (1899–1977) and Aleksandr *Sergeevich* Pushkin (1799–1837). In his first utterance Vladimir Sergeevich identifies himself with Pushkin by emphasizing that they both love winter. Like Pushkin he keeps calling Ira "the genius of pure beauty" (101) and beseeches her to grant his wildest wishes, just as Pushkin's "golden fish" does for an "old fisherman" (46–48).

The Nabokovian theme intervenes when Vladimir Sergeevich declares his deeply Russian love for winter and adds, "In winter we turn the tennis court into a skating rink."[42] From Nabokovian characters (Humbert Humbert, in particular) Vladimir Sergeevich inherits his passion for playing tennis and his love for little girls.[43] As Ira remarks about his playing tennis with Ksiusha when she was still in her early teens: "I know that once, on the tennis court, the power behind her serve made you suddenly realize that she had grown up, and you missed the ball, causing her papa a certain embarrassment, despite your friendship."[44] When Ira analyzes her behavior in Vladimir Sergeevich's presence, she confesses that she "always felt like a shy schoolgirl with stumpy pigtails" (100). Ira's "refusal" to accept a car as a present from her lover brings to mind Lolita's unwillingness to take Humbert's car during their last encounter. In Ira's situation the car is most likely the product of Ira's imagination—"and I didn't need a car, and even if he had given me one, I would have smashed it right up, like an egg! I didn't want a car, I wanted happiness" (94)—but the fact that she thinks along these lines is very revealing. Ira's patronymic—Vladimirovna—suggests an incestuous relationship with her lover.[45]

Erofeev does not bring Pushkin and Nabokov together only to produce laughter. Their joint appearance is only natural. If the Russian Silver Age traced proudly its provenance back to Pushkin, then in Nabokov it had its legitimate heir, or—in Zinaida Shakhovskaia's words—its last representative.[46] Nabokov more than anyone felt this bond and completed the circle by diligently working on his "definitive" translation of, and commentary on, Pushkin's *Eugene Onegin*.

As I have demonstrated, Vladimir Sergeevich does not have only one, but a number of conceivable prototypes. Since he has no surname and it is repeatedly pointed out that he is very old and that reading his books had been compulsory in secondary school—Ira even says, "I had known of you since childhood" (87)—it is possible to identify him not only with one particular person or persons, but with the whole literary tradition, mainly that of the Silver Age. Vladimir Sergeevich's identification with the Renaissance artist is not fortuitous: as we have seen, from the late 1930s onward the Silver Age has been often described as the period of religious, artistic, and spiritual renaissance. Consequently, Vladimir's child harbored in Ira's body can be seen as some form of legacy of that antecedent tradition.

Nadezhda Azhgikhina and Helena Goscilo begin their article on the institution of female beauty in modern Russia with a brief discussion of *Russian Beauty*. They suggest that one of the weaknesses of this novel lies in its pseudo-female narrator, whom Erofeev used to "ventriloquiz[e] . . . his own purely male complexes and problems."[47] The persecuted female heroine mourning her dead lover is only to be expected, however, in a novel apparently devoted to passing on cultural tradition and literary evolution. As Beth Holmgren demonstrates, in Soviet society (particularly at the time of Stalin's purges) gender distinctions were strongly emphasized among intellectuals. In the absence of their dead or prosecuted husbands, brothers, and fathers, Soviet women "were not merely articulate survivors, but eventual powerbrokers enabled by a peculiar overlap of neglect and opportunity; . . . they frequently resurfaced as the guardians and even co-producers of artistic treasure." Hence from the early 1930s on, women found themselves "drawn into the production and maintenance of unofficial culture. It fell to them to preserve the cultural artifacts—the texts, images, and practices—produced in this place."[48] As a matter of fact, prior to his death Vladimir Sergeevich confided in Ira that he had also managed to create "something forbidden" apart from his patently pro-Soviet works (117). It is conceivable, therefore, to picture Ira as such "guardian and co-producer of artistic treasure" in the mode of Nadezhda Mandelstam, Lidiia Chukovskaia, or even Olga Ivinskaia.

Ira, however, conceals the "artistic treasure(s)" of her dead lover neither in saucepans, nor in trunks or baskets, but literally inside her body. Her supernatural pregnancy, therefore, might be perceived as one text or tradition permeating and growing inside another text or tradition, with sexuality being supplanted by intertextuality. The underlying structure of Ira's narrative mirrors the pattern of her submissive sexual behavior. Her narrative is as open and vulnerable to the intrusion of other narratives as is her body to all who want to satisfy their sexual needs. (One of her lovers, the musician Dato, for example, liked attacking Ira from behind and taking her by surprise.)

Ira's inability to pour out her story—"it's quite a burden to carry around" (13)—is linked with her unwanted pregnancy. Thus, the threadbare metaphor of comparing the work of an artist with a child (or to the state of being "pregnant" with art) is turned upside down in Erofeev's novel. Ira's "child," on the contrary, constantly interferes with her writing and threatens her with possible catastrophe: "and this writing summons me, summons, I can't stop writing, fool, and it is as though I am again running through the field, the same shivers and fever, and the fateful child howls in my womb, orders me from the womb not to write, threatens a miscarriage, but I can't not tell, and indeed in any event I'm done for, such now is my fate" (255–56). Moreover, the reprobate fetus starts to rot, a development matched by the texual chaos, reaching its apogee in the last chapter, in which Ira seemingly finds it harder and harder to preserve her own voice.[49] Ira delivers an eloquent speech about erecting a monument to her genitalia that relies heavily on Akhmatova's *Requiem:*[50] "Give my cunt to the poor; . . . if you collect money for a monument to her, don't put it in the middle of a busy square, that's tasteless, don't put it facing Saint Basil's, for it is unbecoming for the Blessed Basil to behold her every day, and also don't put her on the Manezh Square like a Christmas tree! There are in Moscow far cozier corners, the meeting places of lovers" (327–28). Her vengeful thoughts, which suddenly give way to humility ("you'll groan under the weight and die sorry deaths! Let it be! I welcome this grave new world of mass death and grant my permission. . . . But all the same I am not evil, no, and doubts seized me" [325]), are evocative of Rozanov's words: "I could have filled in the world with crimson clouds of smoke. . . . But I don't want to. And everything would have been burnt down. . . . But I don't want to. Let my little grave be peaceful and 'to the side.'"[51]

To restore the cohesiveness of her narrative, Ira has to purge her child by going through a self-inflicted Apocalypse. In *Russian Beauty* the long-prophesied Apocalypse is precipitated, occurs, and is restricted to the level of "writing." The narrator simply asserts her freedom to put an end to her narrative: "Beat it! I composed you in order to compose myself, but when I discompose you I shall dissolve myself as a person" (342). There is no threat that this ghastly finale may turn into a "world" tragedy (or spill over to the "real" world). In accordance with Ira's wishes, it is restricted to her body, for she hangs herself two-thirds through her pregnancy *before* anybody can stop her. The "author," the only witness and survivor of this novelistic Apocalypse, steps forward and says, "Good to see you!"[52]

> And so it's time, good-bye, or else they'll make it in time. I clamber up onto the soapy stool, toward the ceiling, the stool I used for washing clothes, and the soap has caked. I climb up, and Leonardik enters. . . . I take a step toward him. I throw myself into his embrace. Tighter! Hold me tighter, my dear! Enter, enter me, my prince! Oh, how good! . . . Let me come sweetly! *[Dai mne sladko konchit'!]*[53] You are totally choking me, beloved. . . . Oh, no! Don't! That hurts, idiot! I don't w-a-a-a-a-a-a-nnn-nna . . . wa . . . w . . . wa . . .
>
> Light! I see light! It widens. It grows. One bound and I am free. I hear soothing voices, they egg me on approvingly. The gas water heater drones. I see her: she is swinging evenly. And such a generous belly.

Good-bye, froglet! I look at her: she has fallen silent. Awash with happy tears. Mommy opens the doors. The guests flood in. The wedding! The wedding! But where's the bride? And here comes the bride! Good to see you! (343)

One should not take this sad finale too seriously, that is, as the actual death of the female protagonist, for it is suspiciously reminiscent of the famous passage from Roland Barthes's *The Pleasure of the Text*: "The pleasure of the text is like that untenable, impossible, purely *novelistic* instant so relished by Sade's libertine when he manages to be hanged and then cut the rope at the very moment of his orgasm, his bliss."[54]

By bringing together the book of Revelation and Soviet socialist reality of Moscow in 1980, Erofeev daringly explores previously untrodden paths and creates a new version of the Apocalypse. In this revelation, a renowned prostitute is expected to save the nation, while the phallus is mythologized and plays a crucial role in Erofeev's eschatology. Erofeev's Apocalypse, however, is not an act of intellectual sacrilege. In some ways it is an Apocalypse with a human face, so to speak. As is often the case in real life, Erofeev's characters quietly go through with their personal Apocalypses (drugs, alcohol, death, sexual abuse), events that usually escape the eyes of a witness.

In narrowing the sphere of apocalyptic events, Erofeev might have been following in part the lead of artists of the Silver Age. For them private life and art (the public sphere) merged to such an extent that they became virtually indistinguishable.[55] Thus, when in 1929 Andrei Bely searched for the cause of his pervasively apocalyptic moods in the 1900s and 1910s, he found it in his very personal experiences: for most of his childhood he had been torn between his incompatible and constantly arguing parents.[56] Characteristically, Bely sought solutions to his private problems in the world-consuming holocaust that he welcomed in his writings. In *Russian Beauty*, on the contrary, the events of a cosmic order take place not within the whole universe, but within the microcosm of one body (we might add, the body of the book) and manifest themselves through its function and malfunction, such as drinking, bingeing, excessive sexual indulgence, death, unwanted pregnancy, and even flatulence. In the opening portion of the book Ira dismisses contemporary writers on the grounds that they are "always rather agitated, they fuss, and they come very quickly" *(bystro konchaiut)* (14). The Russian text allows this to be interpreted both as that they reach their orgasm too soon or that—to one's disappointment—they stop telling their story halfway through. In her account Ira does not spare any details. She creates her version of a private, intimate Apocalypse in which the size of her toes and the smell of her groin prophesy the approach of the end. It is—to borrow the title of Erofeev's short story—truly a "Pocket Apocalypse" ("Karmannyi apokalipsis").

Erofeev's book of Revelation, although literally pregnant with the literary tradition of the Silver Age, is notably different from the works of his numerous predecessors. He brings to the point of absurdity the preoccupation of Silver Age artists with the internal, private sphere, their obsession with both sex and religion, and their general tendency toward syncretism.[57] Does this actually mean that the Silver Age holds no attraction for Erofeev? On the contrary. His recent literary essays show that he is as preoccupied as ever with the works of his predecessors—after all, Ira was really in love with Vladimir Sergeevich. However, it was precisely because of this love, this almost irresistible attraction, that Erofeev felt the need to ridicule their ideas and thus to purge himself of their influence. Otherwise, as the novel suggests, his "incestuous" relationship with his forefathers would have given birth to a monstrous or simply stillborn child. Erofeev's situation was typical of that of many representatives of alternative prose. On the one hand, in order to legitimatize their subversive and often overtly offensive writings within the Russian cultural tradition, they had to show that they in fact took their roots from one of the most vital periods in cultural history; on the other, to acquire or preserve their own voice they had to distinguish themselves radically from their progenitors. In any case, "strong writers do not choose their prime precursors: they are chosen by them, but they have the wit to transform the forerunners into composite and therefore partly imaginary beings."[58]

9   Coda

THE SILVER AGE UP CLOSE

> To forget is not to lose
> But finally accept—
> Inside onself, at the very bottom, for all eternity . . .
> —Maximilian Voloshin, 1907

During the night of March 15–16, 2004, I dreamed that Anna Akhmatova and I were climbing a very tall mountain, with me acting as a guide. Besides the two of us, there is some boy and Lidiia Korneevna Chukovskaia, whose age is difficult to tell. Out of nervousness, I keep addressing her as "Sofia Petrovna." It takes us forever to climb the mountain, but we keep going. Then we are lying on the brink of a bluff, looking around and down the drop with enjoyment, and suddenly we become aware that we have left Akhmatova somewhere behind us. We begin to retrace our steps mentally and decide, for some reason, that she remained on the subway—never managed to get out of it, having tarried on the escalator. We climb down the mountain (it takes very long in the dream, and Lidiia Korneevna, contrary to my expectations, seems very calm and in no hurry at all). We go down to the subway and find Akhmatova there.

I still feel the intensity of that dream and the elation from the piercing thought that, after all, she *was* my contemporary. I was born before she died. "Who would have thought that I was meant to live for such a long time? And why didn't I know it before?" Akhmatova wrote in 1957.[1] "Pushkin," she told Natalia Roskina a few years ealier, "would have been unthinkable in the 1840s. He would have been utterly forgotten and it would have been terrible."[2] In his analysis of the literary essays that would-be journalists write when applying for admission to Moscow State University, Oleg Lekmanov reveals how little these young people know about Akhmatova in particular and the culture of the first half of the twentieth century in general. Accordingly, Akhmatova is described first as "rejecting the revolution of 1905 [sic!]," then "witnessing the death of her only son," and later "committing suicide" as a desperate "representative of the Silver Age."[3] More so, one of the youngsters endowed Akhmatova with a pair of golden whiskers *(zlatousaia)*, a corruption of Marina Tsvetaeva's famous description— "the golden-mouthed Anna of all Russias" *(zlatoustaia Anna vseia Rusi)*. If Lekmanov's survey reflects the emerging tendencies in Russian cultural education, does this mean that the Silver Age can vanish? Is this ever possible?

High up on the wall of the church in Tarakanovo where Blok was married in 1903, one can still make out the graffito: "Draftees for 1979– 1981 were here." But the times when draftees climb up the scaffolding of a dilapidated church to pay their respects to Blok are now gone. By the end of the 1990s, the legacy of the Silver Age had passed through the stages of being ingested, digested, and assimilated and had entered the inevitable stage of being internalized and eternalized. This was prepared by a series of interconnected events that may be described as the loss of its delectable "outsideness" *(vnenakhodimost')*. A high school student wrote in the visitors' book of the Blok Museum in Tarakanovo:[4]

> Blok is cool!
> Blok is class!
> We love Blok,
> And Blok loves us.

Whereas only recently the Silver Age was considered foreign territory, today it has been reasonably explored and developed and has its own maps and guidebooks. For example, a study of Boris Tukh is marketed as *A Silver Age Guidebook* (*Putevoditel' po Serebrianomu veku*, 2005). These days the Silver Age is not only read and heard about but also seen (as in El'dar Riazanov's melodrama, *The Key to the Bedroom* [*Kliuch ot spal'ni*], 2004) and tasted in the Silver Age restaurant that I visited in Moscow. Whereas in 1993 the idea of re-experiencing the Silver Age appeared both attractive and unattainable, now it seems superfluous and unpalatable. The crux of the matter is not in the sky-high prices at the restaurant—the problem is in the impossibility of entering the same proverbial stream twice. How can you make a regular meal of something that quite recently triggered a million exotic associations (*rasstegai*, hazel-grouse, oysters, artichokes, and asparagus) without its losing its initial fascination? It's a question of anticipation versus the actual taste. As Andrei Makine shows in his *Dreams of My Russian Summers*, the direct transference destroys the magic of the words, and the French *bartavelles* turn into plain partridges, while the "gossamer threads, silvery and light in [the narrator's fin de siècle] fantasy" are transformed into "the new strands of barbed wire" that marked the territory of a Stalinist women's camp.[5]

Today, despite the ongoing publication of contentious works, such as Vera Luknitskaia's publication of her husband's private diary in 2005, interest in the Silver Age is clearly on the wane. This can be seen, for example, in the deserted rooms of the Silver Age Museum in Moscow or in the recent debates about the future of literary museums in Russia held in St. Petersburg in November 2005 on the occasion of the 125th anniversary of Blok's birth. Despite their enviable energy, enthusiasm, and sheer courage, many museum workers complained not only about their meager funding, but also about the low attendance, particularly on the part of the younger generation. The director of the Literary Museum at the Pushkinskii Dom wondered, "How can we present Blok's passing on so that it will not oppress but excite visitors?" *(Kak vyrazit' konets Bloka, chtoby on ne ugnetal, a vozbuzhdal?)*, when asked to share her impressions of the recently unveiled exhibition at the Blok Museum in Petersburg. One student of Blok confessed that after visiting the mansions of some so-called new Russians (the Russian nouveaux riches) she was unimpressed by the living quarters of Russia's past geniuses: "Even Tolstoi's estate in Yasnaia Poliana (which I considered the most beautiful house in the world when I was young) pales in comparison with what you can build nowadays." Other participants in the discussion advocated an interactive approach, suggesting that visitors should be encouraged to write a poem or a story or to make a drawing while listening to the tour guide. In fact, the interactive approach has been successfully employed in the Akhmatova Museum in the Fountain House. Schoolchildren are typically asked to choose among various things from "Akhmatova's chest"—such as an old camera, a pair of glasses, a teddy bear, an old coffee grinder, a theater lorgnette, a picture frame, to name but a few—and comment on what they thought the purpose of this or that object was. As the 2006 visitors' book indicates, most visitors had very good impressions of Akhmatova's communal apartment. The inscriptions range from "It is absolutely overwhelming. I want to come here again and again" to "Very good! I would have liked to live in a similar apartment. Maybe I would have started writing poetry" to "Everything is so cool" to "My dear young romantics wanting to live in such an apartment, how wonderful that you imagine life in this apartment along these romantic lines . . ." to "Oh, God, how this house has changed over the years. While it seems that I left it not long ago." The last was signed "A. A." (Anna Akhmatova).

Clearly, what increases in one place inevitably decreases in another. Insofar as the Silver Age flows into the exhibitions of permanent museums similar to Disneyland, where you can casually visit your favorite fairy-tale characters, the Silver Age loses its erstwhile preeminence in prose fiction, literary criticism, journalism, drama, and even architecture. The "eternalization" of the Silver Age in Russian culture was highlighted by the restoration of the Christ the Savior Cathedral in Moscow, which had been destroyed by the Soviets in 1931.[6] Today the time frames of cultural artifacts that are being restored are shifting both in literature and architecture. In literature, theater, and cinema there is a tilt toward the seventeenth and eighteenth centuries, late Stalinism, and the 1960s.[7] Something very similar has happened in restoration work. The current schedule of restoration projects in Moscow includes the walls of Kitai-Gorod, Borovitskaia Square, Varvarka Street, the "Moskva" Hotel, and the infamous "House on the Embankment," which was allotted its place in the cultural canon in the 1960s and in the 1970s.

The uncertain position of the Silver Age in literary studies has given rise to the myth of the necessity and, what is more significant, the possibility of presenting its true picture completely. According to a literary scholar, Natalia Dzutseva, only a total reconstruction of the ethos of the Silver Age could ensure a "reading" of the prerevolutionary culture that would be "fully commensurate with its content" (*do kontsa, adekvatno [ego] istinnomu soderzhaniiu*).[8] As revealed by the recent debates about a scientific approach to the preparation of a complete (academic) edition of Blok's famous *Notebooks* (*Zapisnye knizhki*), apart from many other reasons, the publication is stalled by the sheer enormity of the enterprise, which would require copious references and footnotes to numerous texts that were written during Blok's lifetime and after his death, not to mention the fact that the specialists are still arguing about how "complete" this complete edition should be. For example, all seemed to agree that Blok's anti-Semitic statements (deleted by Vladimir Orlov from the 1965 publication of the *Notebooks*) should be reinserted into the main body of the text. But what is to be done, for example, with Blok's tedious references to various medications and his meticulous descriptions of his visits to doctors? Should one preserve them? What will they tell us about Blok? Would readers know how to handle this information? Do they actually need all these "insignificant" (but, for commentators, time-consuming) details? These were the questions raised at the 2005 Blok conference in Pushkinskii Dom in St. Petersburg. Ten years earlier, the former director of the Blok Museum in Shakhmatovo stressed the futility of the preservationist approach when it comes to the restoration of writers' homes, such as the Shakhmatovo estate, which was burned down by rioting peasants. Arzamastsev writes, "You can certainly use the painstaking recollections of [Blok's aunt] M. A. Beketova, who traced the sad fate of the estate from beginning to end. But will that bring us closer to Blok? By a conservative reckoning, the house is too small to accommodate all the items Maria Andreevna lists. A scrupulous restoration of such an inventory would most likely lead to creating an antique store rather than an information system about Blok."[9]

The Silver Age institution, which has grown inordinately large, is spinning its wheels in the highly favorable milieu it is unaccustomed to and may be facing a slow death. In the absence of cultural and political upheavals and given the general restoration of the Silver Age, literature ceases to be the only repository of cultural memory, which it has been for so many years. Strange though it may be, despite the seemingly casual ethical standards of representatives of the so-called alternative prose, they happen to be the last Russian writers who still see it as their duty to introduce into their prose allusions to and direct quotations from works by representatives of the Silver Age. In fact, they are proud to call themselves its direct heirs and sometimes even its last representatives. "My *Russian Beauty* is the last product of the Silver Age," Viktor Erofeev told me somberly in spring 2000.

Today prose fiction is unburdening itself of its heavy load of recollection and is reassuming its functions of edifying and entertaining. Present-day writers (and readers) increasingly "return" to the family hearth, from whence, in Pavel Basinskii's words, they begin to "write and speak with their hearts."[10] As is seen from Basinskii's *Novyi Mir* article, heart-to-heart contacts are welcomed not just by writers and readers, but also by "heart-centered" critics, who are beginning to set the goal of raising a "heart-based" culture to the level of a state priority.[11] Likewise, in his novel, *Kablukov* (2005), Anatolii Naiman (once Akhmatova's secretary and a dedicated student of the Silver Age) advocates chastity in deeds and thoughts *(tselomudrie),* as embodied in his main character.[12] Kablukov is a handsome man and a sophisticated cinematographer who comes in contact with many women, but his "complete loyalty to his wife" of many years is "infinitely more important to him than any cheap sexual exploits."[13] In this new cultural environment, the literature of the Silver Age, which has no place for a "philosophy of hope" (in Viktor Erofeev's definition from the 1990s), is acquiring increasingly negative connotations. Notably, in a review of Nancy Andersen's translations of Akhmatova's poems and of her biographical sketch, the cultural historian Aileen Kelly praises Andersen above all for restoring a lovable image of Akhmatova. While in recent years scholars have looked at Akhmatova's creative and personal life "in the light of theories of cultural myth and 'charismatic performance' . . . [and] 'constructed self,'" Andersen has succeeded in "demonstrating convincingly that the key to Akhmatova's performance lies in the moral motivation of her poetry." Endorsing Andersen's mode of interpretation, Kelly concludes that Akhmatova's "obsession with her image sprang from her vision of the unique role and obligations of a Russian poet."[14]

Furthermore, the Silver Age is losing its primary base or "realm of memory," which for many years was embodied in the generation of the 1960s. It was thanks to the efforts of this generation that an active resurrection of the legacy of the Silver Age got under way. Today this generation, whose contribution to the mythology of the Silver Age is so vast, is expending the same amount of enthusiasm on mythologizing itself. They have no more time for the Silver Age. This is clearly evidenced by the number of "round-table discussions" in the "thick journals" devoted to analyzing and interpreting the experiences of the 1960s generation and by the number of memoirs written by its representatives. This seems to be the first generation since the time of "the generation of the Silver Age" that has become aware of its own cultural completeness and finiteness as poignantly as their Silver Age forerunners. The title of Anatolii Naiman's memoirs, *The Glorious End of the Inglorious Generations* (*Slavnyi konets besslavnykh pokolenii*, 1998), and their final words are a case in point: "No matter how close-knit the groups you become part of are, no matter how steadfastly you stick to 'your own kind,' sooner or later, you'll be driven away from society because you have deviated from the expected course by a millimeter, because you've become sick and are no longer as useful as you used to be, because you've grown old and died."[15] Apparently, this acquisition of a sense of closure was brought about in large part by "the death of a poet"—in this case, Joseph Brodsky (1940–1996)—which added to this sense of finality, a kind of metaphysical depth. Given the keen understanding of such finiteness (or "outsideness"), the former object of intense scrutiny (which for many was the Silver Age) must retreat to the background and begin to be perceived as a mere projection of the beholder. For example, Naiman and his friends (according to his memoirs) not only reminded Akhmatova of the days of her youth, which was only natural, given their age difference, but also embodied that youth physically. In Naiman's words, "The ethos of our poetic generation, specifically, of the four of us, characterized by creativity, cheerfulness and energy—and I'm saying this in an unequivocal way, based on observation of concrete facts—reminded her of the 1910s by its direct and indirect correspondences." Naiman explains, "From her frequent comparisons of the way I dressed, behaved, and reacted to things with that of some friends of her youth, for example, I believe that she also found in me a physical resemblance to them."[16]

While the *shestidesiatniki* are wallowing in self-admiration and self-reflection, some prominent representatives of the Silver Age attracted the attention of Aleksandr Solzhenitsyn. In his more than friendly analysis of Bely's *Petersburg*, Solzhenitsyn refers nevertheless to Bely's "unhealthiness" and "mental derangement," adding that "sickliness made a manifold impact on the novel."[17] Wittingly or unwittingly, Solzhenitsyn employs terms well known to the Marxist literary critics of the 1900s, namely, the concepts of the "degeneracy" and "morbidity" of the decadents, drawn from Nordau's classic *Degeneration* (1892). Likewise, in his essay entitled "All That Glitters Is Not Silver: Decadent Poetry at the Turn of the [Twentieth] Century and Modern Times" ("Ne vse to serebro, chto blestit," 1997), a critic, Nikolai Trifonov calls for a reassessment of some allegedly "entrenched history":

> Our century is coming to an end. In summing up its results (both sociopolitical and cultural), it is necessary to reevaluate certain aspects of the entrenched academy and high school–level history of its literary development as well as to correct some traditional assessments. In particular, one should describe the beginning of the twentieth century as the Silver Age of Russian literature not in the direct sense of this term but with reservations—only in a very narrow restricted sense, and in quotation marks.[18]

Until recently the Silver Age occupied a unique place in Russia's collective memory. Its distinct position as a pariah and an enigmatic "other" prevented it from turning into a realm of memory par excellence. It has always been a sleeping volcano, rather than an extinct one. Paradoxically, now that the Silver Age has finally come to occupy its rightful place in the landscape of Russian culture, its future is more bleak and uncertain than it was in the 1920s. On November 4, 2005, Russia for the first time celebrated Day of Popular Unity *(Den' narodnogo edinstva)*. Although not everyone was aware of the exact historical events that made this particular day more memorable than others (most newspapers had to provide short or extended explanations that this was the day Moscow was liberated from the Poles in 1612), this date was chosen by Putin and his government to supplant and erase another "red date" on the calendar, November 7, which for many years had been celebrated as the official annual commemoration of the Bolshevik Revolution. Thus the Bolshevik Revolution is currently being erased from the political and cultural maps of twentieth-century Russia, while the all-pervasive and fundamental cultural role of the Silver Age is being downplayed. Up till now, the revolution of 1917 has been seen as the main enemy of the Silver Age. However, the Silver Age (like the mysterious Atlantis, to which it is often compared) might sink into oblivion not because of the revolution but together with the revolution.

APPENDIX
Original Russian Texts

Translations of these extracts appear in chapter 6.

Александр Блок
Стихотворения

> Явился он на стройном бале
> В блестяще сомкнутом кругу.
> Огни зловещие мигали,
> И взор описывал дугу.
>
> Всю ночь кружились в шумном танце,
> Всю ночь у стен сжимался круг.
> И на заре—в оконном глянце
> Бесшумный появился друг.
>
> Он встал и поднял взор совиный,
> И смотрит - пристальный - один,
> Куда за бледной Коломбиной
> Бежал звенящий Арлекин.

А там - в углу - под образами,
В толпе, мятущейся пестро,
Вращая детскими глазами,
Дрожит обманутый Пьеро.

7 октября 1902

❋ ❋ ❋

... Мелькали жолтые огни
И электрические свечи.
И он встречал ее в тени,
А я следил и пел их встречи.

Когда внезапно смущены,
Они предчувствовали что-то,
Меня скрывали в глубины
Слепые темные ворота. . . .

27 сентября 1902

❋ ❋ ❋

И я, невидимый для всех,
Следил мужчины профиль грубый,
Ее сребристо-черный мех
И что-то шепчущие губы.

При жолтом свете веселились,
Всю ночь у стен сжимался круг,
Ряды танцующих двоились,
И мнился неотступный друг.

Желанье поднимало груди,
На лицах отражался зной.
Я проходил с мечтой о чуде,
Томимый похотью чужой. . . .

Сентябрь 1902

НА СМЕРТЬ ДЕДА
(1 июля 1902 г.)

Мы вместе ждали смерти или сна.
Томительные проходили миги.
Вдруг ветерком пахнуло из окна,
Зашевелился лист Священной Книги.

[...] Но было сладко душу уследить
И в отходящем увидать веселье.
Пришел наш час—запомнить и любить,
И праздновать иное новоселье.
С. Шахматово

❋ ❋ ❋

Не бойся умереть в пути.
Не бойся ни вражды, ни дружбы.
Внимай словам церковной службы,
Чтоб грани страха перейти.

Она сама к тебе сойдет.
Уже не будешь в рабстве тленном.
Манить смеющийся восход
В обличьи бедном и смиренном.

Она и ты—один закон,
Одно веселье Высшей Воли.
Ты не навеки обречен
Отчаянной и смертной боли.
5 июля 1902

Борис Пастернак
Доктор Живаго

Но вместо Фадея Казимировича из-за перегородки вышел кто-то другой. Это был плотный, бритый, осанистый и уверенный в себе человек. Над головою он нес лампу, вынутую из резервуара. Он прошел к столу, за которым спала девушка, и вставил лампу в резервуар. Свет разбудил девушку. Она улыбнулась вошедшему, прищурилась и потянулась. . . . между девушкой и мужчиной происходила немая сцена. Они не сказали друг другу ни слова и только обменивались взглядами. Но взаимное их понимание было пугающе волшебно, словно он был кукольником, а она послушною движениям его руки марионеткой.

Улыбка усталости, появившаяся у нее на лице, заставляла девушку полузакрывать глаза и наполовину разжимать губы. Но на насмешливые взгляды мужчины она отвечала лукавым подмигиванием сообщницы. Оба были довольны, что все обошлось так благополучно, тайна не раскрыта и травившаяся осталась жива.

Юра пожирал обоих глазами. Из полутьмы, в которой никто не мог его видеть, он смотрел не отрываясь в освещенный лампою круг. Зрелище порабощения девушки было неисповедимо таинственно и беззастенчиво откровенно. Противоречивые чувства теснились в груди у него. У Юры сжималось сердце от их неиспытанной силы.

Это было то самое, о чем они так горячо год продолдонили с Мишей и Тоней под ничего не значащем именем пошлости, то пугающее и притягивающее, с чем они так легко справлялись на безопасном расстоянии на словах, и вот эта сила находилась перед Юриными глазами, досконально вещественная и смутная и снящаяся, безжалостно разрушительная и жалующаяся и зовущая на помощь, и куда девалась их детская философия и что теперь Юре делать?

❈ ❈ ❈

От горя, долгого стояния на ногах и недосыпания, от густого пения, и ослепляющего света свечей днем и ночью, и от простуды, схваченной на этих днях, у Юры в душе была сладкая неразбериха, блаженно-бредовая, скорбно-восторженная.

Десять лет тому назад, когда хоронили маму, Юра был совсем еще маленький. Он до сих пор помнил, как он безутешно плакал, пораженный горем и ужасом. Тогда главное было не в нем. Тогда он едва ли даже соображал, что есть какой-то он, Юра, имеющийся в отдельности и представляющий интерес или цену. Тогда главное было в том, что стояло кругом, в наружном. Внешний мир обступал Юру со всех сторон, осязательный, непроходимый и бесспорный, как лес, и оттого-то был Юра так потрясен маминой смертью, что он с ней заблудился в этом лесу и вдруг остался в нем один, без нее. . . .

Совсем другое дело было теперь. Все эти двенадцать лет школы, средней и высшей, Юра занимался древностью и законом Божьим, преданиями и поэтами, науками о прошлом и о природе, как семейною хроникой родного дома, как своею родословною. Сейчас он ничего не боялся, ни жизни, ни смерти, всё на свете, все вещи были словами его словаря. Он чувствовал себя стоящим на равной ноге со вселенною и совсем по-другому выстаивал панихиды по Анне Ивановне, чем в былое время по своей маме. Тогда он забывался, робел и молился. А теперь он слушал заупокойную службу как сообщение, непосредственно к нему обращенное и прямо его касающееся. Он вслушивался в эти слова и требовал от них смысла, понятно выраженного, как это требуется от всякого дела, и ничего общего с набожностью не было в его чувстве преемственности по отношению к высшим силам земли и неба, которым он поклонялся как своим великим предшественникам.

NOTES

Chapter 1. Introduction

1. Tatiana Tolstaya, "Pushkin's Children," in *Pushkin's Children: Writings on Russia and Russians,* trans. Jamey Gambrell (New York: Houghton Mufflin, 2003), 86–87.

2. Omry Ronen, *The Fallacy of the Silver Age in Twentieth-Century Literature* (Amsterdam: Harwood Academic Publishers, 1997), 3.

3. Ibid.

4. Boris Gasparov, introduction to *Cultural Mythologies of Russian Modernism,* ed. Boris Gasparov, Robert P. Hughes, and Irina Paperno (Berkeley and Los Angeles: University of California Press, 1992), 1.

5. Ibid.

6. Ibid., 10.

7. Peter Davidson writes: "A true evaluation of the 'appropriateness' of the term would require a thorough critique of the literature of the Silver Age in the light of an agreed definition of the term and in relation to previous literary periods. Needless to say, such a critique would not depend on the motley usage of the term by various critics, although it might well be prompted by it. Ronen does not attempt this task of evaluation. The extent of his scrutiny is limited to noting the inconsistent usage (and consequent inadequacy) of the term (this is the 'fallacy' of the 'Silver Age' referred to in the book's title), not to arguing or demonstrating its invalidity as a criterion of assessment" (Davidson, review of Omry Ronen, *The Fallacy of the Silver Age, Slavonic Eastern European Review [SEER]* 78 [2000]: 140–41).

8. Petr Pertsov, "Antologiia novoi poezii," review of *The Anthology of New Poetry (Antologia novoi poezii), Novoe vremia* [literary supplement], no. 13775, July 19 (August 1), 1914, 11.

9. The same literary supplement to *Novoe vremia* (see ibid.) features a review of Anna Akhmatova's *Rosary (Chetki).* Akhmatova, who closely followed critical

responses to her work, might have got her idea of the Silver Age from Pertsov's review and not from the later writings of Berdiaev, as is generally believed.

10. Ronen, *The Fallacy of the Silver Age*, 94.

11. Ibid., 93.

12. Richard Gilman exposed the futility of such attempts to exorcise the generally accepted cultural terms: "No decadence? . . . Do we hold a trial, hear evidence and character witness, retire to the jury room, pronounce a verdict, and then watch the guilty one, its poor tattered vague possessions wrapped up in an Art Nouveau bundle on a stick, or thrown into a suitcase held together with cord and bearing stickers from Monte Carlo, Marrakesh, and the liner *Ile de France*, trudge toward the designated border station with an occasional melancholy backward glance? And what land will accept this exile?" (Gilman, *Decadence: The Strange Life of an Epithet* [New York: Farrar, Sraus, and Giroux, 1975], 30).

13. Paul Ricoeur, *Freud and Philosophy: An Essay on Interpretation*, trans. Denis Savage (New Haven: Yale University Press, 1970), 27. I was reminded of Ricoeur's ideas while reading Katerina Clark's introduction to *Petersburg, Crucible of Cultural Revolution* (Cambridge: Harvard University Press, 1995), 26.

14. Apart from Ronen's book and the collection edited by Gasparov et al., see Irene Masing-Delic, *Abolishing Death: A Salvation Myth of Russian Twentieth-Century Literature* (Stanford: Stanford University Press, 1992); Irina Paperno and Joan Delaney Grossman, eds., *Creating Life: The Aesthetic Utopia of Russian Modernism* (Stanford: Stanford University Press, 1994); Bernice Glatzer Rosenthal, ed., *Nietzsche and Soviet Culture: Ally and Adversary* (New York: Cambridge University Press, 1994); Clare Cavanagh, *Osip Mandelstam and the Creation of the Modernist Tradition* (Princeton: Princeton University Press, 1995); Katerina Clark, *Petersburg: Crucible of Cultural Revolution* (Cambridge: Harvard University Press, 1995); Aleksandr Etkind, *Sodom i Psikheia* (Moscow: Its-Garant, 1996); Aleksandr Etkind, *Khlyst* (Moscow: Novoe Literaturnoe Obozrenie, 1998); Stephen Hutchins, *Russian Modernism: The Transfiguration of the Everyday* (New York: Cambridge University Press, 1997); Eric Naiman, *Sex in Public: The Incarnation of Early Soviet Ideology* (Princeton: Princeton University Press, 1997); Irina Gutkin, *The Cultural Origins of the Socialist Realist Aesthetic, 1890–1934* (Evanston: Northwestern University Press, 1999); and Olga Matich, *Erotic Utopia: The Decadent Imagination in Russia's Fin de Siecle* (Madison: University of Wisconsin Press, 2005).

15. See, for example: "Everything came to an end after 1917, with the beginning of the civil war. No Silver Age was in evidence after that, however much some people may have wanted to convince us of the opposite. . . . Every active participant [of that epoch] realized that although the people were still there, the characteristic atmosphere of the epoch, when talents grew like mushrooms after a summer shower, has petered out. What remained was a cold lunar landscape without an atmosphere and creative individuality, with every artist confined to the cell of his creativity" (Vadim Kreyd, "Vstrechi s serebrianym vekom," in *Vospominaniia o serebrianom veke*, ed. Vadim Kreyd [Moscow: Respublika, 1993], 7).

16. William J. Bouwsma, "Anxiety and the Formation of Early Modern Culture," in *A Usable Past: Essays in European Cultural History* (Berkeley and Los Angeles: University of California Press, 1990), 170.

17. Ibid., 2.

18. A. V. Lavrov and John Malmstad, eds., *Andrei Bely i Ivanov-Razumnik: Perepiska* (St. Petersburg: Atheneum/Feniks, 1998), 260.

19. Ibid., 260, 266.

20. Angela Brintlinger, *Writing a Usable Past: Russian Literary Culture, 1917–1937* (Evanston: Northwestern University Press, 2000), 2.

21. Anna Akhmatova, "O posmertnykh sud'bakh poetov," in *Stikhotvoreniia. Poemy. Proza* (Moscow: Ripol Klassik, 1998), 638–39.

22. Kathleen Smith, *Mythmaking in the New Russia: Politics and Memory during the Yeltsin Era* (Ithaca: Cornell University Press, 2002), 4.

23. Thus, in his 1996 version of Sologub's *Petty Demon (Melkii bes,* 1903), the director Nikolai Dostal' makes it clear in the last scenes of his film that there is no other future for Peredonov than to join the ranks of political outlaws, most likely, the Bolsheviks. I am grateful to Olga Glagoleva for sharing this insight.

24. Boris Paramoanov, "Russkuiu zhizn' izurodovali khoroshie knigi: skromnyi nigilizm Borisa Paramonova," *Literaturnaia gazeta*, May 28, 1997.

25. "[Marx or Nietzsche] could not be depended on . . . to affirm once and for all—and God knows it is needed in the distress of today—that history, at least, is living and continuous, that it is, for the subject in question, a place of rest, certainty, reconciliation, a place of tranquillized sleep" (Michel Foucault, *The Archaeology of Knowledge*, trans. A. M. Sheridan Smith [New York: Pantheon Books, 1972], 14).

26. Stephanie Sandler, *Commemorating Pushkin: Russia's Myth of a National Poet* (Stanford: Stanford University Press, 2004), 4.

27. Bouwsma, *A Usable Past*, 2.

28. Gary Taylor, *Cultural Selection* (Basic Books: New York, 1996), 5.

29. Cf. Joseph Brodsky's observation about the popularity of Nadezhda Mandelstam's memoirs: "She was a widow to culture, and I think she loved her husband more at the end than on the day they got married. That is probably why the readers of her books find them so haunting. Because of that, and because the status of the modern world vis-à-vis civilization also can be defined as widowhood" (Brodsky, "Nadezhda Mandelstam [1899–1980]: An Obituary," in *Less Than One* [New York: Farrar, Straus, and Giroux, 1986], 154).

30. Gerstein's *Memoirs* was awarded both the little Russian Booker and the Anti-Booker prizes. This is quite remarkable given that the latter was instituted by *Nezavisimaia gazeta* in opposition to the Russian Booker Foundation. For a critical response to the *Memoirs*, see Galina Bashkirova, "Blagodatnaia pustynia poslednego svidetelia: ia ne khochu znat', chto obozhaemyi mnoi Mandel'shtam byl sadistom!" *Nezavisimaia gazeta* [Kulisa], no. 12, June 1999, 4.

31. Lidiia Chukovskaia, *Dom poeta. Iz arkhiva, Nezavershennoe*, in *Sochineniia v dvukh tomakh* (Moscow: Art-Fleks, 2001), vol. 2.

32. Emma Gershtein, "Na fone vsekh revizii veka," *Pamiat' pisatelia* (St. Petersburg: Inapress, 2001), 587–89.

33. Harold Bloom, *The Anxiety of Influence*, 2nd ed. (New York: Oxford University Press, 1997), xx–xxii.

34. In addition to The *Anxiety of Influence* (1973), see Harold Bloom, *A Map of Misreading* (1975); *Poetry and Repression* (1976); and *The Western Canon* (1994).

35. See Yurii Tynyinov, "Dostoevskii i Gogol," *Arkhaisty i novatory* (Munich: Wilhelm Fink, 1967), 412–55.

36. Bloom, *The Anxiety of Influence*, 19, 5.

37. *Sredi velikikh: Literaturnye vstrechi*, ed. Margarita Odesskaia (Moscow: RGGU, 2001).

38. Acmeists "refused to see symbols everywhere and in everything, instead reveling in the beauty and vigor of the world as perceived by the senses" (Victor Terras, *A History of Russian Literature* [New Haven: Yale University Press, 1991], 386).

39. See Osip Mandelstam, "Stikhi pamiati Andreia Belogo," in *Sobranie sochinenii v chetyrekh tomakh* (Moscow: Terra-Terra, 1991).

40. Osip Mandelstam, "A Letter About Russian Poetry," in *The Collected Critical Prose and Letters*, trans. Jane Gary Harris and Constance Link (London: Collins Harvill, 1991), 156.

41. Paul de Man, review of Harold Bloom, *Anxiety of Influence*, in *Blindness and Insight*, 2nd ed. (Minneapolis: University of Minnesota Press, 1983), 273.

42. Already in 1923 Akhmatova was "outraged" by Ivanov-Razumnik's decision to open his *Critical Miscellany (Kriticheskii sbornik, 1925)* with Blok's "Without a Deity, Without Inspiration" ("Bez bozhestva, bez vdokhnoven'ia," 1921), a polemic piece directed against the acmeist movement in general and against their leader Nikolai Gumilev in particular. Akhmatova was enraged not so much by Blok's caustic and often unfair remarks but by the fact that his article was going to be published *after* Gumilev's premature death (see Ronen, *The Fallacy of the Silver Age*, 67–68). As another example, in 1929–1932, Bely's longtime friendship with Ivanov-Razumnik deteriorated. However, prompted by Ivanov-Razumnik's subsequent arrests, imprisonments, and tragic death, Klavdiia Bugaeva retroactively eliminated most of the negative remarks about him from her memoirs and her husband's records (*Litsa: Biographicheskii Almanakh* [St. Peterburg: Feniks, 2002], 9:119).

43. For a pioneering discussion of this aspect of Russian literature see Dmitrii Segal, "Literatura kak vtorichnaia modeliruyushchaia sistema," *Slavica Hierosolymitana* 4 (1979): 1–35.

44. On how Mandelstam's writing was informed by the preservationist drive, see Clare Cavanagh, *Osip Mandelstam and the Modernist Creation of Tradition* (Princeton: Princeton University Press, 1995).

45. Joseph Brodsky, "Primechanie k kommentariiu," in *Brodsky o Tsvetaevoi: Interviews, Essays* (Moscow: Nezavisimaia gazeta, 1997), 158.

46. Susan Sontag, "Joseph Brodsky," in *Where the Stress Falls* (New York: Farrar, Straus, and Giroux, 2001), 331–32.

47. Bloom, *The Anxiety of Influence*, xxiii.

48. Recall Akhmatova's reaction in October 1940 to an unpublished volume of Khlebnikov that she received from its editor, Nikolai Ivanovich Khardzhiev: "An excellent job, a superb one. But you know what: more and more I come to the conclusion that the history of literature is nothing but hypothetical nonsense! It is evident even here, in this excellent work by Nikolai Ivanovich. Khlebnikov vilifies Sologub, Artsybashev, and Blok. Nikolai Ivanovich explains that this was nothing but a battle with the Symbolists. Rubbish! What kind of a Symbolist is Artsybashev? And Khlebnikov never engaged in a conscious battle with the Symbolists. They fought anyone of renown in order to clear a space for themselves.... By the way, Khlebnikov also attacks Kornei Ivanovich [Chukovskii] here. And this, of course, is also in the framework of a battle with fame. Take Maiakovski. Nowadays they say and write that he liked my poetry. But publicly he always berated me. ... They had to clear the woods, so they chopped the trees that were a little taller" (Chukovskaia, *The Akhmatova Journals*, 170).

49. See the numerous discussions of Pushkin between Akhmatova and Luknitskii in Pavel Luknitskii, *Acumiana: Vstrechi s Annoi Akhmatovoi*, vol. 2: *1926–1927* (Paris: YMCA-Press, Russkii put', 1997).

50. For a reading of the 1917 revolution as a set of cohesive narratives that gave aim and meaning to the Bolsheviks' prerevolutionary activity, see Frederick C. Corney, *Telling October: Memory and the Making of the Bolshevik Revolution* (Ithaca: Cornell University Press, 2004).

51. Sheila Fitzpatrick, *The Russian Revolution* (Oxford: Oxford University Press, 1994), 2.

Chapter 2. Literature and Revolution

1. Stanislav Iur'evich Kuniaev, "Zhivye stranitsy," *Voprosy literatury* 10 (1980): 35.

2. Kuniaev (b. 1932) is now the editor-in-chief of *Nash sovremennik* and a mouthpiece for the Russophiles. If in his youth Kuniaev liked singing Blok's and Yesenin's poems with his friends, in his later years he adopted Blok as a major authority on the specifics of the Russian national character. (Blok is one of the most frequently quoted authors in his books of memoirs.) As Kuniaev records in his memoirs, in the early 1970s he recognized his vocation to fight for the purification of Russian culture from all other influences, particularly the Jewish influence. Blok, with his occasional anti-Semitic statements in his diaries and notebooks, along with his "impartial" insights into the pre- and postrevolutionary literary scenes, became for Kuniaev the embodiment of a true Russian writer and a patriot on a par only with Pushkin, Yesenin, Akhmatova, and Nikolai Rubtsov. See his memoirs, *Poeziia, Sud'ba, Rossiia* (Moscow: Nash sovremennik, 2001). The title of the second book of memoirs, "Est' eshche okean," is an allusion to Blok's diary entry of 1912. Interestingly, another line of Blok made its way into the title of

a semiautobiographical novel by Aleksandr Pavlovich Chudakov, *Lozhitsia mgla na starye stupeni: Roman-idiliia* (Moscow: OLMA-PRESS, 2001). Chudakov (a well-known literary scholar, 1938–2005) and Kuniaev did not belong to the same cultural and political circles, yet they reveal the same sources of reference; this may not be fortuitous, given their shared goal of creating an uplifting picture of Russia and things Russian. Clearly, both writers relied in part on Blok to bridge the gap between Russia's past and present.

3. Kuniaev, "Zhivye stranitsy," 24–50.

4. Mstislav Borisovich Koz'min, "Velikii poet Rossii," *Voprosy literatury* 10 (1980): 3–23.

5. *The Diaries of Nikolai Punin, 1904–1953*, ed. Sidney Monas and Jennifer Greene Kupala, trans. Jennifer Greene Kupala (Austin: University of Texas Press, 1999), 89–90.

6. See Michael Levenson, ed., *The Cambridge Companion to Modernism* (Cambridge: Cambridge University Press, 1999).

7. See Boris Groys, *The Total Art of Stalinism* (Princeton: Princeton University Press, 1992); Omry Ronen, *The Fallacy of the Silver Age in Twentieth-Century Literature* (Amsterdam: Harwood Academic Publishers, 1997); and Oleg Lekmanov, "Kontseptsiia 'Serebrianogo veka' i akmeizma v zapisnykh knizhkakh A. Akhmatovoi," *Novoe literaturnoe obozrenie* 46 (2000): 216–30.

8. See David Perkins, *Is Literary History Possible?* (Baltimore: Johns Hopkins University Press, 1992), esp. 121–73.

9. See Georgii Ivanov, "Tvorchestvo i remeslo," *Russkaia volia*, no. 22 (January 23, 1917); "Al. Blok," *Utro Rossii*, no. 33 (February 2, 1917); D. Vygotskii, "U novoi grani," *Novaia zhizn'*, no. 9 (April 28 [May 11], 1917). I saw these articles in a large folder ("Kritika obo mne") where they had been placed by Blok. Comments about Blok following in the wake of realists were underlined in red and green pencil, either by Blok himself or by the folder's later owner, Vladimir Nikolaevich Orlov (1908–1985), the prominent Blok specialist and custodian of his legacy (RGALI f. 2833, op. 1, d. 502).

10. Vygotskii, "U novoi grani."

11. See E. Blium and V. Gol'tsev, "Bibliografiia (1918–1928)," in *O Bloke*, ed. Evdokiia Fedorovna Nikitina (Moscow: "Nikitinskie subbotniki," 1929), 333–81.

12. See Vladimir Orlov, "Nekotorye itogi i zadachi sovetskogo blokovedeniia," in *Blokovskii sbornik* (Tartu: Tartusskii gosudarstvennyi universitet, 1964), 1:509.

13. See V. Gol'tsev, "Pis'ma Bloka," *Novyi mir*, no. 3 (1926); B. Skvortsov, "Opustoshennaia dusha," *Novyi mir*, no. 11 (1928); Evgeniia Knipovich, "Aleksandr Blok v ego 'Dnevnikakh,'" in *Pechat' i revoliutsiia*, nos. 2–3 (February–March 1929); and Lev Lozovskii, "Blok v otsenke kritikov," in *O Bloke*, ed. Nikitina.

14. "Blokovskie dni v Leningrade," *Literaturnaia gazeta*, August 10, 1946.

15. Pavel Antokol'skii, "Sovest' russkoi poezii," *Literaturnaia gazeta*, August 10, 1946.

16. "Pamiati poeta," *Literaturnaia gazeta*, July 27, 1946; *Aleksandr Blok v pesniakh*

i romansakh sovetskikh kompozitorov (Moscow: Gosudarstvennoe muzykal'noe izdatel'stvo, 1946).

17. "Pamiati Bloka," *Literaturnaia gazeta*, August 3, 1946.

18. Kornei Ivanovich Chukovskii, *Dnevnik, 1901–1969* (Moscow: OLMA-PRESS, 2003), 2:237.

19. Lidiia Ginzburg, *Zapisnye knizhki* (Moscow: Zakharov, 1999), 437.

20. See V. A. Kamenskaia and Zara Grigor'evna Mints, "Pervyi Blokovskii (dialog-vospominaniia)," in *Blokovskii sbornik* (Tartu: Tartusskii gosudarstvennyi universtiet, 1989), 9:11–21.

21. P. V. Kupriianovskii, "D. E. Maksimov—issledovatel' russkoi poezii," in *Blokovskii sbornik* (Tartu: Tartusskii gosudarstvennyi universtiet, 1989), 9:6.

22. Pavel Reifman, "Istoriia odnogo posviashcheniia," in *Blokovskii sbornik* (Tartu: Tartusskii gosudarstvennyi universitet, 1998), 14:43.

23. The folders can be found in the library of the Muzei-kvartira A. Bloka in St. Petersburg.

24. The fact that Blok and nonconformist behavior became somewhat synonymous in the eyes of Soviet intellectuals is ridiculed (albeit gently) in Viktor Erofeev's novel *Russian Beauty (Russkaia krasavitsa,* 1982–1990). When Irina Tarakanova (a prostitute-cum-Russia's national savior) goes into hiding from the authorities, she suddenly turns into an avid reader of Blok: "'I drag out my life in loneliness, with a book, I've fallen in love with Blok.' 'With whom?' 'Blok, you know! The poet. I've learned some poems by heart'" (Erofeev, *Russian Beauty*, trans. Andrew Reynolds [Harmondsworth: Penguin Books, 1992], 108–9).

25. Andrei Bely, Razumnik Vasil'evich Ivanov-Razumnik, and Aaron Zakharovich Shteinberg, *Pamiati Aleksandra Bloka* (Petrograd: Vol'fila, 1922), 54.

26. Mikhail Kuzmin, "Dnevnik 1921 goda," *Minuvshee* 13 (1993): 475.

27. Vladimir Vladimirovich Maiakovskii, "Umer Aleksandr Blok" [1921], in *Sochineniia v dvukh tomakh* (Moscow: Pravda, 1988), 2:630.

28. Evgenii Zamiatin, "Vospominaniia o Bloke," in *Russkii sovremennik* (1924), 3:187, 190; Kornei Chukovskii, *Aleksandr Blok kak chelovek i poet* (Petrograd: Izdatel'stvo "A. F. Marks," 1924), 24.

29. Andrei Bely, "K materialam o Bloke" [1921], in *Literaturnoe nasledstvo: Aleksandr Blok: Novye materialy i issledovaniia*, ed. S. S. Grechishkin and A. V. Lavrov, vol. 92, bk. 3 (Moscow: Nauka, 1982), 795.

30. Interestingly, a book about the art historian Nikolai Vrangel' draws parallels between his death and the death of Blok, claiming that both men died from the premonition of a great catastrophe. "[Vrangel'] died during World War I, while working for the Red Cross—not from a bullet but from an illness. However, was it just the virus that caused the death of thirty-five-year-old Vrangel'? No, his heart was gradually worn out by the premonition of a great catastrophe. Aleksandr Blok also died slowly several years later, and his doctors were powerless" *(Baron i Muza: Nikolai Vrangel': Pallada Bogdanova-Bel'skaia*, ed. A. A. Murashev and A.Yu. Skakov [St. Petersburg: Kolo, 2001], 7).

31. Bely, "K materialam o Bloke," 804, 810; see also Zinaida Gippius, "Moi lunnyi drug" [1922], *Zhivye litsa: Vospominaniia* (Tbilisi: Merani, 1991), 2:36.

32. Bely, "K materialam o Bloke," 807–10. It is not accidental that the titles of Andrei Bely's trilogy, which were initially conceived as memoirs about Blok, all highlight the notion of a boundary or watershed: *On the Border of Two Centuries; The Beginning of the Century;* and *Between Two Revolutions*.

33. Bely, "K materialam o Bloke," 796.

34. Bely, Ivanov-Razumnik, and Shteinberg, *Pamiati Aleksandra Bloka*, 54.

35. Vladimir Weidle, "Po povodu dvukh statei o Bloke," *Zavtra*, no. 1 (Berlin: Petropolis, 1923), 113.

36. Boris Eikhenbaum, "Blok's Fate" [1921], in *Blok: An Anthology of Essays and Memoirs*, ed. and trans. Lucy Vogel (Ann Arbor, MI: Ardis, 1982), 130.

37. Ibid., 136, 143.

38. Ibid., 131.

39. Ibid., 138.

40. Valerii Briusov, "Vchera, segodnia i zavtra russkoi poezii," *Pechat' i revoliutsiia*, bk. 7 (September–October 1922): 50, 67–68.

41. Dmitrii S. Mirskii, "O sovremennom sostoianii russkoi poezii" [1922], in *Uncollected Writings on Russian Literature*, ed. G. S. Smith (Berkeley, CA: Berkeley Slavic Specialities, 1989), 90–91.

42. Yurii Tynianov, "Promezhutok" [1924], in *Arkhaisty i novatory* (Munich: Wilhelm Fink Verlag, 1967), 542–43, 547.

43. Leon Trotskii, *Literature and Revolution* (New York: Russell and Russell, 1957), 14, 28.

44. Ibid., 116.

45. Ibid., 120.

46. Frederick C. Corney, "Narratives of October and the Issue of Legitimacy," in *Russian Modernity: Politics, Knowledge, Practices*, ed. David Hoffmann and Yanni Kotsonis (New York: Macmillan, 2000), 185–203.

47. Trotskii, *Literature and Revolution*, 12.

48. *Voprosy Literatury i dramaturgii (Disput v Gosudarstvennom Akademicheskom Malom teatre v Moskve 26 maia 1924 goda pod predsedatel'stvom A. V. Lunacharskogo)* (Leningrad: Academia, 1924), 27.

49. Trotskii, *Literature and Revolution*, 125.

50. Dmitrii Maksimov writes: "Blok was developing in the direction of realism, but he did not reach the heights of true realism [in art]. . . . While studying Blok we also notice that all his development and evolution, albeit very slow and contradictory, but nevertheless moving in a constant direction, were ultimately bringing him to the same foundations that served as the basis for our building of revolutionary art. That is why a correct understanding of Blok can only invigorate us in our struggle for socialist culture. Blok's artistic development is just another proof that there is no other way apart from the one already chosen" (Maksimov, "Along the Road to Realism"["Na puti k realizmu"], *Rezets*, no. 15 [1936]: 22.).

51. *Literaturnaia entsiklopediia*, ed. Vladimir Maksimovich Friche (Moscow: Izdatel'stvo Kommunisticheskoi akademii, 1930), 1:507.

52. See Max Nordau, *Entartung*, 2 vols. (Berlin: C. Duncker, 1892–1893). The first Russian translation of *Degeneration* appeared in 1894.

53. Anatolii Vasil'evich Lunacharskii, "Aleksandr Blok," in Aleksandr Blok, *Sobranie sochinenii* (Leningrad: Izdatel'stvo pisatelei, 1932), 1:20, 51, 54. For fictional accounts of Blok's alleged pathologies, see Aleksei Tolstoi, *Sestry* (1921) and Mikhail Zoshchenko, "Michel Siniagin" (1930). Tolstoi and Zoshchenko came up with unflattering portrayals of poet-decadents in their works. Both Aleksei Bessonov (in *Sestry*) and Siniagin (in "Michel Siniagin") were conspicuously modeled after Blok and bear clear signs of degeneracy.

54. "Pokhorony A. A. Bloka: Ot nashego korrespondenta iz Peterburga," *Rul'* [Berlin], no. 232 (August 23, 1921). Cf. the artist Aleksandr Benua's immediate reaction to Blok's death: "[Blok] was a man with a kindly soul but limited intelligence. The revolution destroyed him. He failed to internalize it. Like most members of the intelligentsia, he felt it his duty to be in awe of the revolution *an und für sich*, but when he found himself caught unawares by its real essence, he was first totally taken aback and then thrown into deep depression and desperation. His poem 'The Twelve' is, in my view, a reflection of this 'hysteria of desperation.' It was the result of his efforts to 'come to love them, black though they were,' a kind of convulsion of acceptance of something that 'revolted his soul.' The efforts could only make him grow silent and then become extinct" ("Dnevnik Benua za 1921 god," *Nashe Nasledie* 74 [2005]).

55. Georgii Adamovich, "S. Yesenin" [1926], in *Literaturnye besedy* (St. Petersburg: Aleteia, 1998), 2:29–30.

56. See the appendix to Abram Terts [Andrei Siniavskii], *Progulki s Pushkinym* [1966–1968] (Paris: Syntaxis, 1989).

57. For example, Selivanovskii was surprised to find that Blok used words such as *"zhidovka"* and "a nice human being" with regard to the same woman (Aleksei Pavlovich Selivanovskii, "Dnevnik Al. Bloka," *Na literaturnom postu*, January 1929, 47–58). Kuniaev found similar passages in Blok's diaries "prophetically mysterious" (*Poeziia, Sud'ba, Rossiia*, 1:191).

58. Lev Lozovskii, "Blok v otsenke kritikov," in *O Bloke*, ed. Nikitinka, 187. In 1980 Mints also started her programmatic article by reinstating the many-sidedness of Blok's creativity: "Blok can be seen as someone who continued and became the apotheosis of the traditions of great Russian literature of the nineteenth century. At the same time, Blok can be viewed as the vanguard of the new Russian poetry of the twentieth century. [He can be interpreted both] as a realist and as an heir and a champion of romantic traditions; as an author of inspired 'eschatological' prophecies about the end of the old world—and as the author of the first long poem about the October Revolution. All these approaches are rooted in the richness and multifaceted character of Blok's legacy" (Mints, "Blok i russkii simvolizm," in *Aleksandr Blok: Novye materialy i issledovaniia. Literaturnoe nasledstvo*

[Moscow: Nauka, 1980], 1:98). As recent debates reveal, Blok's legacy is as open to contradictory interpretations today as ever. The same statements allow some critics to celebrate Blok as a great thinker and a prophet (Kuniaev, *Poeziia, Sud'ba, Rossiia*, 1:221–22) and others to denounce him as a Russian fascist (Aleksandr Etkind, "Final 'Dvendtsati'—vzgliad iz 2000 goda," *Znamia* 11 [2000]: 203–4).

59. Nina Berberova, "25 let smerti A. A. Bloka," in *Neizvestnaia Berberova* (St. Petersburg: Limbus Press, 1998), 135–36.

60. "Pamiati Bloka," *Literaturnaia gazeta*, August 3, 1946.

Chapter 3. The Russian Silver Age

1. Vitalii Shentalinskii, "Oskolki serebrianogo veka," *Novyi mir* 5 (1998): 180. Shentalinskii's sentiment was rearticulated by Tolstaya's younger friend and collaborator Dunia (Avdot'ia) Smirnova. Smirnova (b. 1969) is a talented script writer in her own right and, along with Tolstaya, the founder of a popular literary talk show, *The School for Scandal (Shkola zlosloviia)*. In a 2006 interview Smirnova said that "the Silver Age was the last light of the bright, full-blooded Russian day the country had enjoyed. It had been in darkness for a long time, then the nineteenth century came, a new day gradually dawned over the country, and then, at a certain moment, Russia seemed to shine brightly. After that, darkness descended on it again and it has been in darkness ever since" (Smirnova, *Sviaz', Kinostsenarii* [St. Petersburg: Amfora, 2006], 346).

2. Gr. Novopolin, *V sumerkakh literatury i zhizni: 80 i 90-ye gody* (Kharkov: Izdatel'stvo E. A. Golovinoi, 1902), 5. The first chapter of Nordau's *Degeneration* is entitled "The Dusk of the Nations."

3. Ibid., 12, 14.

4. R. I. Sementkovskii, "Nazad ili vpered?" (1894), in Maks Nordau, *Vyrozhdenie: Sovremennye frantsuzy* (Moscow: Respublika, 1995), 5.

5. A. Volynskii, "Literaturnye zametki," *Severnyi vestnik* 12 (1896): 240, 250–51.

6. See Olga Matich, *Erotic Utopia: The Decadent Imagination in Russia's Fin de Siecle* (Madison: University of Wisconsin Press, 2005).

7. Sementkovskii, "Nazad ili vpered?" 15.

8. See *Literaturnyi raspad: Kriticheskii sbornik*, 2 vols. (St. Petersburg: Tovarishchestvo Izdatel'skoe biuro/EOS, 1908–1909), esp. the introduction by Yurii Steklov, "Sotsial'no-politicheskie usloviia literaturnogo raspada," 1:5–58.

9. *Kuda my idem? Nastoiashchee i budushchee russkoi intelligentsii, literatury i iskusstv. Sbornik statei i otvetov na anketu "Zari"* (Moscow: Zaria, 1910).

10. S. A. Vengerov, "Etapy neoromanticheskogo dvizheniia," in *Russkaia literatura XX veka (1890–1910)*, ed. S. A. Vengerov (Moscow: XXI vek-Soglasie, 2000), 1:32–33.

11. Ibid., 34.

12. Irina Paperno, introduction to *Creating Life: The Aesthetic Utopia of Russian Modernism*, ed. Irina Paperno and Joan Delaney Grossman (Stanford: Stanford University Press, 1994), 7.

13. Bernice Glatzer Rosenthal, *Dmitri Sergeevich Merezhkovsky and the Silver Age: The Development of the Revolutionary Mentality* (The Hague: Martinus Nijhoff, 1975), 6–7.

14. V. I. Lenin, "Partiinaia organizatsiia i partiinaia literatura," in *O literature i iskusstve* (Moscow: Khudozhestvennaia literatura, 1957), 43.

15. See Boris Groys, *The Total Art of Stalinism: Avant-Garde, Aesthetic Dictatorship, and Beyond*, trans. Charles Rougle (Princeton: Princeton University Press, 1992).

16. See Katerina Clark, *Petersburg, Crucible of Cultural Revolution* (Cambridge: Harvard University Press, 1995).

17. Roman Jakobson, "The Dominant," in *Language in Literature*, ed. Krystyna Pomorska and Stephen Rudy (Cambridge: Harvard University Press, 1987), 44.

18. Valerii Briusov, "Vchera, segodnia i zavtra russkoi poezii," *Pechat' i revoliutsiia* 7 (September–October 1922): 48. In "About Bunin" (1924) Georgii Adamovich follows in Briusov's wake, this time, however, using Briusov's "talent" as a yardstick for his "comparative evaluation." Adamovich describes the earlier works of Briusov and Ivan Konevskoi as charming but obsolete and concludes that "nowadays modernism has given up all of its leading positions [in Russian culture] and that we [already] know how empty its rhetoric turned out to be and how poor its heritage is" (Georgii Adamovich, "O Bunine," in *Sobranie sochinenii: Literaturnye besedy* [St. Petersburg: Aleteia, 1998], 1:56–57).

19. Boris Eikhenbaum, "Sud'ba Bloka" ("Blok's Fate," 1921), in *Blok: An Anthology of Essays and Memoirs*, ed. and trans. Lucy Vogel (Ann Arbor, MI: Ardis, 1982), 42.

20. One of the most striking responses came from Anna Akhmatova, who reportedly described *The Trout* as "a highly bourgeois book" with an unnecessarily complicated plot (quoted in Lidiia Ginzburg, *Chelovek za pis'mennym stolom* [Leningrad: Sovetskii pisatel', 1989], 108).

21. Mikhail Osorgin's story "Tat'ianin den'" is quoted in Viacheslav Kostikov, "Izgnanie iz raia," *Ogonek* 24 (June 1990): 16.

22. Vasilii Rozanov, "Apokalipsis nashego vremeni" (1918), in *Izbrannoe* (Munich: A. Neimanis, 1970), 447.

23. Nikolai Berdiaev, *Smysl istorii*, 2nd ed. (Paris: YMCA-Press, 1969), 186–87, 206, 211, 213–14.

24. Cf. "Anyway, we are going to write like Lev Tolstoi and not like Leonid Andreev" (Georgii Adamovich, "O Bunine" [1924], 1:57). As is well known, in the 1920s and 1930s the Soviet literary establishment demonstrated a similar infatuation with the cultural legacy of Lev Tolstoi, inviting Soviet writers to turn themselves into "red Tolstois."

25. The labels *sanintsy* and *ogarki* were an invention of the boulevard press, being derived from currently popular works of literature, Mikhail Artsybashev's novel *Sanin* (1907) and a short story by Skitalets (Petrov) entitled "Ogarki" ("Candle Stubs," 1905). Although evidence is scarce, members of both "secret organizations" reportedly indulged in a hedonistic lifestyle, advocating "free love" and disregard

for political activisim. Members of *ogarki* were particularly notorious for their sexual orgies and prodigious consumption of alcohol. (I am grateful to Otto Boele for sharing this information.)

26. Vladislav Khodasevich, "Muni," in *Nekropol'. Literatura i vlast': Pis'ma B. A. Sadovskomu* (Moscow: SS, 1996), 74. In "The End of Renata" ("Konets Renaty," 1928) Khodasevich insisted that he could no longer understand the language of some of his contemporaries such as Nina Petrovskaia. However, the following excerpt from Petrovskaia's memoirs (1923) demonstrates that Khodasevich and Petrovskaia not only shared the same language, but also the same vision of the cultural situation in late imperial Russia: "Somewhere one could detect distinct claps of thunder from the approaching year 1905. And the pillar of deadly green and oily fumes was hanging above Moscow, a Moscow that was indulging itself in overly refined caprices and was wallowing in wine, flowers, and exotic music. . . . That's how—chaotically, by leaps and bounds, amid the caricature [lifestyle] the new Russian literature was making its name in history. . . . That dying and decaying lifestyle *[byt]* was yielding at the seams and was reflecting the existing aesthetic chaos in the most comic details" (Petrovskaia, "Vospominaniia," published by E. Garetto, *Minuvshee* 8 [1992]: 41–42). Petrovskaia's contemporary, Margarita Sabashnikova, in her otherwise intimate account of her life also could not resist the temptation of seeing the breakup of her marriage to Maximillian Voloshin in 1907 within the broader cultural and political context of Russia on the brink of the Bolshevik Revolution: "I find everything that happened and all of my anxieties typical of prerevolutionary Russia and characteristic of the 'Luciferian' culture that, in my view, had reached its peak in Russia by that time. . . . Divorced from practical activity, immersed in their inner world separated from the realities of life, which inevitably led to a reassessment of their own personalities, members of the Russian intelligentsia indulged in all kinds of crankiness, flamboyant and characteristic" (Margarita Voloshina [M. V. Sabashnikova], *Zelenaia zmeia [The Green Snake]*, trans. M. N. Zhemchuzhnikova [Moscow: Enigma, 1993], 145).

27. Vladislav Khodasevich, "Ob Annenskom," in *Literaturnye stat'i i vospominaniia* (New York: Izdatel'stvo imeni Chekhova, 1954), 172.

28. Yurii Terapiano, "Chelovek 30-kh godov," *Chisla* (Paris), nos. 7–8 (1933): 211. Cf. Georgii Adamovich's evocation of Tolstoi in his earlier essay, "Oscar Wilde" (1925): "In *What Is Art?* Tolstoi made a thousand outrageous assertions but he can be justified in one essential respect—in that he fanatically loathed 'decadence.' Recall the names Maeterlinck, Przybyszewski, D'Annunzio, Leonid Andreev, Hauptmann. . . . At times one feels totally amazed that after everything that people read, saw, or knew they could embrace as a revelation what was offered them by those writers. There is only one consolation—the deception didn't last long, and the reign of false masters of people's thoughts was short-lived. . . . Like Krylov's frog, modernism 'overstrained itself, burst and kicked the bucket'" (Adamovich, "Oskar Uail'd," in *Sobranie sochinenii: Literaturnye besedy* [St. Petersburg: Aleteia, 1998], 1:355–57).

29. Yurii Terapiano, "Chelovek 30-kh godov," 211.
30. Ibid., 212.
31. Fedor Stepun, "Pamiati Aikhenval'da" (1929), in Yurii Aikhenval'd, *Siluety russkikh pisatelei* (Moscow: Respublika, 1998), 1:12.
32. Cf. "The impressions gained from reading Kuprin . . . are rather dull. He possesses one extremely precious quality, however. This quality is simplicity. That's why he should be immediately and without reservation placed above a whole group of writers who are unable 'to utter one word without being pretentious'" (Georgii Adamovich, "O Kuprine" [1924], in *Sobranie sochinenii. Literaturnye besedy,* 1:61). Cf. also the letter of Nina Petrovskaia: "There is only one comforting piece of news, which is the new Russian literature. There are books that were born by the revolution, absolutely wonderful. They are thrusting upward—healthy, hearty, fragrant, just like saffron milk-caps after a good rain. And [they thrust upward] without pose or pretension—without formality and in good order—as if [they know] that one should simply be large and simple" (Petrovskaia, "Vospominaniia," 42–44).
33. Clifford Geertz, "Art as a Cultural System," in *Local Knowledge: Further Essays in Interpretive Anthropology* (New York: Basic Books, 1983), 103.
34. Nikolai Otsup, "Ob Andree Belom. K piatidesiatiletiiu so dnia rozhdeniia," *Chisla,* no. 4 (1930–1931): 214.
35. Ginzburg, *Chelovek za pis'mennym stolom,* 95–96. Compare this excerpt with the letter that Khodasevich sent in 1925 to a younger poet, Mikhail Froman, who continued to reside in Soviet Russia. Khodasevich wrote in response to a letter that he and Nina Berberova received from Froman's wife, Ida Napel'baum, describing the contemporary literary scene. Note that Khodasevich saw pro-Bolshevik developments as a natural continuation of the decay in literature and society that had started in 1911–1912: "To my mind, the streak of esthetic (and, of course, more deeply—spiritual) degradation that began around 1911–1912 has to come to an end relatively soon. Had it not been for some external and 'rejuvenating' circumstances, this streak would have probably ended already. But the circumstances are still present and the microbes that cause decomposition are still at work. [However,] I. M.'s letter has proved yet again that the disease hasn't affected the whole organism and that there still exist healthy cells in it, all the more valuable for being young and, consequently, capable of resistance. It is to those cells that I'd like to send my 'futuristic best wishes,' as I often think that the future belongs to 'my way of being' and, in that sense, I call myself a futurist" (Vladislav Khodasevich, *Sobranie sochinenii v chetyrekh tomakh* [Moscow: Soglasie, 1997], 4:496).
36. Khodasevich, "Gumilev i Blok," in *Nekropol',* 87.
37. Ibid., 90–91.
38. Ibid., 87.
39. Andrei Bely, *Vospominaniia o Bloke* (Moscow: Respublika, 1995), 16.
40. See Irina Paperno, "Pushkin v zhizni cheloveka serebrianogo veka," in *Cultural Mythologies of Russian Modernism,* 26–28.

41. Valentin Asmus, "Filosofiia i estetika russkogo simvolizma," in *Literaturnoe nasledstvo* 27–28 (Moscow: Zhurnal'no-gazetnoe ob'edinenie, 1937): 1–53.

42. Nikolai Bogomolov, "Predislovie," in Vladislav Khodasevich, *Nekropol'*, 10.

43. "As if feeling that he had done everything that could be done, Dostoevskii abandoned life—he died. L. Tolstoi continued to live. But *Anna Karenina* became for him, like *The Brothers Karamazov* for Dostoevskii, the fateful frontier beyond which he couldn't go. . . . It has taken us twenty years since Dostoevskii's death and L. Tolstoi's renouncing creative literary work to realize that we are currently witnessing not an accidental 'degeneration,' not a temporary 'decline,' and not inspired, as it were, by the West's 'decadence,' but a long-prepared, natural, and overdue *demise of Russian literature*" (Dimitri Merezhkovskii, "L. Tolstoi i Dostoevskii," in *L. Tolstoi i Dostoevskii: Vechnye sputniki* [Moscow: Respublika, 1995], 349).

44. Andrei Bely, "A. P. Chekhov," *Arabeski* (Moscow: Musaget, 1911), 395–400.

45. Zinaida Gippius, "Literaturnyi dnevnik (1899–1907)," *Dnevniki* (Moscow: NPK "Intelvak," 1999), 1:233–35.

46. Zinaida Gippius, "Oderzhimyi (O Val. Briusove)," *Okno* (Paris) 2 (1923): 203–4.

47. Andrei Levinson, "Parizhskaia vetv' russkoi literatury," *Zveno* (Paris), August 13, 1923, 2.

48. Yurii Mandel'shtam, "Nekropol'," *Vozrozhdenie* (Paris), no. 4175, March 17, 1939.

49. Ronen, *The Fallacy of the Silver Age*, 13–15.

50. See Vladimir Weidle, "Tri Rossii," *Sovremennye zapiski* 65 (1937): 304–22.

51. The term "realms of memory" (*les lieux de memoire*) was coined by Pierre Nora in the early 1980s to outline "sites" that have come to constitute French national/collective memory, such as "Vichy," the "Tour Eiffel" and "Bastille Day." Nora explains, the goal was "to pass French identity through a prism, to relate the symbolic whole to its symbolic fragments" (*Realms of Memory: Rethinking the French Past*, ed. Pierre Nora, trans. Arthur Goldhammer [New York: Columbia University Press, 1996], 1:xvii).

52. Weidle in "Tri Rossii" explicitly states that the Silver Age of Russian culture was terminated by the Bolshevik Revolution of 1917.

53. See Aleksandr Blok, "Bez bozhestva, bez vdokhnoven'ia" (1921), in *Sobranie sochinenii* (Moscow-Leningrad: Khudozhestvennaia literatura, 1962), 6:174–84. Blok's criticism was aimed primarily at Nikolai Gumilev, whose "uninspired" literary and theoretical writings Blok held responsible for bringing on the decline of Russian literature.

54. K. Mochul'skii, *Aleksandr Blok, Andrei Bely, Valerii Briusov* (Moscow: Respublika, 1997), 252.

55. Ronen, *The Fallacy of the Silver Age*, 65–80.

56. See Barry Schwartz, "The Reconstruction of Abraham Lincoln," in *Collective Remembering*, ed. David Middleton and Derek Edwards (New York: Sage Publications, 1990), 104.

57. M. M. Bakhtin, *Speech Genres and Other Late Essays*, ed. Caryl Emerson and Michael Holquist, trans. Vern W. McGee (Austin: University of Texas Press, 1986), 7.

Chapter 4. No "Room of Her Own"

1. See *The Diary of Nikolai Punin, 1904–1953*, ed. Sidney Monas and Jennifer Greene Krupala, trans. Jennifer Greene Krupala (Austin: University of Texas Press, 1999); and Nikolai Nikolaevich Punin, *Mir svetel liubov'iu, Dnevniki, Pis'ma*, ed. L. A. Zykov (Moscow: Artist. Rezhisser. Teatr, 2000).
2. *The Diary of Nikolai Punin*, 88, 121.
3. Emma Gerstein, *Moscow Memoirs*, trans. John Crowfoot (New York: Overlook Press, 2004), 218–19.
4. Lidiia Chukovskaia, *The Akhmatova Journals, 1938–1941*, trans. Milena Mikhalski and Sylvia Rubashova (Evanston: Northwestern University Press, 1994), 148.
5. See Irina Punina, "Pod krovlei Fontannogo Doma," in *Anna Akhmatova i Fontannyi Dom*, ed. N. I. Popova and O. E. Rubinchik (St. Petersburg: Nevskii Dialekt, 2000), 147.
6. See V. A. Chernykh, *Letopis' zhizni i tvorchestva Anny Akhmatovoi*, vol. 3, *1935–1945* (Moscow: Editorial URSS, 2001), 39–40.
7. Chukovskaia, *The Akhmatova Journals*, 143.
8. Anna Akhmatova, *The Word That Causes Death's Defeat*, ed. and trans. Nancy K. Andersen (New Haven: Yale University Press, 2004), 49.
9. Nancy Andersen writes: "Precise accounts of how many poems she wrote in a given year are difficult because some of her poems may be lost or misdated, but it is safe to say that she wrote fewer poems between 1923 and 1935 than in the single year 1921" (ibid., 54).
10. Nikita Struve suggests that every great poet experiences an extended period of poetic silence ranging from two to four years (as was the case with Pushkin and Blok) to five to seven years (Tiutchev, Pasternak, and Mandelstam). An extreme case was Marina Tsvetaeva, who could not write poetry for almost fifteen years (Struve, "Marina Tsvetaeva's Creativity Crisis" ["Tvorcheski krizis Tsvetaevoi," 1982], in *Pravoslavie i kul'tura* [Moscow: Russkii put', 2000], 340–47).
11. Carol Shields, *Jane Austen: A Life* (New York: Penguin, 2001), 85.
12. Ibid., 99.
13. L. D. Blok, *I byli i nebylitsy o Bloke i o sebe*, in *Dve liubvi, dve sud'by: Vospominaniia o Bloke i Belom* (Moscow: Izdatel'skii dom XXI vek-Soglasie, 2000), 74–75.
14. See, for example, M. A. Beketova, *Aleksandr Blok: Biograficheskii ocherk* (Leningrad: Academia, 1930).
15. In the winter of 1902–1903, unknown to their families, Blok rented a furnished room on Serpukhovskaia Street for their clandestine meetings. Shortly after declaring love, Blok was consigned to bed with a sexually transmitted disease and Liubov' Dmitrievna used the room as her private thinking and writing space. She wrote to him: "My darling, my joy, what are you doing now? Are you very sick?

As for me, I'm sitting in our room, rereading your verses but mostly remembering, remembering.... I've now decided to get a good grip on myself and always put on a false front—I'll act happy, go to the theater with the Mendeleevs.... But it is here, to our room, that I'll be coming, whenever I have a spare minute, in order to rest, think about you, wait for you, and remember." She did not learn the nature of Blok's sickness until their marriage (see *Aleksandr Blok: Pis'ma k zhene, Literaturnoe nasledstvo* [Moscow: Nauka, 1978], 89:74–77).

16. Dmitrii Merezhkovski, *L. Tolstoi i Dostoevskii: Vechnye sputniki* (Moscow: Respublika, 1995), 377.

17. Olga Matich discusses L. D. Blok's immodest descriptions of her own body in the broader context of fin de siècle erotic prose, notably, as a spoof on Fedor Sologub's character Liudmila (*Petty Demon*) with her "blossoming flesh," meant to signify "the awakening of her and Sasha's desires" (Matich, *Erotic Utopia: The Decadent Imagination in Russia's Fin de Siècle* [Madison: University of Wisconsin Press, 2005], 105).

18. Vladimir Gavrilov, "Tri vstrechi s blizkimi Bloka," in V. P. Yenisherlov, *Nashe Nasledie* 74 (2005): n. 12.

19. Kornei Chukovskii, *Dnevnik 1901–1969* (Moscow: Olma-Press, 2003), 1:385.

20. Ibid., 1:440–41.

21. Vadim Gaevskii, "Istoriia baleta i L. D. Blok," *Nashe nasledie* 70 (2004): 60.

22. This work was first published in 1987 with an introduction by Vadim Gaevskii, who is largely responsible for the belated rediscovery of L. D. Blok's writings. See L. D. Blok, *Klassicheskii tanets: istoiia i sovremennost'* (Moscow: Iskusstvo, 1987).

23. The first smuggled copy was published in Bremen in 1970. See L. D. Blok, *Byli i nebylitsy*, ed. I. Paul'man and L. S. Fleishman (Bremen: Verlag K-Press, 1970).

24. Chukovskaia, *The Akhmatova Journals*, 150–51.

25. Lidiia Chukovskaia, *Zapiski ob Anne Akhmatovoi* (Moscow: Soglasie, 1997), 1:465.

26. See, for example, invariably negative comments about L. D. Blok in David Samoilov and Lidiia Chukovskaia, *Perepiska: 1971–1990* (Moscow: Novoe literaturnoe obozrenie, 2004), 90, 158–60, 170.

27. See Beth Holmgren, *Women's Works in Stalin's Time: On Lidiia Chukovskaia and Nadezhda Mandel'shtam* (Bloomington: Indiana University Press, 1993).

28. See the discussion of Rudakov and the Mandelstams in Gerstein, *Moscow Memoirs*.

29. Chukovskaia, *The Akhmatova Journals*, 138.

30. Joseph Brodsky, "Nadezhda Mandelstam (1899–1980): An Obituary," in *Less Than One* (New York: Farrar, Straus, and Giroux, 1986), 146. In "In a Room and a Half " (1985), describing his growing up in a Leningrad communal apartment, Brodsky came up with an interesting crossbreed between the cesspit of a communal apartment and L. D. Blok's vision of an ideal living space: "Of course, we all shared

one toilet, one bathroom, and one kitchen. But the kitchen was spacious, the toilet very decent and cozy" (ibid., 454).

31. Chukovskaia, *The Akhmatova Journals*, 10.

32. When in October 1957 Chukovskaia visited Akhmatova in Moscow, where she stayed at the Ardovs, she happily noted that "now [her] room had a more Akhmatovian look: a [copy of] Modigliani, an icon in the corner, an old round mirror over a bedside table, and a 'chipped [Venetian] flacon' on the book shelf, not the actual flacon but a drawing of it" (*Zapiski ob Anne Akhmatovoi*, 2:268).

33. The following quoted passages are from ibid., 2:365–66 .

34. Kornei Chukovskii, "Iz vospominanii," in *Vospominaniia ob Anne Akhmatovoi* (Moscow: Sovetskii pisatel, 1991), 48–49.

35. In the late 1950s, her summer house in Komarovo apparently gave Akhmatova an outlet for her rediscovered passion for acquisition. Quickly, she filled it with various odd-looking pieces of dead wood that she picked up in the nearby forest.

36. For example, in 1923, the literary critic Boris Arvatov described Akhmatova's poetry as "narrow, cozy, suitable for a boudoir, and homey: love [extending] from the bed to the croquet lawn" ("Grazhd. Akhmatova i tov. Kollontai," *Molodaia gvardiia*, nos. 4–5 [1923]: 151). In 1926, a literary chronicler, Innokentii Basalaev visited Akhmatova in the apartment which she shared with her former husband Vladimir Shileiko at the Marble Palace in Leningrad. He observed: "Akhmatova's quarters are cramped and uncomfortable. The place is cluttered up. The tables, chairs, and couch are of the most ordinary kind. There's a white tablecloth on one of the tables. This table, contrary to the fashion of the day, isn't round but rectangular. And her life is also cramped, and restricted *[I zhizn' ee tesnaia, neshirokaia]*. She has a special kind of life of her own, incomprehensible to us, with its own customs and its own yardsticks for rapture and for grief" (Basalaev, "Zapiski dlia sebia," *Minuvshee* 19 [1996]: 369–70). The famous dancer Tatiana Vecheslova described her first visit to Akhmatova at the Fountain House in 1944: "I sat looking at Anna Akhmatova and her austere room and thinking that a poet of her caliber should indeed live in a way different from that of other people. She had a world of her own, her own special fate, her own heroes, her own ideas, and shadows. . . . A cot covered with a simple gray blanket, two or three rare antiques, already falling apart, and she herself—calm, quiet and wearing black. Proud as a queen, but simple and defenseless at the same time" (Vecheslova, "Ob Anne Akhmatovoi," in *Vospominaniia ob Anne Akhmatovoi* [Moscow: Sovetskii pisatel, 1991], 460).

37. Elizaveta Kuz'mina-Karavaeva, "Vstrechi s Blokom" [1936], in *Ravnina russkaia* (St. Petersburg: Iskusstvo-SPb, 2001), 622.

38. Elizaveta Kuz'mina-Karavaeva, "Poslednie rimliane" [1924], in ibid., 569; Kuz'mina-Karavaeva, "Vstrechi s Blokom," in ibid., 623.

39. Kuz'mina-Karavaeva, "Poslednie rimliane," 567, emphasis added.

40. Ibid., 567–70.

41. "Decisive for the Acmeist conception of culture is its lack of a consciousness of thresholds; accumulation and points of collection are conceived as being in flux,

as being duration in the sense of Henry Bergson's duree.... For the Acmeists, duration is the present state of a continually new merging of the horizon of the past into the horizon of the future. Here, thresholds and discontinuities cannot be thought as markers, as in this conception such temporal markers do not exist. The Acmeist entry into a new chronotope aims above all to recall past culture, to traverse its stratifications, and to conceive this process of recalling and traversing as a new stratum itself" (Renate Lachmann, *Memory and Literature: Intertexuality in Russian Modernism* [Minneapolis: University of Minnesota Press, 1997], 231).

42. Chukovskaia, *Zapiski ob Anne Akhmatovoi*, 2:103.

43. Anna Akhmatova, *The Poem Without a Hero,* in *The Word That Causes Death's Defeat*, 163.

44. Gerstein, *Moscow Memoirs*, 144.

45. In 2000 and 2001 I met Irina Nikolaevna Punina. To my questions about Akhmatova's silence in the late 1920s and early 1930s, Irina Nikolaevna and her daughter, Anna Genrikhovna Kaminskaia, repeatedly gave the same answer: "She didn't write poems because she was extremely happy with Punin at the time. There was nothing to write about. She was simply very content and wallowed in her happiness."

46. Chukovskaia, *The Akhmatova Journals,* 69.

47. Kuz'mina-Karavaeva, "Poslednie rimliane," 567.

48. M. L. Kozyreva's recollections of her meetings with Akhmatova in the 1940s are quoted in Olga Rubinchik, "Das Ewig Weibliche v sovetskom adu," *Nashe nasledie* 71 (2004): 112.

49. Kornei Chukovskii, "From My Diary," in *Anna Akhmatova and Her Circle*, 94–96.

50. Kornei Chukovskii, *Dnevnik 1901–1969* (Moscow: Olma-Press, 2003), 1:282.

51. Quotations in the following paragraph are from Kornei Chukovskii, "Akhmatova i Maiakovskii," in *Anna Akhmatova: Pro et contra* (St. Petersburg: Izdatelstvo Russkogo Khristianskogo gumanitarnogo instituta, 2001), 1:210–15, 217.

52. Ibid., 1:234.

53. Ibid., 1:235.

54. Together with Boris Eikhebaum's *Anna Akhmatova, Opyt analiza* (1923), Chukovskii's article was continuously mined by Soviet critics to buttress their attacks on Akhmatova and her poetry and eventually inspired the party official Andrei Zdanov to accuse her in 1946 of being "wretchedly limited" and of "constantly dashing from drawing-room to chapel" (*Pravda*, no. 225, September 21, 1946).

55. Although Chukovskaia was very much affected by Akhmatova's death, she nevertheless had enough energy to discuss the possibilities of Akhmatova having affairs with Blok and the minor poet Vsevolod Kniazev shortly after the funeral (Chukovskaia, "Posle kontsa. Iz 'akhmatovskogo dnevnika,'" *Znamia* 1 [2003]: 157).

56. Chukovskaia, *Zapiski ob Anne Akhmatovoi*, 2:455.

57. Chukovskii, "From My Diary," 94–95.

58. Ibid., 95. In his review of Akhmatova's collection *Anno Domini* (1921),

Mikhail Kuzmin cautioned her about possible dangers of repeating herself, particularly in the absence of such literary giants as Blok. "Of course, the great, melancholy poetess had long enjoyed well-deserved popularity in her own right. It may have coincided with Blok's death by accident. It's not a question of some substitution or betrayal; it would seem that the heart, even a collective one, is afraid of a vacuum. This adoration is neither Akhmatova's personal fault nor achievement, but there is a danger in it, or it may conceal a danger. The public is lazy and demands from its favorites repetitions and variations on the same theme, which signal stagnation and, as a result, the death of creativity." This review was first published as "Parnasskie zarosli" in the Berlin newspaper *Zavtra* in 1923, but was known to Akhmatova and the reading public since its conception in 1921 (quoted in Svetlana Kovalenko, "Anna Akhmatova [Lichnost', Real'nost', Mif]," in *Anna Akhmatova, Pro et Contra: Antologia* [St. Petersburg: Izdatel'stvo Russkogo Khristianskogo gumanitarnogo instituta, 2001], 1:20).

59. In 1924, the Gumilev scholar Lev Gornung recorded in his diary Sofia Parnok's story of her visit to Akhmatova. A poet herself, she was surprised to see Akhmatova get her poetry notebook from under a mattress. "The poems were written in pencil, . . . [and] in order to change a word or a line, Anna Andreevna rubbed them out with an eraser and then wrote in new words." Parnok sensed that Akhmatova was afraid of her future biographers. "After Aleksandr Blok's death," Akhmatova explained, "his drafts became accessible to strangers who rummaged through them, trying to make sense of them, just a few days after Blok died." In Gornung's account, "Parnok wanted to give Akhmatova a book of her poetry, signing it in ink, but Akhmatova couldn't find any ink." When Parnok finally succeeded in getting "an ancient pen in the shape of a goose feather," the pen broke when she attempted to sign. In 1926, Gornung recorded his own conversation with Akhmatova about Maxim Gorky, who, according to Akhmatova, "was so famous that every remark and written note of his would be remembered and published somewhere." Gornung confesses, "I had the impression that while talking about Gorky, Akhmatova was thinking about herself. . . . In general, during those years, she was so cautious that she didn't even write any letters or speak over the phone" (Gornung, "Zapiski ob Anne Akhmatovoi," in *Vospominaniia ob Anne Akhmatovoi* [Moscow: Sovetskii pisatel', 1991], 180, 188).

60. Samoilov and Chukovskaia, *Perepiska*, 75.

61. Chukovskaia, *The Akhmatova Journals*, 152–53.

62. John Malmstad and Nikolai Bogomolov, *Mikhail Kuzmin: A Life in Art* (Cambridge: Harvard University Press, 1999), 222. A thorough analysis of intertextual parallels was first performed by R. D. Timenchik, V. N. Toporov, and T. V. Tsiv'ian in "Akhmatova i Kuzmin," *Russian Literature* 6 (1978): 213–305.

63. Malmstad, *Mikhail Kuzmin*, 222–23.

64. Akhmatova's comment, "How could the Russian prerevolutionary renaissance have been entrusted to the vicious and totally ignorant pederast?" is

from *Sobranie sochinenii v shesti tomakh* (Moscow: Ellis Lak, 2001), 5:107. Viacheslav Vs. Ivanov described a meeting in 1964 as follows: "On May 10 I went to see Anna Andreevna. She was in bed, not well, and two women were helping her. Despite her ill health, she sat up and spoke contemptuously of Viacheslav Ivanovich Ivanov: 'Fraud! As much a charlatan as those of the eighteenth century—like those who talked like they lived at the time of Christ, like Cagliostro. . . . This is what he did: brought me to his room and asked me to read. Praising me, he wiped the tears from his eyes. Then he led me out to everyone else and there began to criticize me. What a traitor'" (V. V. Ivanov, "Meetings with Akhmatova," in *Anna Akhmatova and Her Circle*, 206).

65. Akhmatova typically criticized Kuzmin not for his works but for his "amoral" behavior, even when his intended "victim" deserved to be punished, as with Olga Glebova-Sudeikina, who openly cheated on Kuzmin with his lovers. "Kuzmin was a very nasty, malevolent, and rancorous person," Akhmatova said in 1940. "He couldn't stand Blok, because he envied him. . . . He left a diary, which he sold to Bonch, but Olenka, who was friends with Kuzmin, told me that it was something monstrous. . . . My Olenka used to fall in love very often. Once she fell in love with a young composer and brought his works to show Kuzmin. Kuzmin knew perfectly well of her love, but chose to mock the young composer's efforts mercilessly. Tell me, why did he have to do that?" (Chukovskaia, *The Akhmatova Journals*, 138). "He was a very spiteful and unpleasant person, a real Satanist," she said in 1962 (M. I. Budyko, "Rasskazy Anny Akhmatovoi," in *Ob Anne Akhmatovoi*, ed. Mikhail Kralin [Leningrad: Lenizdat, 1990], 491).

66. See Irina Paperno and Joan Delaney Grossman, eds., *Creating Life: The Aesthetic Utopia of Russian Modernism* (Stanford: Stanford University Press, 1994); and Matich, *Erotic Utopia*.

67. *Balaganchik* (a diminutive of *balagan* and a theatrical term for the Russian puppet show) was also the title of Blok's famous play of 1906 in which he ridiculed his immediate family and his friends, specifically his tangled relationship with Andrei Bely, who was madly in love with L. D. Blok.

68. Citations in the following paragraph are from Chukovskaia, *The Akhmatova Journals*, 146–47.

69. Beth Holmgren, *Women's Works in Stalin's Time: On Lidiia Chukovskaia and Nadezhda Mandel'shtam* (Bloomington: Indiana University Press, 1993), 87–88.

70. Chukovskaia, *The Akhmatova Journals*, 28.

71. Jerome Bruner, *Acts of Meaning* (Cambridge: Harvard University Press, 1990), 113.

72. Ibid., 112.

73. Patricia Meyer Sparks, *Gossip* (New York: Knopf, 1985), 7. I am grateful to Eric Naiman for bringing this work to my attention.

74. Chukovskaia, *The Akhmatova Journals*, 9. Chukovskaia could be described as one of Akhmatova's Muses. She was definitely responsible for maintaining and intensifying Akhmatova's awareness of Stalinist terror in the late 1930s. By

1942, however, Chukovskaia was no longer instrumental in Akhmatova's creative development. Akhmatova was finishing her first version of *Poem Without a Hero*, which at that time focused on the year 1913, with its opulent decadence and irresponsible characters. Chukovskaia, with her moral stance and expectation that Akhmatova would continue to develop the prison theme, was apparently no longer a source of inspiration, which might explain Akhmatova's unaccountable ruthlessness toward Chukovskaia at that time. No matter how guilty Akhmatova might have felt, she had to break away. As Otto Rank contends, "This feeling is, however, not only ethical and concerned with the loved companion, but inner and psychical, since it concerns his own development and his loyalty to himself" (*Art and Artist* [New York: Agathon Press, 1968], 380). By the time she reestablished their friendship in 1952, Chukovskaia had become indispensable once again, since Akhmatova was about to plunge into rewriting her *Poem* with an eye to new cultural and political developments.

75. Chukovskaia, *The Akhmatova Journals*, 147.
76. Ibid., 74.
77. Ibid., 136.
78. Chukovskaia, *Zapiski ob Anne Akhmatovoi*, 1:456. In a similar interpretive mode, Osip Mandelstam reduced Chekhov to an insignificant chronicler of communal apartment conflicts. Chekhovian characters could easily resolve their problems by sorting out their living arrangements. "Why are they all together?" Mandelstam wondered in a review of a performance of *Uncle Vanya*. "A biologist would describe the Chekhovian principle as ecological. For Chekhov, cohabitation is the determining factor. His dramas have no action; they only have cohabitation with all the consequent trouble. Chekhov scoops imaginary samples of human 'scum' [as if] with a dip net. People are living together and cannot manage to move away from each other and live separately. End of story. Provide them—the 'three sisters,' for example—with train tickets and the play will be over" (Mandelstam, "O p'iese A. Chekhova 'Diadia Vania,'" in *Sobranie sochinenii v chetyrekh tomakh* [Moscow: Terra-Terra, 1991], 4:521–22).
79. Chukovskaia, *Zapiski ob Anne Akhmatovoi*, 1:414.
80. Pavel Luknitskii, *Vstrechi s Annoi Akhmatovoi* (Paris: YMCA-Press Russkii put'', 1997), 2:5, 7.
81. "I don't really know Akhmatova," Blok told Kornei Chukovskii in May 1921. "Once she came to see me at my place on Sunday because she had been taking a stroll in my neighborhood, [and] because she was wearing a nice shawl—the one she later sat in for Altman. . . . Her poetry never touched me. . . . In her *Plantain* collection, I only liked one poem—'When in Suicidal Melancholy,' and then he began reciting it. . . . The rest of Akhmatova's poems were rejected with contempt" (*Dnevnik 1901–1969*, 1:189).
82. In 1960, Viacheslav Vs. Ivanov observed Akhmatova's reaction to the publication of the third volume of Blok's works: "Akhmatova for the first time discovered several versions of a poem and outlines of a poem devoted to her. That

day at the Ardovs' this was all she could talk about. She discussed the various interpretations of the line: 'But I am not so simple / Not so complex'" (Viacheslav Vs. Ivanov, "Meetings with Akhmatova," 201).

83. A. V. Lavrov and John Malmstad, eds., *Andrei Bely i Ivanov-Razumnik: Perepiska* (St. Petersburg: Atheneum/Feniks, 1998), 588.

84. Ibid., 591–92.

85. Ibid., 595.

86. Ibid., 672. Akhmatova's rather ambiguous portrayal of Blok in her *Poem Without a Hero* could mean that her provocative title is somehow related to Beethoven's title-page destruction episode and to the above-quoted letter by Bely. The Akhmatova-Beethoven connection seems plausible because Beethoven was later praised by his friends for his prophetic abilities, manifested in the funeral march in the *Eroica*, which they later interpreted as symbolizing Napoleon's demise and isolation. See Alessandra Comini, *The Changing Image of Beethoven: A Study in Mythmaking* (New York: Rizzoli, 1987), 87–88. The first stanza of *Poem* also refers to a funeral march, that of Chopin.

87. Bely, *Andrei Bely i Ivanov-Razumnik*, 672.

88. "I hate the first chapter of Blok's *Retribution*—pop, mom, aunties, and uncles—but Warsaw is delightful—and I can't bear a city with its obligatory prostitute," Akhmatova confessed in 1942 (Chukovskaia, *Zapiski ob Anne Akhmatovoi*, 1:456). "Two persons lived inside Blok," she said fifteen years later. "One of them was a poet of genius, a visionary, the prophet Isaiah; the other—the son and nephew of the Beketovs and also Lyuba's husband. 'Auntie likes this,' 'Mom doesn't like that,' 'Liuba said . . .' And Liuba was a total idiot. . . . Blok was in Paris and was looking at the city and the arts through the eyes of Liuba and his aunt. . . . What a disgrace! Referring to Matisse, a genius, when the painter was visiting Russia, he calls him in his diary 'a wretched little Frenchman from Bordeaux'" (ibid., 2:230).

89. Chukovskaia, *The Akhmatova Journals*, 146.

90. Chukovskaia, *Zapiski ob Anne Akhmatovoi*, 3:203. Compare Akhmatova's description of L. D. Blok's disproportionately big legs, arms, and body with Brodsky's sympathetic portrayal of the "weightless" Nadezhda Mandelstam: "She was a small woman of slim build, and with the passage of years she shriveled more and more, as though trying to turn herself into something weightless, something easily pocketed in the moment of flight" (Brodsky, "Nadezhda Mandelstam [1899–1980]: An Obituary," 147).

91. Lidiia Ginzburg, "Brief Reminiscences on Anna Akhmatova," in *Anna Akhmatova and Her Circle*, 121.

92. Akhmatova prudently avoided any printed criticism of Blok by maintaining her discontent within the limits of communal apartment gossip. Likewise, she said of Bely's memoirs in 1940: "They are mendacious, consciously mendacious memoirs, in which everything is distorted—the roles people played as well as events." But she allowed herself to disapprove only of Bely's tactless behavior;

his integrity had been compromised by his affair with L. D. Blok. "It used to be considered improper to write about someone if your relationship with the person was that of Bely to Blok. . . . After all, they wouldn't have published D'Anthes's memoirs of Pushkin, would they?" (Chukovskaia, *The Akhmatova Journals*, 173).

93. Akhmatova said after reading Dostoevskii's letters in April 1959: "It follows from his letters that Anna Grigorievna was frightening. I always hated the wives of great people and thought that she was better. But no, even Sofia Andreevna [Tolstaia] was better. Anna Grigorievna was stingy and miserly. . . . It was Punin who told me about Lilia Yurievna," Akhmatova said in 1959. "He loved her and thought that she loved him, too. Looking back today, I have this theory: Lilia always loved 'the top dog'—Punin, when he was the big boss,' Krasnoshchokov, Agranov, Primakov. . . . That was her system" (Chukovskaia, *Zapiski ob Anne Akhmatovoi*, 2:352–53). Using the same strategy, in 1942 Chukovskaia voiced her pain and frustration at Akhmatova's betrayal of their friendship and creative collaboration by criticizing her imperfect companions, such as the famous actress Faina Ranevskaia, whom Chukovskaia suspected of having an affair with Akhmatova and whom she invariably portrayed as crude and perpetually drunk (Lidiia Chukovskaia, "Iz 'Tashkentskikh tetradei,'" in ibid., vol. 1).

94. Dmitrii Maksimov recorded Akhmatova's recollection of two meetings with Tsvetaeva in prewar Moscow. She pointedly focused on Tsvetaeva's appearance, saying nothing about her poetry. "Marina's hair," Akhmatova recalled, "was already gray. Her erstwhile healthy complexion was all gone. She was 'démodée' ('old-fashioned,' a French adjective, which was definitely uttered [Maksimov interjected]). She reminded [me of] one of the Moscow symbolist ladies of the 1900s" (Dmitrii E. Maksimov, "Ob Anne Akhmatovoi, kakoi pomniu," in *Vospominaniia ob Anne Akhmatovoi* [Moscow: Sovetskii pisatel, 1991], 122). "I learned that in her last year Marina Tsvetaeva was madly in love with Villiam-Vilmont while he openly mocked her," Akhmatova told Chukovskaia in 1942. "He showed her letters to his acquaintances and told his housemaid, 'When the scrawny old lady comes, I'm not home.' . . . No, I'm sure that a woman in love shouldn't be active. Nothing but disgrace ever comes of it" (Chukovskaia, *Zapiski ob Anne Akhmatovoi*, 1:455).

95. "Boris didn't know the first thing about women," Akhmatova said in October 1960. "Perhaps he was simply unlucky with them. His first wife, Yevgeniia Vladimirovna, was nice and refined, but, you see, she fancied herself a great artist, and, as a consequence, it was Boris who had to cook soup for the whole family. Zina, is a seven-legged dragon, coarse, shallow, and anti-art incarnate. After he began living with her, Boris stopped writing poetry, but she, at least, raised their sons and is a woman of integrity—not a thief like Olga" (ibid., 2:429).

96. Chukovskaia, *The Akhmatova Journals*, 123.

97. The following quotations are from Chukovskaia, *Zapiski ob Anne Akhmatovoi*, 2:76, 2:233, 2:203, 2:271.

98. Viacheslav Vs. Ivanov, "Meetings with Akhmatova," 211.

99. Akhmatova described her recollection of Zinaida Gippius at the Tenishev

College Hall in 1918 in this way: "Zinaida Nikolaevna was wearing a red wig, her face looked enameled, she was wearing a dress from Paris. . . . [The Merezhkovskiis] kept trying to get me to visit, but I avoided it because they were nasty—in the simplest, most elementary sense of the word" (Chukovskaia, *The Akhmatova Journals*, 61–62). Commenting on L. Yu. Brik's appearance in 1960, Akhmatova said, "I saw her at a performance of the play *Merchants of Glory*, when she was thirty. She had a worn look, dyed hair, and brazen eyes on a debauched face" (Chukovskaia, *Zapiski ob Anne Akhmatovoi*, 2:416). Note that the main feature of the heroine of the *Poem* is her inherent falsehood. She is both a "Petersburg doll, acclaimed on stage" and the narrator's "double," who changed to such an extent that nobody could guess that originally her family came from the provincial town of Pskov.

 100. Chukovskaia, *Zapiski ob Anne Akhmatovoi*, 1:141–43.

 101. In 1957, in her autobiographical sketch, Akhmatova highlighted her kinship with this particular work by Tolstoi: "I was born the same year as Charlie Chaplin, Tolstoi's *Kreutzer Sonata*, the Eiffel Tower, and, it seems, T. S. Eliot" (Anna Akhmatova, *My Half-Century*, trans. Ronald Meyer [Evanston: Northwestern University Press, 1997], 1).

 102. Nadezhda Mandelstam's letters to Boris Kuzin and many other memoirs, including Chukovskaia's long-suppressed "From the Tashkent Notebooks" and Pavel Luknitskii's more personal accounts of his meetings with Akhmatova in the 1950s and the 1960s, reveal that she often suffered from Akhmatova's insensitivity and authoritarian control of her life, exercised under the pretext of taking care of her best poet-friend's widow. She was careful to hide her resentment but apparently shed her inhibitions after Akhmatova died. Her second book of memoirs, *Hope Abandoned*, which feature her notorious "misreading" of Akhmatova's *Poem Without a Hero*, can be read as her response to Akhmatova on behalf of other mistreated wives and companions.

 103. Brodsky, "Nadezhda Mandelstam (1899–1980): An Obituary," 155.

 104. Akhmatova, *The Word That Causes Death's Defeat*, 40.

 105. Vera Luknitskaia, *Liubovnik, Rytsar', Letopisets* (St. Petersburg: Sudarynia, 2005).

 106. Ibid., 32–33.

 107. Akhmatova, *The Word That Causes Death's Defeat*, 39–40; According to Chukovskaia, Akhmatova often impressed her by her familiarity with memoirs written by writers' widows and companions. See their exchange in 1942 about women associated with Alexander Herzen and about Avdot'ia Panaeva, mistress of the poet Nikolai Nekrasov (Chukovskaia, *Zapiski ob Anne Akhmatovoi*, 1:388–89). Yet her harsh criticism of Panaeva was followed by her creative adaptation of one of Nekrasov's poems dedicated to Panaeva. Akhmatova's line, "I didn't get my gray crown for nothing" ("Sedoi venets dostalsia mne nedarom"), from her famous poem of June 1942, "The Way I Am, I Wish You Someone New" *("Kakaia est', zhelaiu vam druguiu")*, is redolent of Nekrasov's "She got her heavy cross to carry through" *("Tiazhelyi krest dostalsia ei na doliu")*.

108. "She was indifferent to her literary success in the beginning, believing with Gumilev that they would share the same fate as the Brownings—in life the wife was famous; after death she was forgotten and the husband was celebrated" (Nadezhda Mandelstam, "Akhmatova," in *Anna Akhmatova and Her Circle*, 121).

109. Stephanie Sandler singles out two impulses for Akhmatova's Pushkin essays, which are "the search for source texts and the accretion of a partial biography" (*Commemorating Pushkin: Russia's Myth of a National Poet* [Stanford: Stanford University Press, 2004], 203).

110. Luknitskii, *Vstrechi s Annoi Akhmatovoi*, 1:267.

111. In Gerstein's memoirs she describes an intimate gathering at the Punins' in 1938: "Supper was not ready, and people sat around, Akhmatova [sat] on the little divan in the corner. 'I've written a novel that no-one will ever read,' said Luknitskii. Not to be outdone, Lyova [Gumilev] declared that he had written a short story no one would ever read. Even Punin joined in this ludicrous competition and, pointing to one of his articles, said that no one would ever read it either. At that moment, Akhmatova's sonorous and musical voice came from the corner of the room: 'But they will read me'" (Gerstein, *Moscow Memoirs*, 219).

112. I. N. Punina, "Iz arkhiva Nikolaia Nikolaevicha Punina," in *Litsa, Biograficheskii al'manakh* (Moscow/St. Petersburg: Feniks/Athenium, 1992), 1:437.

113. Quoted passages in this paragraph are from Luknitskii, *Vstrechi s Annoi Akhmatovoi*, 2:161–62, 2:214–15, 1:303.

114. Chukovskaia, *The Akhmatova Journals*, 165. I changed the translator's "and appropriated" to "and got possession of."

115. The poet Larisa Vasilieva relates her discussion with Akhmatova's friend Salomeia Andronikova and Isaiah Berlin in the 1970s about how to describe somebody who inspires women poets. Was it a "hero" or a "muse"? They finally decided on the facetious "muz." The discussion was in Russian, so "muz" was coined as an abbreviation and a grammatically masculine equivalent of the feminine "muza" (muse). "Muz" in Russian also sounds very much like "muzh" (husband). "So you're Akhmatova's 'muz'?" Vasilieva asked Berlin. "One of the 'muzes'? [Odin iz muzov?]" she clarified. "He understood the joke immediately and smiled himself," Vasilieva continued. "Never considered myself as such. But I did play a certain role in her life," was Berlin's prompt reply (Vasilieva, "Salomeia," in *Taina vremeni* [Moscow: Eksmo-Press, 2001], 366–67).

116. Natalia Roskina, "Anna Akhmatova," in *Chetyre glavy* (Paris: YMCA-Press, 1980), 25–26.

117. Luknitskii, *Vstrechi s Annoi Akhmatovoi*, 1:187, 2:181.

118. M. I. Budyko, "Rasskazy Anny Akhmatovoi," 484.

119. Chukovskaia, *The Akhmatova Journals*, 148.

120. *Zapisnye knizhki Anny Akhmatovoi* (Moscow-Torino: Guido Einaudi editore, 1996), 625, emphasis in original.

121. Chukovskaia, *The Akhmatova Journals*, 192.

122. Chukovskaia, *Zapiski ob Anne Akhmatovoi*, 2:429.

123. "Tell me, which was Tatiana?"
"Oh, she's the one, who, melancholy
and silent like Svetlana,
entered and sat down by the window."
"How come you're with the younger one in love?"
"Why, what's the matter?" "I'd have chosen the other,
If I had been like you a poet."
Aleksandr Pushkin, *Eugene Onegin, A Novel in Verse*, trans. Vladimir Nabokov (Princeton: Princeton University Press, 1990), 151.

124. M. I. Budyko, "Rasskazy Anny Akhmatovoi," in *Ob Anne Akhmatovoi*, 497.

125. Akhmatova, *Sobranie sochinenii*, 5:125.

126. Chukovskaia, *The Akhmatova Journals*, 156.

127. Akhmatova apparently recognized a similar transformation in Mikhail Bulgakov's *Master and Margarita*, with its communal apartment serving as a stage for Satan's annual ball in Moscow. This explains her puzzling comment to Chukovskaia about her discovery that Bulgakov did not know Dante's work. "Our sources of influence are different," she stated in 1942 (Chukovskaia, *Zapiski ob Anne Akhmatovoi*, 1:484). See also Margaret Atwood's insight into the relationship between Dante's "woods" and Virginia Woolf's "room": "Dante begins the *Divine Comedy*—which is both a poem and a record of the composition of that poem—with an account of finding himself in a dark, tangled wood, at night, having lost his way, after which the sun begins to rise. Virginia Woolf said that writing a novel is like walking through a dark room, holding a lantern which lights up what is already in the room anyway" (Atwood, *Negotiating with the Dead* [New York: Anchor Books, 2003], xxiii).

Chapter 5. The Winged Eavesdropper

The epigraph is translated from the following: *Vzdokhnut' poglubzhe i do plech / v kryl'ia vdev raspravlennye ruki, / s podokonnika na vozdukh lech' / i letet' naperekor nauke . . . / Boius' ne vynesu poleta . . . / Net, vynes. Na polu sizhu vpot'makh, / i v glazakh pestro, i shum v ushakh, / i blazhennaia v plechakh lomota.*

1. Aleksandr Dolinin, *Istinnaia zhizn' pisatelia Sirina. Raboty o Nabokove* (St. Petersburg: Akademicheskii proekt, 2004), 13.

2. Vladimir Nabokov, *Speak, Memory* (London: Penguin Books, 1967), 220.

3. In the late 1960s, to Alfred Appel's question, "In which of your early works do you think you first begin to face the possibilities that . . . reach an apotheosis in the 'inviolate abode' of *Pale Fire*?"—Nabokov gave the least expected answer: "Possibly in *The Eye*" (Vladimir Nabokov, *Strong Opinions* [New York: McGraw-Hill, 1973], 74).

4. Georgii Ivanov, "V. Sirin, *Mashen'ka;. Korol', dama, valet. Zashchita Luzhina; Vozvrashchenie Chorba*," in *Sobranie sochineniy v trekh tomakh* (Moscow: Soglasie, 1994), 3:524–25.

5. Ivanov's negative opinions were shared by Georgii Adamovich and the Merezhkovskii-Gippius circle; see Nina Berberova, *Kursiv moy* (Moscow: Soglasie, 1996), 286. Ivanov retained his negative view of Nabokov throughout his life. See his attack on Nabokov's famous memoirs as a non-Russian product: "A grown-up dunce's passion for butterflies is as revolting to me as someone's showing off their wealth or phony noble origins and high rank. . . . And whoever in Russian literature ever flaunted wealth? Those who were wealthy felt rather ashamed of it. Even in the quiet times nobody held forth on their footmen and diamonds" (Georgii Ivanov, letter to Roman Gul' [July 1954], in *Klassik bez retushi*, ed. N. G. Mel'nikov [Moscow: Novoe Literaturnoe obozrenie, 2000], 614).

6. See, for example, David M. Bethea, "Nabokov and Blok," in *The Garland Companion to Vladimir Nabokov*, ed. Vladimir Alexandrov (New York: Garland, 1995), 374–81.

7. Vladimir Nabokov, *The Gift* (New York: Vintage Books, 1991), 115.

8. John E. Malmstad, "Mixail Kuzmin: A Chronicle of His Life and Times," in Mikhail Kuzmin, *Sobranie stikhov*, ed. John Malmstad and Vladimir Markov (Munich: Wilhelm Fink, 1977), 3:99.

9. Mikhail Kuzmin,*Wings,* in *Selected Prose and Poetry*, ed. and trans. Michael Green (Ann Arbor, MI: Ardis, 1980), 10; subsequent page references are given in parentheses.

10. See Gennadii Shmakov, "Blok i Kuzmin (Novye materialy)," in *Blokovskii sbornik* (Tartu: Tartusskii Universitet, 1972): 2:341–64; see also Klaus Harer, *"Kryl'ia* M. A. Kuzmina kak primer 'prekrasnoi legkosti'," in *Amour et Erotisme dans la littérature russe du XXe siècle*, ed. Leonid Heller, *Slavica Helvetica* 41 (1992): 45–56.

11. Aleksandr Blok, *O literature* (Moscow: Federatsiia, 1931), 135.

12. Aleksandr Benua, *Moi vospominaniia v piati knigakh* (Moscow: Nauka, 1990), 5:477.

13. Vladimir Markov, "Poeziia Mikhaila Kuzmina," in Mikhail Kuzmin, *Sobranie stikhov*, 3:409.

14. G. Ivanov, *Sobranie sochinenii v trekh tomakh*, 3:98–108.

15. Vladislav Khodasevich, *Nekropol', Literatura i vlast', Pis'ma B. A. Sadovskomu* (Moscow: SS, 1996), 19–29.

16. Laura Engelstein, *The Keys to Happiness* (Ithaca: Cornell University Press, 1994), 67–71. Several members of V. D. Nabokov's family, including his son Sergei, were homosexuals.

17. Andrew Field, "Notes on a Decadent Prose," *Russian Review* 20 (1963): 300; Gennadii Shmakov, "Dva Kaliostro," in Mikhail Kuzmin, *Chudesnaia zhizn' Iosifa Bal'zamo grafa Kaliostro* (New York: Russica, 1982); Vladimir Markov, "Beseda o proze Kuzmina," in Mikhail Kuzmin, *Proza (pervaia kniga rasskazov)*, ed. Vladimir Markov (Berkeley, CA: Berkeley Slavic Specialities, 1984), vii–xviii; Olga Skonechnaia, "Liudi Lunnogo sveta v russkoi proze Nabokova," *Zvezda* 11 (1996): 207–14.

18. John A. Barnstead, "Nabokov, Kuzmin, Chekhov and Gogol': Systems of Reference in 'Lips to Lips,'" in *Studies in Russian Literature in Honor of Vsevolod*

Setchkarev, ed. Julian W. Connolly and Sonia I. Ketchian (Columbus, OH: Slavica, 1986), 59n.

19. Kuzmin's use of the name of Dostoevskii's character is explained in A. G. Timofeev, "M. Kuzmin v polemike s F. M. Dostoevskim i A. P. Chekhovym (*Kryl'ia*)," in *Serebrianyi vek v Rossii* ed. Viach. Vs. Ivanov, V. N. Toporov, and T. V. Tsiv'ian (Moscow: Radiks, 1993), 211.

20. Vladimir Nabokov, *The Eye* (London: Weidenfeld and Nicolson, 1966), 85; subsequent page references are given in parentheses.

21. Ibid., 37; "Mona Vanna" can be traced back to Maeterlinck's *Monna Vanna* (see Susan Fromberg Schaeffer, "The Editing Blinks of Vladimir Nabokov's *The Eye*," *University of Windsor Review* 8 [1972–1973]: 28).

22. D. Barton Johnson, "The Books Reflected in Nabokov's Eye," *SEEJ* 29 (1985): 399–400.

23. "Petropolis" reprinted the following works by Kuzmin when Nabokov moved to Berlin: *Plavayushchie-puteshestvuyushchie*, 3rd and 4th eds. (1923); *Kryl'ia*, 4th ed.(1923); and *Glinianye golubki*, 2nd and 3rd eds. (1923); see John Malmstad, commentary to the "Letter of M. A. Kuzmin to Ja. N. Blox," in *Studies in the Life and Works of Mixail Kuzmin*, ed. John Malmstad, *Wiener Slawistischer Almanach* 24 (1989): 178n.

24. Mikhail Kuzmin, *Podzemnyie ruch'i: Romany, povesti, rasskazy* (St. Petersburg: Severo-Zapad, 1994), 397. Matilda's parting with her husband and immediately starting an affair with Smurov evokes the reckless tone of Kuzmin's poem "Ariadna" (from *Parabolas*, 1923): "*U platana ten' prokhladna / Tesny terema tsarei,— / Ariadna, Ariadna, / Uplyvaet tvoi Tezei!// . . . Cheredoiu plod za tsvetom, / Sinii purpur kruzhit vniz,— / I uvenchan vechnym svetom, / Zhdet nevesty Dionis.*"

25. Nabokov, *The Eye*, 17–18. This passage probably alludes also to Kuzmin's novella *The House of Cards* (*Kartonnyi domik*, 1907), where the name Matilda Petrovna appears for the first time: "If you find it amusing when Matilda sits on your stomach and says she's a chimera, when in one evening you have ten of the silliest tête-à-têtes of the most compromising kind, when you listen to as many as twenty poets—then we've had a very good time. But, between ourselves, all that has palled to a considerable degree" (Kuzmin, *The House of Cards*, in *Selected Prose and Poetry*, 143).

26. On references to *Travelers by Land and Sea* in Nabokov's "Lips to Lips," see Barnstead, "Nabokov, Kuzmin, Chekhov, and Gogol.'"

27. My ideas were influenced by Irina Paperno's discussion of a similar love triangle in Kuzmin's *The Trout Breaking through the Ice* (*Forel' razbivaet led*, 1929). See Irina Paperno, "Dvoinichestvo i liubovnyi treugol'nik: poeticheskii mif Kuzmina i ego pushkinskaia proektsiia," in *Studies in the Life and Works of Mixail Kuzmin*, ed. Malmstad, 57–83.

28. G. Ivanov, *Peterburgskie zimy*, 101–2.

29. Mikhail Kuzmin, *The Diary (1905–1906)*, ed. George Cheron, *Wiener Slawistischer Almanach* 17 (1986): 417.

30. See, for example, Blok, *O literature*, 189; G. Ivanov, *Peterburgskie zimy*, 104–5; Markov, "Poeziya Mikhaila Kuzmina," 402–5; and Zinaida Shakhovskaia, *V poiskakh Nabokova. Otrazheniya* (Moscow: Kniga, 1991), 40–41.

31. Nikolai Bogomolov and John Malmstad, *Mikhail Kuzmin: iskusstvo, zhizn', epokha* (Moscow: Novoe literaturnoe obozrenie, 1996), 96–97.

32. On *Wings*, see Markov, "Beseda o proze Kuzmina."

33. See Olga Matich, "The Symbolist Meaning of Love: Theory and Practice," in *Creating Life: The Aesthetic Utopia of Russian Modernism*, ed. Irina Paperno and Joan Delaney Grossman (Stanford: Stanford University Press, 1994), 24–50.

34. Donald Gillis, "The Platonic Theme in Kuzmin's *Wings*," *SEEJ* 22 (1978): 336–47.

35. The following quotations from *Phaedrus* are from Plato, *The Symposium and The Phaedrus: Plato's Erotic Dialogues*, trans. William S. Cobb (Albany: State University of New York Press, 1993), 253D, 253E, 255A.

36. Ibid., 255C–D.

37. Ibid., 255A.

38. Halfway through the narrative, Vanya is told that Stroop "can be reached at the Four Seasons Hotel" in Munich (75).

39. Plato stipulates, "Each person selects his love from the ranks of the beautiful according to his own style" (*Phaedrus*, 252D); on keenness of sight, see ibid., 250D.

40. Ibid., 251A–C.

41. Paperno, "Dvoinichestvo i liubovnyi treugol'nik," 60.

42. Plato, *Phaedrus* 255D; see also Gillis, "The Platonic Theme in Kuzmin's *Wings*."

43. Sigmund Freud, "On Narcissism: An Introduction," in *Freud's "On Narcissism: An Introduction,"* ed. Joseph Sadler, Ethel Spector Person, and Peter Fonagy (New Haven: Yale University Press, 1991), 18–19.

44. On Kuzmin's Smurov as an outsider, see Franz Schindler, "Otrazhenie gomoseksual'nogo opyta v *Kryl'iakh* M. Kuzmina," in *Amour et Erotisme dans la littérature russe du XXe siècle*, 57–63.

45. Freud, "On Narcissism," 3.

46. Ibid., 3, 18.

47. Quoted in Havelock Ellis, *Studies in the Psychology of Sex* (New York: Random House, 1936), 3:363–64.

48. See ibid., 3:347–75; Otto Rank, *The Double: A Psychoanalytic Study*, ed. and trans. Harry Tucker Jr. (Chapel Hill: University of North Carolina Press, 1971), 69–86; and Heinz Kohut, *The Search for the Self* (New York: International Universities Press, 1978), 2:615–17. The studies by Ellis and Rank were published before Nabokov wrote *The Eye*.

49. Hermann Hesse's *Narcissus and Goldmund*, about the spiritual and sensual progression in life of the young Goldmund, was published in the same year as Nabokov's *The Eye*.

50. Kohut, *The Search for the Self*, 623. On Nabokov as Narcissus, see Andrew

Field, *Vladimir Nabokov*, 12, 27–30, 58, 80–81, 82, 139. However, Field does not consider *The Eye* in the light of the myth. Nabokov's 1965 foreword to *The Eye* betrays his intimate links with his protagonist. In it, Nabokov describes Mukhin, Smurov's lucky rival for Vanya's attention, as "a nasty prig, fought in 1919 under Denikin, and under Wrangel, speaks four languages, affects a cool, worldly air, and will probably do very well in the soft job into which his future father-in-law is steering him" (8–9). The text does not support such an "unfair" characterization, unless we assume that this foreword was written by the aging Smurov himself. The foreword finishes almost with a threat: "The plot will not be reducible in the reader's mind—if I read that mind correctly—to a dreadfully painful love story in which a writhing heart is not only spurned, but humiliated and punished" (10).

51. Thomas M. Greene, *The Light in Troy* (New Haven: Yale University Press, 1982) 40, emphasis in original.

52. See, for example, Johnson, "The Books Reflected in Nabokov's *The Eye*"; and Field, *Vladimir Nabokov*.

53. Vladimir Nabokov, *The Gift* (New York: Vintage, 1991), 350.

54. Susan Sontag, *Illness as Metaphor* (New York: Farrar, Straus, and Giroux, 1977).

55. I borrow the term "target text" from Linda Hutcheon, *A Theory of Parody* (New York: Routledge, 1991).

56. Vladimir Nabokov, *Pnin* (New York: Vintage Books, 1989), 125, 183.

Chapter 6. The Silver Age in Translation

1. On Pasternak's striving to become a truly contemporary writer in the 1920s and 1930s, see Christopher Barnes, *Boris Pasternak: A Literary Biography*, vol. 1, *1890–1928* (Cambridge: Cambridge University Press, 1989), 348–80; and ibid., vol. 2, *1928–1960*, chaps. 1–3.

2. Boris Pasternak, *Safe Conduct*, in *The Voice of Prose*, vol. 1, *Early Prose and Autobiography*, ed. and trans. Christopher Barnes (Edinburgh: Poligon, 1986), 81.

3. Boris Pasternak, *Liudi i polozheniia*, in *Sobranie sochinenii v piati tomakh* (Moscow: Khudozhestvennaia literatura, 1989–1992), 4:307.

4. Boris Pasternak, "Shopen," in ibid., 4:404.

5. All quotations are from Boris Pasternak, *Doctor Zhivago*, trans. Max Hayward and Manya Harari (London: Collins Harvill, 1988), 394. Subsequent references are given in parentheses.

6. Olga Carlyle, "Tri vizita k Borisu Pasternaku," in *Vospominaniia o Borise Pasternake*, ed. E. V. Pasternak and M. I. Feinberg (Moscow: Slovo, 1993), 654.

7. See letter to O. M. Freidenberg, in *Sobranie sochinenii*, 5:395–96. I am grateful to Christopher Barnes for bringing this to my attention.

8. Boris Pasternak, "To S. N. Durylin," January 27, 1946, in ibid., 3:651. The title of the novel underwent various mutations until it finally crystallized in 1948 as *Doctor Zhivago*.

9. Lidiia Chukovskaia, "Otryvki iz dnevnika," in *Vospominaniia o Borise Pasternake*, 410.

10. Boris Pasternak, "To G. I. Gudz' [V. Shalamov]," March 7, 1953, in *Perepiska Borisa Pasternaka*, ed. E. V. Pasternak and E. B. Pasternak (Moscow: Khudozhestvennaia literatura, 1990), 537.

11. Dmitrii Sergeevich Merezhkovskii, *Polnoe sobranie sochinenii* (Moscow: Sytin, 1914), 17:5–6, emphasis in original.

12. Konstantin Fedin, *Sochineniia v shesti tomakh* (Moscow: Khudozhestvennaia literatura, 1954), 6:552–53.

13. Katerina Clark, *Petersburg, Crucible of Cultural Revolution* (Cambridge: Harvard University Press, 1995), 304–5.

14. Cf. Pasternak's letter in *Sobranie sochinenii*, 5:226.

15. Katerina Clark, *Petersburg, Crucible of Cultural Revolution*, 201–23. See also Mikhail Zoshchenko's description of his attempts to turn himself into a new writer whose work is appreciated by the masses. "My first literary steps after the revolution were erroneous," Zoshchenko recalled in the early 1930s. "I began to write long stories in the old style using the old, threadbare language that, true enough, even today is occasionally used in works supposed to be the last specimens of real/big literature. It wasn't until a year later that I became aware of my mistake and started regrouping along the whole front. The mistake might have been expected. I was born into a family of members of the intelligentsia. In actual fact, I wasn't a specimen of New Man, nor was I a new writer. For a while, my innovation in literature was purely an invention of my own. Subsequently, I had to work on my language very hard. My whole syntax had to be overhauled in order to make a literary piece simple and accessible to new readers" (Zoshchenko, "Avtobiografiia," *Litso i maska Mikhaila Zoshchenko*, ed. Yu. V. Tomashevskii ([Moscow: Olimp.PPP, 1994], 12).

16. See Konstantin Mochul'skii, *Andrei Bely* (Paris: YMCA-Press, 1955), 269; and Lazar Fleishman, "Bely's Memoirs," in *Andrei Bely: Spirit of Symbolism*, ed. John Malmstad (Ithaca: Cornell University Press, 1987), 231.

17. Fleishman, "Bely's Memoirs," 241.

18. Andrei Bely, *Nachalo veka* (Moscow: Soiuzteatr, 1990), 17–18.

19. Vladislav Khodasevich, *Literaturnye stat'i i vospominaniia* (New York: Izdatel'stvo imeni Chekhova, 1954), 225.

20. Boris Pasternak, "To V. T. Shalamov," July 9, 1952, letter 292 of Boris Pasternak, *Sobranie sochinenii*, 5:498.

21. Boris Pasternak, "To O. M. Freidenberg," February 4, 1941, letter 215, and "To T. V. and V. V. Ivanov," April 8, 1942, letter 231, in *Sobranie sochinenii*, 5:392–93, 413–15.

22. See Andrei Bely, "Vospominaniia ob Aleksandre Aleksandroviche Bloke," in *Aleksandr Blok v vospominaniiakh sovremennikov v dvukh tomakh*, 1:252, 322. Images of Christ, Hamlet, and Faust also played an important role in Blok's own writings; see Avril Pyman, *The Life of Aleksandr Blok* (Oxford: Oxford University Press, 1979–1980). Harold Bloom writes, "The ultimate shock . . . comes when we realize

that the Western worship of God—by Jews, Christians, and Moslems—is the worship of a literary character" (Bloom, *The Western Canon* [New York: Riverhead Books, 1995], 5).

23. All unrhymed prose translations of Blok's poetry in this chapter were generously made by Timothy Sergay. For the Russian originals, see the appendix.

24. Aleksandr Blok, *Sobranie sochinenii v vos'mi tomakh* (Moscow/Leningrad: Khudozhestvennaia literatura, 1960), 1:227.

25. Ibid., 1:224.

26. Ibid., 1:221.

27. Pasternak-Blok parallels have been studied by a number of scholars. See Henry Gifford, "Pasternak and the 'Realism' of Blok," *Oxford Slavonic Papers* 18 (1967); and Irene Masing-Delic, "Zhivago's 'Christmas Star' as Homage to Blok," in *Aleksandr Blok: Centennial Conference*, ed. Walter N. Vickery and Bogdan B. Sagatov (Columbus, OH: Slavica Publishers, 1984), 207–24; Timothy Sergey, "'Blizhe k suti, k miru Bloka': The Mise-en-Scène of Boris Pasternak and Pasternak's Blokian-Christological Ideal," *Russian Review* 64 (July 2005): 401–21. I do not intend to point out yet more parallels, but to explore Pasternak's strategies of assimilation of any "foreign" text in his novel.

28. Boris Pasternak, "K kharakteristike Bloka," in *Sobranie Sochinenii*, 4:706.

29. Lidiia Ginzburg, *Chelovek za pis'mennym stolom* (Leningrad: Sovetskii pisatel, 1989), 118.

30. A. Toporov, *Krest'iane o pisateliakh* (Moscow/Leningrad: Gosudarstvennoe izdatel'stvo, 1930), 236–37.

31. The fact that peasants had problems with this particular work is significant because in it (as well as in other long narrative poems of this period) Pasternak hoped to reach new artistic heights by combining the events of one personal life with those in the history of the nation (see Barnes, *Boris Pasternak*. 1:348–80).

32. Toporov, *Krest'iane o pisateliakh*, 267–69.

33. Evgenii Dobrenko, "The Disaster of Middlebrow Taste, or, Who 'Invented' Socialist Realism?" in *Socialist Realism Without Shores*, ed. Thomas Lahusen and Evgenii Dobrenko (Durham: Duke University Press, 1997), 135–64.

34. See Barnes, *Boris Pasternak*, vol. 2. It is not fortuitous that Zhivago dies in 1929, more or less when Pasternak himself felt the urge for a drastic change of his style and mode of poetic expression.

35. Pasternak, *Sobranie sochinenii*, 3:659. The fact that Pasternak was at times prepared to go quite far in an effort to make his novel accessible can be illustrated with the following poem. In the drafts, it was composed by Zhivago while sawing wood with his third wife Marina (ibid., 3:618):

> Raz u nuvorisha
> V prazdnik Rozhdestva
> S bednoiu Marishei
> Ia pilil drova.

36. This scene might have been inspired by a similarly unsuccessful attempt of Nina Petrovskaia (1884–1928) to kill her former lover, Andrei Bely, during his lecture at the Polytechnical Museum in Moscow in 1905.

37. Aleksandr Blok, "Na smert' deda," in *Sobranie sochinenii v vos'mi tomakh*, 1:202–3.

38. George Steiner reflects on "understanding as translation" in *After Babel* (Oxford: Oxford University Press, 1992), 1–51.

39. Pasternak, "O Shekspire," in *Sobranie sochinenii*, 4:386.

40. Varlaam Shalamov, "Pasternak," in *Vospominaniia o Borise Pasternake*, 618. As many scholars have noted, some of Zhivago's poems can be related directly to specific episodes in the prose sections of the novel.

41. When in 1947 Pasternak claimed that Blok's prose (rather than his poetry) was particularly inspiring to his endeavor, he most likely had in mind Blok's long poem *Retribution* (*Vozmezdie*). This poem (which took Blok over ten years to write and never finished) is usually published along with its drafts and various prose outlines. The latter—apart from providing an insight into Blok's creative method—contain a key to understanding the obscure, fragmentary portions in the poetic text. The first publications from *Retribution* ensured Blok's status, for some critics, as an accomplished realist on a par with the mature Pushkin a few months before the Bolshevik Revolution. As Vygotskii notes, *Retribution* "is no longer [an example] of decadent art, it is completely comprehensible and, most important, is of general significance" (D. Vygotskii, "U novoi grani," *Novaia zhizn'*, April 28 [May 11, 1917]).

42. In their comments on *Doctor Zhivago*, V. M. Borisov and E. B. Pasternak observe that the following passage relates to Blok (in Boris Pasternak, in *Sobranie sochinenii*, 3:703). The text they quote to support their statement, however, does not account either for Pasternak's choice of a specific social background for Galuzina or for the intensely visual imagery that pervades this excerpt. The other possible "sources" might have been Mikhail Vrubel' or Scriabin; the color lilac/mauve/violet was a general "period" color.

43. Dmitrii Merezhkovskii, *The Romance of Leonardo da Vinci*, trans. Bernard Guilbert Guerney (New York: Modern Library, 1955), 522–24.

44. Ibid., 543.

45. Ibid.

46. Ibid., 544–45. Compare this passage with Pasternak's remark about Yurii and Misha Gordon's different responses to the philosophical ideas of Yurii's uncle Nikolai Vedeniapin: "Yura advanced and developed under the influence of his uncle's theories but Misha was cramped by them" (68).

47. Merezhkovskii, *The Romance of Leonardo da Vinci*, 544.

48. On intertextuality in *Doctor Zhivago*, see Neil Cornwell, "Perspectives on *Doctor Zhivago*" in *Essays in Poetics Publications* 2 (1986): 40–44; see also Christopher Barnes, "Pasternak, Dickens and the Novel Tradition," *Forum for Modern language Studies* 24 (1990): 326–41; Savelii Senderovich, "K geneticheskoi eidologii 'Doktora

Zhivago': Doktor Zhivago i poet Chekhov," *Russian Language Journal (RLJ)* 45 (1991): 3–16; Edith Clowes, "From Beyond the Abyss: Nietzschean Myth in Zamiatin's *We* and Pasternak's *Doctor Zhivago*," in *Nietzsche and Soviet Culture: Ally and Adversary*, ed. Bernice Glatzer Rosenthal (Cambridge: Cambridge University Press, 1994), 313–37; I. P. Smirnov, *Porozhdenie interteksta (elementy intertekstual'nogo analiza s primerami iz tvorchestva Pasternaka)* (St. Petersburg: Iazykovoi tsentr SPbGU, 1995); Jerome Spencer, "'Soaked in *The Meaning of Love* and *The Kreutzer Sonata*': The Nature of Love in *Doctor Zhivago*," in *Doctor Zhivago: A Critical Companion*, ed. Edith W. Clowes (Evanston: Northwestern University Press, 1995), 76–88; and Aleksandr Etkind, *Tolkovanie Puteshestvii* (Moscow: Novoe literaturnoe obozrenie, 2001).

49. Vsevolod Ivanov, *Pri vziatii Berlina, Novyi mir,* nos. 1–6 (1945).

50. Yurii's inability to carry out his intention recalls a similar episode in the life of the painter Pavel Dmitrievich Korin (1892–1967), who was commissioned in the late 1920s to produce a grand-scale painting under the title "Russia Receding" ("Rus' ukhodiashchaia"). Like Mikheev and Zhivago, Korin was provided by Maxim Gorky with a gigantic studio in the heart of Moscow and with an extraordinary large canvas. Aside from producing numerous sketches, Korin did not accomplish his task (Vladimir Soloukhin, *Chasha, Nash Sovremennik* 7 [1997]: 92).

51. This period is discussed in detail in Barnes, *Boris Pasternak*, vol. 1, chaps. 1–2.

52. See Klavdiia Bugaeva, *Vospominaniia ob Andree Belom*, in *Vospominaniia o Bloke i Belom* (Moscow: Izdatel'skii dom XXI vek-Soglasie, 2000), 171–76.

53. I believe that a considerable gap was consciously observed and maintained between Pasternak and his character. Zinaida Pasternak observes: "For me Doctor Zhivago, in contrast to Boria, was no hero at all. Boria was a more accomplished person as compared with his hero. He portrayed Zhivago as an average member of the intelligentsia with limited aspirations and his end was typical of such a person" (in Boris Pasternak, *Vtoroe rozhdenie. Pis'ma k Z. N. Pasternak. Z. N. Pasternak, Vospominaniia*, ed. N. Pasternak and M. Feinberg [Moscow: GRIT Dom-muzei Pasternaka, 1993], 359). Placing Zhivago's coffin on his writing desk is another sign pointing to the lifelessness of his last project.

54. Pasternak, "To M. G. Vatagin," December 15, 1955, letter 320, in *Sobranie sochinenii*, 5:543–44.

55. In the late 1940s, Pasternak stressed that he had been writing and putting some of his poems aside for his character Yurii Zhivago (see Olga Ivinskaia, *Gody s Borisom Pasternakom. V plenu vremeni* [Moscow: Libris, 1992], 212). These poems became commonly known either as Zhivago's poems or as "poems from the novel."

Chapter 7. Braving the Thaw

1. Solomon Volkov, "Vspominaia Akhmatovu: osen' 1981–zima 1986," *Dialogi s Iosifom Brodskim* (Moscow: Eksmo, 2003), 342.

2. Mikhail Levidov, "Tema poeta," *Literaturnaia gazeta* 65 (November 24, 1935).

3. Gleb Struve, "Anna Akhmatova," in Anna Akhmatova, *Sochineniia* (Munich: Inter-Language Literary Associates, 1965), 1:5.

4. Boris Pasternak, *Doctor Zhivago*, trans. Max Hayward and Manya Harari (London: Collins Harvill, 1988), 439. Akhmatova's diary entry in the winter of 1966, when she was recovering from her last heart attack, suggests a sad crossbreed between Mademoiselle Fleury and Yurii Zhivago: "The ambassador asked to tell me that France is open to me at any moment. The attempt (a second one) to raise me from my bed today failed: a damp forehead, giddiness and a three-hour sleep" (*Zapisnye knizhki Anny Akhmatovoi* [Moscow-Torino: Guido Einaudi editore, 1996], 691).

5. Roman Jakobson, "On a Generation That Squandered Its Poets," *Language in Literature*, ed. Krystina Pomorska and Stephen Rudy (Cambridge: Harvard University Press, 1987), 299.

6. Kornei Chukovskii, "Chitaia Akhmatovu," *Moskva* 5 (1964): 23.

7. Anna Akhmatova, "O posmertnykh sud'bakh poetov," in *Stikhotvoreniia, Poemy, Proza* (Moscow: RIPOL KLASSIK, 1998), 638–39.

8. Cf. "Anna Andreevna Akhmatova (Gorenko) is one of those few poets who seem to be living links, as it were, connecting the 'Silver Age' of Russian poetry to the present time" (introduction to Anna Akhmatova, *Izbrannye stikhotvoreniia* [New York: Izdatel'stvo imeni Chekhova, 1952], v).

9. Natalia Roskina, "Good-bye Again," in *Anna Akhmatova and Her Circle*, comp. Konstantin Polivanov, trans. Patricia Beriozkina (Fayetteville: University of Arkansas Press, 1994), 191–92.

10. Akhmatova, *Zapisnye knizhki*, 318.

11. Theodor W. Adorno, *Beethoven*, ed. Rolf Tiedmann, trans. Edmund Jephcott (Stanford: Stanford University Press, 1998), 123.

12. See Alexander Zholkovsky, "Anna Akhmatova: Scripts, Not Scriptures," *Slavic and East European Journal* 40 (Spring 1996); and "The Obverse Stalinism: Akhmatova's Self-Serving Charisma of Selfishness," in *Self and Story in Russian History*, ed. Laura Engelstein and Stephanie Sandler (Ithaca: Cornell University Press, 2000).

13. Zholkovsky, "The Obverse Stalinism," 46.

14. Apart from providing a sensitive and "usable" account of the 1900s and the 1910s in Russia, Berdiaev was critical and suspicious of the Russian emigration. Both aspects of Berdiaev's work appealed to Akhmatova and gave her critical ammunition.

15. Stanislav Kuniaev, *Vyzyvaiu ogon' na sebia* (Moscow: Voennoe izdatel'stvo, 2001), 258–59.

16. The story is not mentioned even in Roman Timenchik's comprehensive coverage of Akhmatova in the 1960s, *Anna Akhmatova v 60-e gody* (Moscow: Vodolei, 2005).

17. Nadezhda Mandelstam, "Akhmatova," in *Anna Akhmatova and Her Circle*, 128–29.

18. Natalia Roskina recalled, "As she grew older, the most insignificant things could evoke her anger. Often she was irritated without any reason" ("Good-bye Again," 176).

19. Otto Rank, *Art and Artist* (New York: Agathon Press, 1968), 373–74.

20. Larisa Vasilieva, "Salomeia," *Taina vremeni* (Moscow: Eksmo-Press, 2001), 397.

21. See also Klavdiia Bugaeva's testament to her husband's "utter reluctance to get down to work" before Bely started a new novel. He "would procrastinate, resisting the need with every fiber of his being. He would put off the beginning of work until the very last moment and use any excuse if only 'still' not to write. From all of his past experience, he knew only too well of all the consequences and would get scared in advance. He had a clear vision of the enormous amount of moral and physical energy such work would call for and envisaged the state of desolation and 'crushed consciousness' he would end up in" after completing his work. She describes their four-month stay in Koktebel' (the Crimea) in 1924 when Bely kept postponing his writing first under the pretext that he had to devote himself to obtaining a perfect suntan and then collecting pebbles. Not until they were back in Moscow in late autumn was he able to commit himself to writing (Klavdiia Bugaeva, *Vospominaniia ob Andree Belom*, in *Vospominaniia o Bloke i Belom* [Moscow: Izdatel'skii dom XXI vek-Soglasie, 2000], 276–80).

22. See Il'ia Ehrenburg, *Liudi, gody, zhizn'* (Moscow: Sovetskii pisatel', 1961–1966). Even though the accuracy of some of Ehrenburg's reconstructions may be questioned, he nevertheless helped to restore a greater cultural picture of the first half of the twentieth century than had been admitted. His narrative moves freely from one epoch to another, between various European countries and Russia or the Soviet Union, bringing together seemingly disconnected people and weaving a single cultural blanket covering the whole of Europe.

23. Vladimir Toporov outlines three ways in which Akhmatova used to rearrange her poetic output. First, she moved her poems around to organize them into different poetic cycles; second, she changed their dates and attributions; and third, she gave them new epigraphs (*Akhmatova i Blok* [Berkeley, CA: Berkeley Slavic Specialties, 1981], 13–14).

24. Akhmatova, *Zapisnye knizhki*, 10–18.

25. Nadezhda Mandelstam, *Vtoraia kniga* (Moscow: Sovetskii rabochii, 1990), 360.

26. Lidiia Chukovskaia, *Zapiski ob Anne Akhmatovoi* (Moscow: Soglasie, 1997), 2:434.

27. Ibid., 2:376–77.

28. In the late 1960s, commenting on Akhmatova's repeated statements that she hadn't written any poetry for thirteen (in some other versions, six) years while living with Punin, Chukovskaia rushed to explain that Akhmatova's words should be read metaphorically, signifying the degree of her unhappiness with Punin. They can be "explained by her vehemence: there were no such periods in her life when

Akhmatova didn't write any poetry at all" (Chukovskaia, *The Akhmatova Journals,* 148).

29. What was hidden from Akhmatova and members of her immediate circle was clear to Vladimir Orlov, who in his overview of the turn-of-the-century Russian poets presented Ivanov as one of Gumilev's most loyal friends: "One of the significant episodes in the ideological and literary struggle in the early twenties was when Gumilev and his henchmen (G. Ivanov, G. Adamovich, N. Otsup), who were hostile to the revolution and the new social order, in a thinly veiled way attempted to establish a hegemony of their own in poetry. . . . A vivid example of a shameless distortion of history is G. Ivanov's preface to a posthumous collection of Gumilev's poetry (1922), in which this totally second-rate poet is presented in the following way: 'N. Gumilev was the first representative of the period of maturity in Russian poetry . . . and even if among our contemporaries there were poets more captivating than he, it is still Gumilev who is considered the most important figure in the Russian poetry of the first quarter of the twentieth century because he not only produced specimens of unsurpassed poetic mastery but also indicated the fate and directions of development of Russian poetry.'" Orlov concludes about Ivanov's laudatory remarks: "A more unwarranted and false conclusion cannot be imagined, but this 'struggle for Gumilev' in itself has deep significance" (Vladimir Orlov, "Poety nachala veka" [1972], in *Izbrannye raboty* [Leningrad: Khudozhestvennaia literatura, 1982], 1:378).

30. See numerous references to Kafka in Akhmatova, *Zapisnye knizhki,* esp. 145.

31. The following reviews are from RGALI f. 2833, op. 1, d. 349.

32. Ibid.

33. Jean-Paul Sartre, *The Words* (New York: Vintage Books, 1981), 205–6.

34. Amanda Height wrote the first full-length English biography of Akhmatova (*Anna Akhmatova: A Poetic Pilgrimage* [New York: Oxford University Press, 1976]).

35. Proust, whom Akhmatova admired, claimed in *A la recherche du temps perdu* that deafness was a precondition for creativity.

36. On Akhmatova's interpretation of *The Stone Guest,* see Stephanie Sandler, *Commemorating Pushkin: Russia's Myth of a National Poet* (Stanford: Stanford University Press, 2004), 202–10.

37. Pushkin is quoted in Anna Akhmatova, "Pushkin's *Stone Guest,*" in *My Half Century: Selected Prose,* ed. and trans. Ronald Meyer (Evanston: Northwestern University Press, 1997), 209.

38. This episode is in many ways similar to the one described by Kuniaev, when he and his friend Peredreev listened in Akhmatova's presence to her recorded voice.

39. Chukovskaia, *Zapiski ob Anne Akhmatovoi,* 3:222.

40. Anna Akhmatova, "A Little About My Life," in *Anna Akhmatova and Her Circle,* 5–6.

41. Akhmatova, *Zapisnye knizhki,* 643.

42. Ibid., 669.

43. Ibid., 687.

44. Chukovskaia, *Zapiski ob Anne Akhmatovoi* (Moscow: Soglasie, 1997), 3:294–95.
45. Struve, "Anna Akhmatova," 13–14.
46. Akhmatova, *Zapisnye knizhki Anny Akhmatovoi*, 701.
47. Ibid., 706–7.
48. R. D. Timenchik, V. N. Toporov, and T. V. Tsiv'ian, "Akhmatova i Kuzmin," *Russian Literature* 6 (1978): 213–305.
49. Vladimir Nabokov, *Pnin* (New York: Vintage Books, 1989), 117.
50. Viktor Erofeev, introduction to *The Penguin Book of New Russian Writing*, ed. Victor Erofeev and Andrew Reynolds (Harmondsworth: Penguin Books, 1995), xxii.
51. Andrei Bitov, *Pushkin House*, trans. Susan Brownsberger (New York: Farrar, Straus, and Giroux, 1987) 24. *Pushkinskii dom* was not published in the Soviet Union until 1987, when it appeared in *Novyy mir*.
52. Ibid., 31.
53. Ibid., 24.
54. Ibid., 24–26, emphasis added.
55. Ibid., 29–32, emphasis added.
56. Ibid., 25.
57. Ibid., 27.

Chapter 8. The Apocalypse Revisited

1. Viktor Erofeev, "Russia's *Fleurs du Mal*," in *The Penguin Book of New Russian Writing*, ed. Victor Erofeev and Andrew Reynolds (Harmondsworth: Penguin Books, 1995), xiii.
2. Ibid.
3. Ibid., x–xi; Viktor Erofeev, "Razgovor po dusham o virtual'nom budushchem literatury," in *Sobranie sochinenii* (Moscow: Soiuz fotokhudozhnikov Rossii, 1994–1996), 3:560.
4. See Viktor Erofeev, introduction to *Nesovmestimye kontrasty bytiia* by V. V. Rozanov (Moscow: Iskusstvo, 1990), 6–36, in which Erofeev admits to owning Rozanov's own copy of *The Apocalypse of Our Time* (1918), which Erofeev obtained in his youth in exchange for the rare lifetime edition of Pushkin's *Boris Godunov*. His joy was doubled when he discovered that the latter was one of the books that Rozanov really valued in his own library. Oleg Dark was the first to note Erofeev's affinity with Rozanov (see Dark, "Chernovoe pis'mo," *Strelec* 1 [1992]: 183).
5. Vasiliy Rozanov, "Pis'ma k E. F. Gollerbakhu," in *Izbrannoe* (Munich: A. Neimanis, 1970), 552–53; Erofeev, "Zhizn' s idiotom," in *Sobranie sochinenii*, 1:295.
6. Erofeev, "Galoshi," in ibid., 3:373; Erofeev, *Strashnyi sud*, in ibid., 3:215.
7. Vladimir Nabokov, *Otchaianie*, *Sobranie sochinenii v chetyrekh tomakh* (Moscow: Pravda, 1990), 3:401.
8. Erofeev, "Iadrena Fenia," in *Sobranie sochinenii*, 3:333.
9. Erofeev, "Russia's *Fleurs du Mal*," xvi.

10. See Dark, "Chernovoe pis'mo," 177–87; and Robert Porter, *Russia's Alternative Prose* (Oxford: Berg, 1994), 147–62. *Russian Beauty* and its critical reception is discussed in N. N. Shneidman, *Russian Literature, 1988–1994* (Toronto: University of Toronto Press, 1995), 180–82.

11. Linda Hutcheon, *A Theory of Parody* (New York: Routledge, 1991).

12. David Bethea quotes Nikolai Berdiaev as saying, "There are two dominant myths which can become dynamic in the life of a people—the myth about origins and the myth about the end. For Russians it has been the second myth, the eschatological, that has dominated" (Bethea, *The Shape of Apocalypse in Modern Russian Fiction* [Princeton: Princeton University Press, 1989], xiii).

13. For a summary of their ideas, see ibid., 28–61.

14. Rozanov, *Apokalipsis nashego vremeni*, in *Izbrannoe*, 444.

15. On the "*Metropolis* affair," see Erofeev, "Vremia Metropolia," in *Sobranie sochinenii*, 3:493–506.

16. Erofeev, "Razgovor po dusham o virtual'nom budushchem literatury," in ibid., 3:560.

17. Like Luke, Ira arranges her narrative in the form of a letter addressed to her friend Ksiusha (Luke was writing to "the most excellent Theophilus") and divides it into twenty-four chapters.

18. On the structure of apocalyptic narratives, particularly in Russian literature, see Bethea, *The Shape of Apocalypse in Modern Russian Fiction*. The idea that part of the New Testament and the book of Revelation were written by the same person belongs to Lev Shestov (1866–1938), a philosopher whose works are familiar to Erofeev. In "Speculation and the Apocalypse" he suggests that John, author of the fourth Gospel, was "punished" for his exaggerated Hellenic belief in Logos ("In the beginning was the Word") by being made the author of the Apocalypse: "And if that [person] who wrote the fourth testament was not the author of the Apocalypse, then he must have become its author as the fates decree" (Shestov, *Umozreniye i otkrovenie* [Paris: YMCA-Press, 1964], 63). See Erofeev, introduction to Lev Shestov, *Izbrannye sochineniia* (Moscow: Renessans, 1993), 33.

19. Viktor Erofeev, *Russian Beauty*, trans. Andrew Reynolds (Harmondsworth: Penguin Books, 1994); subsequent references are given in parentheses.

20. A. Flegon, *Za predelami russkikh slovarei* (London: Flegon, 1973), 155.

21. See Aleksandr Etkind, *Sodom i Psikheia* (Moscow: Its-Garant, 1996), esp. 59–270; and Eric Naiman, *Sex in Public: The Incarnation of Early Soviet Ideology* (Princeton: Princeton University Press, 1997), 27–45.

22. Rozanov, *Apokalipsis nashego vremeni*, 454.

23. John J. Collins, quoted in Bethea, *The Shape of the Apocalypse in Modern Russian Fiction*, 7.

24. Bethea, *The Shape of the Apocalypse in Modern Russian Fiction*, 8.

25. Another possible source is the teaching of Nikolai Fedorov, who praised Mary Magdalene above all women and expected fallen women (after giving up

their profession) to contribute greatly to the fulfillment of the "common task," that is, the resurrection of the "dead fathers" (see Irene Masing-Delic, *Abolishing Death* [Stanford: Stanford University Press, 1992], 96).

26. V. V. Rozanov, *Liudi lunnogo sveta* (Moscow: Druzhba narodov, 1990), 62–68.

27. Erofeev, *Russian Beauty*, 336; in *The Last Judgment (Strashnyi sud)* Sisin tells his girlfriend: "j'écris avec ma bite" (Erofeev, *Sobranie sochinenii*, 3:275).

28. Nikolai Berdiaev, *Sobranie sochinenii* (Paris: YMCA-Press, 1989) 3:509–11, emphasis added.

29. Erofeev, *Russian Beauty*, 121; this was suggested to me by Joseph Schallert.

30. Challenging this popular image of Solov'ev, Olga Matich regards Solov'ev's long-suppressed "obscene writings" as pointing to his "life-long lusting for the 'cunt,' no less powerful . . . than was Tolstoi's" (Matich, *Erotic Utopia: The Decadent Imagination in Russia's Fin de Siecle* [Madison: University of Wisconsin Press, 2005], 79).

31. See Olga Matich, "The Symbolist Meaning of Love: Theory and Practice," in *Creating Life: The Aesthetic Utopia of Russian Modernism*, ed. Irina Paperno and Joan Delaney Grossman (Stanford: Stanford University Press, 1994), 28.

32. Solov'ev is quoted in ibid., 28; prior to her meeting with Vladimir Sergeevich, Ira was declared barren by a number of gynecologists, making her pregnancy a total shock both to her and to her family doctor.

33. One sees, for example, a miraculously resurrected General Vlasov brought back to life—presumably at the common will of a Fedorovian-like *kollektiv*—to bear witness at Ira's mock trial.

34. This is illustrated by the dust jackets of Erofeev's books. The jacket of his third volume of collected works shows a naked man and woman from Lucien Freud's "And the Bridegroom" (1993). Even that image is not as simple as it might appear, since the "bridegroom" was in fact a homosexual artist, Leigh Bowery, who died of AIDS in 1994. Under the jacket, surprisingly, one sees three singing angels from Gérard David's "Nativity" (1510–1523).

35. Masing-Delic, *Abolishing Death*, 85.

36. Erofeev, *Russian Beauty*, 118; Fedorov foresaw resurrection as a process that should be always accompanied by moral improvement (even crooks and murderers were expected to be transformed beyond recognition).

37. It is repeatedly stated that Vladimir Sergeevich belongs to the generation of the fathers; he was a bosom friend of the father of Ira's best friend. One of Ira's friends is named Yura Fedorov (some sort of hybrid between Yurii Zhivago and Nikolai Fedorov). Fedorov accompanies Ira to the battlefield and volunteers to write a new testament about her deeds.

38. Masing-Delic, *Abolishing Death*, 96.

39. On Leonardo's relationship with Mona Lisa in Merezhkovskii's novel, see Irene Masing-Delic, "Creating the Living Work of Art: The Symbolist Pygmalion and His Antecedents," in *Creating Life*, ed. Paperno and Grossman, 65–75.

40. *Russian Beauty* evokes the title of Pasternak's unfinished play, *The Blind Beauty*, which tells the story of the blind pregnant housemaid in mid-nineteenth-century Russia (Porter, *Russia's Alternative Prose*, 150).

41. Cf. the opening lines of *Revival*: "The grass managed to push its way through the iron and crushed stone; from far away it was possible to hear the howling of the dogs that have gone wild; and around me there were only ruins and the black nests of crows were hanging down from the branches of burnt trees. I recall seeing a similar picture after the civil war, but at that time it was frightening to listen to the dead silence of the plants—this time the plants were turned into the dust" (Leonid Brezhnev, *Vozrozhdenie* [Moscow: Politizdat, 1978], 3).

42. Erofeev, *Russian Beauty*, 40; the outline of Erofeev's novel—an attractive Russian woman, marrying a considerably older man and her subsequent death as a result of her pregnancy—brings to mind Nabokov's short story "Krasavitsa," translated as "A Russian Beauty."

43. He starts eyeing the Siamese twins when they are only nine years old.

44. Erofeev, *Russian Beauty*, 89. The last name of Vladimir Sergeevich's best friend and Ksiusha's father is Mochul'sky. The literary historian Konstantin Mochul'sky was one of the first to recognize Nabokov's talent in 1926 in his laudatory article on *Mary* (Andrew Field, *VN: The Life and Art of Vladimir Nabokov* [London: Macdonald Queen Anne Press, 1987], 111).

45. Ira's father, Vladimir, is reported to have forced Ira into an incestuous relationship when she was about twelve; at the time of the narrative he falls sick and to everybody's surprise insists on calling his wife "Vera" (the name of Nabokov's wife) instead of her actual name. Erofeev, who wrote scholarly articles on Nabokov, appears to have a peculiar attitude toward his predecessor. Thus, the writer Sisin (a reference to Sirin?), the protagonist of Erofeev's *Last Judgment*, is nearly killed in Geneva by "Nabokov's relative" as a result of her seeing something offensive in his writings.

46. See *Cultural Mythologies of Russian Modernism*, ed. Boris Gasparov, Robert P. Hughes, and Irina Paperno (Berkeley and Los Angeles: University of California Press, 1992); and Zinaida Shakhovskaia, *V poiskakh Nabokova. Otrazheniia* (Moscow: Kniga, 1991), 44.

47. Nadezhda Azhgikhina and Helena Goscilo, "Getting Under Their Skin: The Beauty Salon in Russian Women's Lives," in *Russia—Women—Culture*, ed. Helena Goscilo and Beth Holmgren (Bloomington: Indiana University Press, 1996), 94.

48. Beth Holmgren, *Women's Works in Stalin's Time: On Lidiia Chukovskaia and Nadezhda Mandel'shtam* (Bloomington: Indiana University Press, 1993), 2.

49. Such a peculiar sensation as that of harboring "rotting" literature has been experienced previously, although by a man. Vasilii Rozanov wrote in *Fallen Leaves* (*Opavshie list'ia*, 1913): "Sometimes it seems to me that the decomposition of literature—of its very essence—takes place inside my body. And, maybe, this is my ultimate 'emploi.' . . . And I have a fleeting sensation, that I am the last writer,

through whom literature will come to its end, apart from the rubbish, which will soon come to an end as well. . . . This is my personal feeling. And how difficult it is to live with it" (Rozanov, *Opavshie list'ia*, in *Izbrannoe*, 220–21). See Erofeev, "The World Scholars [Speak] about Andrei Bely, or the Decomposition of Literary Studies Takes Place Inside My Body" in *Sobranie sochinenii*, 2:599–613.

50. Porter, *Russia's Alternative Prose*, 150. More general allusions to Akhmatova can be seen in Ira's responsibility for the death of her lover, which is similar to Akhmatova's blaming herself for Gumilev's death and to her resolution to preserve his legacy for posterity. Ira's visit to the gynecologist who informs her of her supernatural pregnancy could refer to Leon Trotskii's criticism of the female poets such as Akhmatova, Tsvetaeva, Radlova, and Shkapskaia in *Literature and Revolution*, in particular, his attack on their religious beliefs. Their "god," Trotskii insisted, "is a very convenient and portable third person, quite domestic, a friend of the family who fulfills from time to time the duties of a doctor of female ailments." For Shkapskaia, "who is so organic, so biologic, so gynecologic . . . , God is something in the nature of a go-between and a midwife" (Trotskii, *Literature and Revolution* [New York: Russell and Russell, 1957], 41).

51. Rozanov, *Opavshie list'ia*, 222.

52. The fact that the novel opens with the description of Ira's gynecologist literally sliding along her genitalia—the medical checkup is presented as a difficult trip of an explorer of new territories—points to the presence of an *extradiegetic* narrator who positions himself inside Ira's body. It is possible to speak about the *extradiegetic* narrator because Ira cannot see inside her own body.

53. In Russian this can mean to die, to reach orgasm, or to stop writing.

54. Roland Barthes, *The Pleasure of the Text*, trans. Richard Miller (New York: Hill and Wang, 1975), 7, emphasis in original.

55. See Paperno and Grossman, eds., *Creating Life*.

56. Andrei Bely, *Na rubezhe dvukh stoletii* (Chicago: Russian Language Specialities, 1966), 72–73.

57. See Lev Kamenev's critique of the fin de siècle culture in 1933: "Against the background of intricately interwoven social relationships in Russia of the beginning of the twentieth century . . . the thoughts of the bourgeois intelligentsia made a brilliant display of unprecedented eclecticism, which would often give way to ideological trickery. One could compile a curious catalogue of such tricks, in which the incompatible notions and viewpoints were glued together by the unsettled minds and verbose lechery typical of the intelligentsia: [thus] mysticism [is combined] with anarchism; the third Testament with *narodnichestvo*; Nekrasov with Verlaine; Marx either with Kant, or with Nietzsche, or with the Fathers of the Church, or with Dostoevskii" (Kamenev, introduction to Andrei Bely, *Nachalo veka* [Moscow: Soiuzteatr, 1990], 12–15).

58. Harold Bloom, *The Western Canon* (New York: Riverhead Books, 1995), 10.

Chapter 9. Coda

The epigraph is translated from the following: *Zabyt' ne znachit poteriat': / A okonchatel'no priniat'— / V sebia, na dno, navek . . .*

1. Anna Akhmatova, *Sobranie sochinenii v shesti tomakh* (Moscow: Ellis Lak, 2001): 5:163.
2. Natalia Roskina, "Anna Akhmatova," in *Chetyre glavy* (Paris: YMCA-Press, 1980), 41.
3. Oleg Lekmanov, "Zlatousoi Anne vseia Rusi," *Russkii zhurnal*, May 11, 2006. I am grateful to Irina Paperno for bringing this article to my attention.
4. *Blok—eto kruto! / Blok—eto klass! / My liubim Bloka, / i Blok liubit nas.*
5. See Andrei Makine, *Dreams of My Russian Summers (Testament francais*, 1995), trans. Geoffrey Strachan (New York: Simon and Schuster, 1998), esp. 239.
6. It is appropriate that in Semyon Aranovich's film *The Anna Akhmatova File (Lichnoe delo Anny Akhmatovoi*, 1989), the end of the Silver Age is visually marked by the destruction of Christ the Savior Cathedral and not some of the buildings or institutions associated with Akhmatova in Leningrad.
7. One indication of the transitional period was the simultaneous staging of two exhibitions at the Tretyakov Gallery in Moscow in 1998–1999: one was devoted to "The World of Art" and the other to Peter the Great. See also numerous recent debates in the Russian press surrounding the excavations and identification of the skull of Ivan Susanin, a heroic peasant allegedly responsible for saving the czar Mikhail Romanov during the Polish invasion at the beginning of the seventeenth century, whom Vladimir Putin now wants to declare a new Russian national hero. Quite unexpectedly, in 2006 Gleb Panfilov's film *In the First Circle (V kruge pervom*, 2005) eclipsed in popularity the long-awaited adaptations of *Master and Margarita* (Vladimir Bortko, 2005) and *Doctor Zhivago* (Aleksandr Proshkin, 2006).
8. Natalia Dzutseva, "I vse zh ne uidu ia iz zhizni," review of S. Kissin *(Muni): Legkoe bremia. Stikhi i proza, Perepiska s V. F. Khodasevichem, Znamia* 12 (1999).
9. V. P. Arzamastsev, "Sovmeshchenie memorial'no-bytovykh i istoriko-literaturnykh podkhodov v ekspozitsiiakh vosstanavlivaemykh ob"ektov," *Shakhmatovskii vestnik* 5 (1995): 11.
10. Pavel Basinskii, "'Kak sertdstu vyskazat' sebia' O russkoi proze 90-kh godov," *Novyi mir* 4 (2000): 185–92.
11. Like works from the 1940s, the introduction to the first *Complete Works and Correspondence* of Blok, published in 1997, places special emphasis on the civic significance of Blok's creative work: "For us Blok is inseparable from notions of the high worth, civic responsibility, and moral courage of a Russian artist. Blok's works and his artistic and civic authority are an effective force in the contemporary literary process and the spiritual life of our society" ("Ot redaktsii," in A. A. Blok, *Polnoe sobranie sochinenii i pisem v dvadtsati tomakh* [Moscow: Nauka, 1997], 1:5).
12. Naiman's emphasis on *tselomudrie* (being virtuous) reads as a counter-discourse to Sergei Trubetskoi's correspondence with Vladimir Solov'ev in the

mid-1890s, in which he jokingly referred to Solov'ev as *tselkomudrennyi* (as opposed to *tselomudrennyi*), knowing full well that Solov'ev was not as indifferent to women as many people thought he was. Trubetskoi's pun, Olga Matich observes, "is appropriately ambiguous, connoting both virginity and knowledge of virgins" (Matich, *Erotic Utopia: The Decadent Imagination in Russia's Fin de Siecle* [Madison: University of Wisconsin Press, 2005], 79).

13. Anatolii Naiman, "O krupnom i tsel'nom," interview, *Na Nevskom* 12 (December 2005–January 2006): 14–15.

14. Aileen Kelly, "A Great Russian Poet," review of Anna Akhmatova, *The Word That Causes Death's Defeat*, ed. and trans. Nancy K. Andersen (New Haven: Yale University Press, 2004), *New York Review of Books*, November 3, 2005, 63.

15. Anatolii Naiman, *Slavnyi konets besslavnykh pokolenii* (Moscow: Vargius, 1999), 316.

16. Ibid., 257.

17. Aleksandr Solzhenitsyn, "*Peterburg* Andreia Belogo," *Novyi mir* 5 (1999): 191.

18. Nikolai Trifonov, "Ne vse to serebro chto blestit: dekadentskaia poeziia nachala veka i sovremennost'," *Knizhnoe obozrenie*, August 12, 1997.

INDEX

"About Annenskii" (Khodasevich), 54
acmeists, 88, 220n38; attachment to material culture, 80, 83–84, 233n41; Blok's critique of, 62–63; Blok set in opposition to, 58, 220n42; preservation project of, 81–84; symbolists and, 15–16, 37
Adamovich, Georgii, 41, 109, 227n18, 243n15
Ada (Nabokov), 174
Adorno, Theodor, 157
"Aerial Ways" (Pasternak), 127
aesthetics: simplicity and austerity in, 55–57
Aikhenval'd, Yurii, 56
Akhmatova, Anna, 17, 164, 221n48, 251n4, 258n50; anxiety about legacy, 102, 167, 171, 235n59; anxiety about perceptions of, 87, 156–57, 165, 171–73, 206, 217n9; anxiety about *Poem Without a Hero*, 20, 162; anxiety about status, 88–89, 156–57; anxiety of, 83, 87–88, 105, 162; attacks on other writers, 88–89, 93–94, 96, 99, 105–6, 157–58, 227n20, 235n64, 236n65, 239n94; attacks on wives and companions of writers, 22, 97–99, 239n93, 239n99; biographies of, 94, 100–101, 168–71, 173, 253n34; Blok and, 50, 95–96, 238n86, 238n88; on Blok's poetry, 237n82, 238n88; Chukovskaia and, 90–93, 236n74, 239n93, 240n102; communal apartments of, 66–71, 93, 158–59, 203; crafting life story, 91–92, 162–63, 167–68, 171; criticisms of poetry of, 11, 85, 87, 233n36, 234n54, 234n58; on deaths of contemporaries, 50, 82, 154; efforts to preserve Gumilev's memory, 100–103, 258n50; gossip about other writers, 89–92, 96; Gumilev and, 19–20, 100, 103–4, 169, 241n108; influence of, 18, 104;
influences on, 87–88, 93, 102, 104–5, 169, 241n115, 242n127; Khrushchev Thaw and, 155, 158, 165; legacy of, 155–56, 201, 241n111; as link between pre- and postrevolutionary culture, 17, 108, 154–55, 161–62, 169; living conditions of, 69–71, 77–81, 84–85, 158–59, 233n32, 233n36; Maiakovskii and, 85–86, 221n48; marriage to Shileiko, 68, 100; memoirs of other people and, 13–14, 76, 164, 170–72, 240n107; Nadezhda Mandelstam and, 13–14, 99–100, 159–60, 240n102; Pasternak and, 97–98, 154–55; personality of, 97–98, 159–61, 252n18; poetry of, 70–71, 80–81, 84, 155–56, 168, 171–73, 206, 237n81, 252n23; poetry's relation to living conditions, 69–71, 78–80, 83, 233n36; possessions/poverty of, 79–80, 82, 85, 233n35; private life of, 86–87, 105; public vs. private in poetry of, 80–81, 83; Punin and, 66–70, 83–84, 90, 101–2, 234n45; Pushkin and, 19, 97, 102; rearrangements of poetry of, 162, 206, 252n23; relations with contemporaries, 13, 98, 100, 103–5, 164–65, 201, 251n14; separation from Punin, 78, 83, 91; silent periods of, 67–70, 82–83, 100, 102, 159–62, 164, 231n9, 234n45, 252n28; Silver Age and, 4–5, 9, 163; Stalinist terror and, 100, 168–70; status of, 87, 155–56; studies of Pushkin by, 101–2, 241n109
"Akhmatova and Kuzmin" (Timenchik, Toporov, Tsivian), 173–74
Aksenov, Vasilii, 19, 174–75, 183
Aleksandr Blok Literary Heritage Committee, 75–76
alienation: as theme, 123–24

— 261

alternative prose: influences on, 180–81; relation to cultural traditions, 179–80, 199, 205; as shocking, 181–82; Soviet repression of, 183–84. *See also Russian Beauty* (Erofeev)
Among the Great, 15
Andersen, Nancy, 71, 100, 101, 206, 231n9
Andronikova, Salomeia, 161, 241n115
The Anna Akhmatova File (Semen Aranovich film), 259n6
Anna Karenina (Lev Tolstoi), 53, 99
Annenskii, Innokentii, 54, 102, 105, 109
Anno Domini (Akhmatova), 234n58
The Anthology of New Poetry, 5
anti-Semitism: Blok's, 204–5, 221n2
Antokol'skii, Pavel, 29
anxiety: management of, 7, 105; sources of, 6–7, 12, 14, 32; writers', 125–26. *See also under* Akhmatova, Anna
"Anxiety and the Formation of Early Modern Culture" (Bouwsma), 7
anxiety of influence, 19
Anxiety of Influence (Bloom), 16
Apocalypse, 198; in *Russian Beauty*, 182–90, 197–99; in Russian literature, 182–83, 189–90, 255n18
The Apocalypse of Our Time (Rozanov), 183, 187, 254n4
Aranovich, Semen, 259n6
Arbenina-Gildenbrandt, Olga, 103
Ardov, Mikhail, 173
Art and Artist (Rank), 160–61
artists, 129–30, 152, 162; as characters, 106, 147, 149–51; need for pacing, 160–61; predecessors and, 14–16, 59; prerevolutionary, 16–17, 49; relations among, 15–16; Silver Age, 198–99; striving for freedom, 174–75. *See also* poets; writers
arts, 3, 14, 19; modern, 52; prerevolutionary, 48; Soviet, 24
Artsybashev, Mikhail, 227n25
Arvatov, Boris, 233n36
Aseev, Nikolai, 102
Asmus, Valentin, 60
"As Soon as the Velvety Blackness of the Sky Begins to Twinkle" (Blok), 140
"At a New Threshold," 26–27
Austen, Jane, 71–72, 84
autobiography: as genre, 164, 167–68
avant-garde movement, Russian, 10
Azhgikhina, Nadezhda, 195

Bakhtin, Mikhail, 64
Balaganchik (Blok), 236n67
Barnstead, John, 112–13

Basalaev, Innokentii, 233n36
Basinskii, Pavel, 205–6
Beethoven, 95, 238n86
The Beginning of the Century (Bely), 95, 134, 224n32
Beketova, Mariia Andreevna, 74–75
Bely, Andrei, 17, 131, 220n42; apocalyptic symbolism of, 183, 198; Blok and, 33–36, 94–95, 236n67; Blok in memoirs of, 8, 95, 134–35, 137, 224n32; on Chekhov's legacy, 60–61; criticisms of, 16, 38, 50, 52, 152; Eternal Feminine and, 190–91; intellectuals and, 16, 134–35; Pasternak and, 128–29, 152; *Petersburg* by, 52, 174–75; private life of, 151–52, 238n92, 249n36; procrastination by, 252n21; status of, 9, 16, 56–57, 166; symbolism and, 28, 183, 198; trying to bridge pre- and postrevolutionary cultural gap, 135–36
Benua, Aleksandr, 111, 225n54
Berberova, Nina, 43, 109, 229n35
Berdiaev, Nikolai, 10–11, 49, 158, 183, 189–90, 251n14, 255n12; on cultural traditions, 52, 62; use of "Silver Age," 4–5, 217n9
Berlin, Isaiah, 241n115
Between Two Revolutions (Bely), 134, 224n32
Beyond the Boundary of Bygone Days (Blok), 50
Bible, 184–85, 255n18. *See also* Revelation
Biblioteka poeta (Poet's Library), 165–67
bildungsroman, *The Eye* as, 115–17, 122
Bitov, Andrei, 19, 175–78
Blagoi, Dmitrii, 40
The Blind Beauty (Pasternak), 257n40
Blok, Aleksandr, 2, 183, 230n53; acmeists vs., 58, 220n42; Akhmatova on, 89–90, 237n82, 238n86, 238n88; Akhmatova's relationship with, 87, 93–94, 97, 234n55; Bely and, 33, 95, 236n67; in Bely's memoirs, 8, 137, 224n32; biographies of, 32–33, 62–63; Bolsheviks and, 30–31, 37; contemporaries and, 35, 90–91, 109, 150; correspondence of, 33, 75–76; criticisms of, 30–31, 37–39, 42–43, 93–96, 140–41, 238n88; as cultural intermediary, 24, 26, 135–36, 221n2; death as dividing line, 33, 39, 42; death of, 7, 41, 51, 172–73, 223n30; degeneracy of, 40–41, 94, 225n53, 231n15; Eternal Feminine and, 190–91; influence of, 23–24, 128; as inspiration for *Doctor Zhivago*, 136–45, 249n42; legacy of, 35, 36–37, 130, 201–2, 225n58, 259n11; marriage of, 73–76, 89–90, 93, 95–97; on other poets, 94, 103–4, 237n81; poetry of, 36–38, 50, 237n82, 238n88, 249n41; popularity of, 27–29, 33, 201–3; portrayals of, 43, 58–59, 223n24, 225n58,

238n86; reactions to death of, 33–35, 40, 43, 75, 87, 225n54; realism and, 26–27, 222n9, 224n50, 249n41; status of, 24–25, 27–31, 35–36, 42, 50, 109, 130, 201–3, 221n2; struggle for control of legacy of, 35–36, 43, 94; studies of, 23–25, 27–28, 30–31, 62–63, 150; writings of, 33, 37, 95–96, 204–5, 231n10
Blok, Liubov' Dmitrievna, 68, 91, 231n15, 232n17; Akhmatova on, 90, 96, 238n88; Bely and, 236n67, 238n92; husband and, 94–95, 95–96; living space of, 72–75, 232n30; marriage of, 73–74, 93; writings of, 75–76, 232n22
Blok Museum (Petersburg), 31, 203
Blok Museum (Shakhmatovo), 205
Blok's Creative Life (Maksimov), 32
Bloom, Harold, 15, 18, 21–22, 247n22; on literary influence, 14, 16, 19–20, 95
Bolshevik Revolution, 51; Apocalypse symbolism and, 182–83; debate over time frame of, 20–21; effects of, 6–7, 10, 46; meaning read into, 39, 53, 62, 163; in memoirs, 76–77; poets and, 27, 253n29; reevaluation of, 10, 53; Silver Age and, 7–8, 63
Bolsheviks, 11; blamed for interrupting Silver Age, 62, 64; Blok and, 37, 41, 62–63; cultural traditions and, 42, 51–52, 60, 62–63; life under, 34, 41; writers and, 19, 49, 53, 85–86
Boris Godunov (Pushkin), 254n4
Bouwsma, William J., 7
Brezhnev, Leonid, 193
Brik, L. Yu., 97, 239n99
Brik, Osip, 40
Brintlinger, Angela, 8–9
Briusov, Valerii, 2, 28, 37, 50, 131, 227n18
Brod, Max, 165
Brodsky, Joseph, 18, 77, 154, 207, 232n30
The Brothers Karamazov (Dostoevskii), 113
Bruner, Jerome, 92
Bugaeva, Klavdiia, 152, 220n42, 252n21
Bukharin, Nikolai, 33
Bulgakov, Mikhail, 8–9, 242n127
Bulgakov, Sergei, 49
The Burn (Aksenov), 174–75

Chekhov, Anton, 15, 60–61, 146–47, 237n78
Christianity: disillusionment with, 186–87
Chudakov, Aleksandr Pavlovich, 221n2
Chukovskaia, Elena, 13–14
Chukovskaia, Lidiia: Akhmatova and, 83, 90–93, 169–71, 234n55, 236n74, 239n93; Akhmatova crafting life story and, 91–92, 163, 169–70; Akhmatova's gossip about other writers and, 89–90, 96; on

Akhmatova's living conditions, 69, 78–79, 159, 233n32; on Akhmatova's poetry, 70–71, 163; on Akhmatova's silences, 164, 252n28; memoirs of, 76, 240n102
Chukovskii, Kornei, 86; on Akhmatova, 79–80, 84–85, 156, 234n54; on Blok, 29, 34, 75–76
church: as cultural institution, 51
civil war, 6, 218n15
Clark, Katerina, 132–33
Classical Dancing: History and Modernity (L. D. Blok), 75
A Cloud in Trousers (Maiakovskii), 44
communal apartments, 237n78; Akhmatova and, 66–70, 93, 103, 158–59, 203; of Bloks, 93, 232n30; *Poem Without a Hero* set in, 106–7; Soviet institution of, 71, 73, 232n30
"Confession of a Heathen" (Blok), 136
Cooley, Charles, 63
Corney, Frederick, 39, 233n50
Critical Miscellany (Ivanov-Razumnik), 220n42
critics, literary, 180; on Akhmatova, 81, 86–87, 156, 173–74, 234n54, 234n58; on Blok, 24–27, 29–31, 37–38, 43, 249n41; essays in *Signposts*, 48–49; on Nabokov, 109, 257n44; on new vs. older poetry, 165–66; Nordau's influence on, 46–47
Cultural Mythologies of Russian Modernism (Gasparov, Hughes, and Paperno), 4–5
cultural renaissance: Blok as last representative of, 62–63
cultural selection, 12
cultural traditions, 17, 199; Akhmatova as keeper of, 19–20, 100, 108, 157–58; Blok as intermediary to, 23–24; Bolsheviks campaigning against, 51–52; influences on, 64–65; keepers of, 81–82, 195–96, 205; of Silver Age, 179; writers reinterpreting, 131–32, 150. *See also* past
cultural upheavals: after October Revolution, 5–6, 46
culture, Russian: alternative prose questioning, 181–82; archaeology of, 8–9; attempts to change, 60–61, 111, 135, 221n2, 259n7; Blok's influence on, 23–24, 28–29, 36; Bolsheviks and, 11, 60; continuity of, 63, 84; decadence of prerevolutionary, 179–80, 228n26, 229n35; efforts to preserve, 14, 16–17, 21; evolution of, 3, 6, 25–26, 40, 59–60, 64; fin de siècle, 258n57; gap between pre- and postrevolutionary, 26, 38, 55, 86, 180; independent (1960s and 1970s), 175; influence of Leonardo da Vinci in, 192–93; intellectuals in, 51–52, 134–35; interpreta-

INDEX —263

tions of, 7, 9, 36, 233n41; links between pre- and postrevolutionary, 8, 86, 129, 132–34, 156, 169, 221n2; October Revolution in, 39–40, 51; prerevolutionary, 19–20, 38, 42, 54–55, 60, 62, 64, 112, 134–35; public vs. private in, 80–81, 198; Pushkin's legacy in, 59; reclaiming forbidden or forgotten aspects of, 129, 176–77, 204; renaissances in, 52, 180–81; 1880s, 54; of 1960s generation, 206–7; Silver Age in, 57, 201–2; 1930s man in, 57–59; Soviet, 42, 59; stagnation in, 81, 180–81

Dante, 87, 105–7, 242n127
Dark, Oleg, 182
Davidson, Peter, 217n7
da Vinci, Leonardo, 147-49, 192–93
"The Death of Ivan Il'ich" (L. Tolstoi), 53, 55
deaths: in changing of culture, 60–61
Decomposition of Literature (Russian Marxists), 47
The Defense (Nabokov), 110
Delmas, Liubov', 90–91
de Man, Paul, 16
democracy: Silver Age and, 174–75
Denis'eva, Elena, 189
Diaghilev, Sergei, 131
Diaries (Blok), 94
Diary (Luknitskii), 100
The Divine Comedy (Dante), 106–7
Dmitrieva, Yelizaveta, 103
Dobrenko, Evgenii, 141
Doctor Zhivago (Pasternak), 18, 174, 248n34; Akhmatova and, 98–99; Bely's streetcar accident in, 151–52; Blok as inspiration for, 136–45, 249n41, 249n42; Blok's poetry translated into, 137–44; criticisms of, 98, 129; influences on, 99, 145–49; Pasternak's goals in, 131, 141, 248n35; Punin's similarity to character of, 67–68; writing of, 17, 127, 130, 246n8
Doctor Zhivago (Proshkin film), 259n7
Dolinin, Aleksandr, 109
Dostal', Nikolai, 219n23
Dostoevskii, Fedor, 15, 230n43; Akhmatova and, 87, 97, 239n93; Nabokov and, 14, 109

Early Joys (Fedin), 132
Ehrenburg, Il'ia, 158, 252n22
Eikhenbaum, Boris, 36–37, 50
Eisenstein, Sergei, 131, 135
emigration, 122–24, 174, 251n14
emigre circles, 8, 109, 157
The Endless Dead End (Galkovskii), 9

"The End of Renata" (Khodasevich), 60, 112, 228n26
Engelgart, Anna, 100, 102
Entartung (Degeneration, Nordau), 46–47
Erofeev, Venedikt, 175
Erofeev, Viktor, 223n24, 254n4, 256n34, 257n45; on Russian alternative prose, 180–81; *Russian Beauty* by, 20, 182–90, 205; on Silver Age, 19, 199, 205; writing style of, 181–82
Yesenin, Sergei, 93
Eternal Companions (Fedin), 132
The Eternal Companions (Merezhkovskii), 60, 74, 131–32
Eternal Feminine, 190–91
Eugene Onegin (Pushkin), 195
exhibitionism: in Russian memoirs, 74
experimentation: Silver Age signifying, 59
The Eye (Nabokov), 109; alienation and narcissism in, 120–24, 245n50; as bildungsroman, 115–17, 122; criticism of, 114–15; homosexuality in, 118–19; Kuzmin's influence on, 110, 113–15; names in, 113–14; photographic quality of, 114–15; *Wings* and, 120–23, 125

Facts and Fables about Blok and Myself (L. D. Blok), 73–74
Fadeev, Aleksandr, 70
The Fallacy of the Silver Age (Ronen), 4, 63
Fallen Leaves (Rozanov), 257n49
family: as cultural institution, 51
Fedin, Konstantin, 29, 131–32
Fedorov, Nikolai, 183, 191–92, 255n25, 256n36
Fet, Afanasii, 173
Field, Andrew, 112, 245n50
First Writers' Congress, 33
Fitzpatrick, Sheila, 20–21
Fleishman, Lazar, 134
The Flight of Time (Akhmatova), 172
Fountain House (Sheremetiev Palace), 233n36; Akhmatova Museum in, 203; Punins' communal apartment in, 68, 70, 83
Frank, Semen, 49
freedom: Silver Age and, 174–75
Free Philosophical Association, 35–36
Freud, Sigmund, 91, 122
Froman, Mikhail, 229n35
"From the Tashkent Notebooks" (Chukovskaia), 240n102
"From You I Hid My Heart" (Akhmatova), 83
"A Funeral Feast for Soviet Literature" (Erofeev), 181
futurists, 37, 229n35

Gaevsky, Vadim, 232n22
Galkovskii, Dmitrii, 9
Gandlevskii, Sergei, 11, 108
Gasparov, Boris, 4–5
Geertz, Clifford, 56
gender, 22; in *Doctor Zhivago*, 147; in *Russian Beauty*, 182, 195; Solov'ev on, 190–91
The Gentle Night (Kuzmin), 113–14
Gershenzon, Mikhail, 49
Gerstein, Emma, 13–14, 68–69, 219n30
Gide, André, 125
The Gift (Nabokov), 110, 124–25, 150
Gillis, Donald, 117
Gilman, Richard, 218n12
Ginzburg, Lidiia, 29–30, 57, 140
Gippius, Tatiana, 75
Gippius, Zinaida, 34, 61, 239n99
Glebov, Anatolii, 40
Glebova-Sudeikina, Olga, 82, 85, 88
The Glorious End of the Inglorious Generations (Naiman), 207
Gogol, Nikolai, 15
Golden Age, 6, 62
Gollerbakh, Erikh, 103
Gorky, Maxim, 47, 131–33
Gornung, Lev, 235n59
Gorodetskii, Sergei, 29
Goscilo, Helena, 195
Gray Morning (Blok), 50
Greene, Thomas, 123
Groys, Boris, 10
Gumilev, Lev, 164
Gumilev, Nikolai, 19, 58, 230n53; acmeists and, 58, 220n42; Akhmatova's efforts to preserve memory of, 100–103, 156–57, 258n50; Akhmatova's marriage to, 100, 104; Akhmatova's relationship with, 19–20, 87, 103–4, 164; biographers of, 102–4; Bolsheviks and, 165, 253n29; death of, 51, 87, 172–73; influence on Akhmatova's poetry, 102, 104–5, 169; influences on poetry of, 81, 104; legacy of, 241n108, 241n111; living spaces of, 69, 81; marriage to Anna Engelgart, 100, 102; Punin and, 67, 69
"Gumilev and Blok" (Khodasevich), 58–59

Hamlet (Shakespeare), 144–45
Height, Amanda, 168–71, 253n34
history, Russian, 9, 38, 84; events defining periods of, 25–26; revisionism of, 27, 76, 162; revolutionary, 38, 76
Holmgren, Beth, 91, 195
homosexuality, 122; in *The Eye*, 115, 118–20, 123–24; in *The Gift*, 124–25; Kuzmin on, 88–89, 110–11, 117; Nabokov and, 112, 123–24; in *Wings*, 116–18, 121
Hope Abandoned (N. Mandelstam), 13, 240n102
Hope Against Hope (N. Mandelstam), 77
The House of Cards (Kuzmin), 244n25
"How I Love You" (Nabokov), 125
Hughes, Robert, 4–5
humanism, crisis of, 52

"I Drink to My Ruined Home" (Akhmatova), 83
"I Heard a Voice Call Consolingly" (Akhmatova), 159
individualism, 59, 74
intellectuals, Russian, 36, 47, 84, 87; apocalyptic symbolism of, 182–83; Bely justifying, 134–35; Blok and, 34–35; on cultural traditions, 51–52, 62; life of, 53–54; October Revolution and, 40, 51, 64, 225n54; portrayed as irresponsible, 53, 163; pre- and postrevolutionary cultural gap and, 132–34; Silver Age and, 59, 62, 64; Soviets and, 32, 59
intelligentsia: criticisms of, 49, 258n57; reevaluation of, 48
In the First Circle (Panfilov film), 259n7
Ivanov, Georgii, 253n29; Akhmatova and, 89, 157, 164–65; criticism of Nabokov, 109–10, 114–15, 243n15; on Kuzmin, 111–12; memoirs of, 17, 157
Ivanov, Viacheslav Ivanovich, 9–11, 89, 115, 235n64
Ivanov, Viacheslav Vsevolodovich, 99, 237n82
Ivanov, Vsevolod, 141, 150–51
Ivanov-Razumnik, R. V., 220n42; on Blok, 8, 33, 35–36, 94–95; use of "Silver Age," 5, 63
Ivan the Terrible, 135
Ivinskaia, Olga, 98–99

Jakobson, Roman, 6, 49–50, 155

Kablukov (Naiman), 206
Kafka, Franz, 165
Kamenev, Lev, 258n57
Kaminskaia, Anna Genrikhovna, 234n45
Kelly, Aileen, 206
The Key to the Bedroom (Riazanov melodrama), 202
Khardzhiev, Nikolai Ivanovich, 13, 221n48
Khlebnikov, Velimir, 221n48
Khodasevich, Vladislav, 9, 54, 135, 228n26; on Blok, 58–59; *Necropolis* by, 8, 58–62; on prerevolutionary cultural traditions, 112, 229n35

Khrushchev Thaw: Akhmatova during, 155, 158, 165
King, Queen, Knave (Nabokov), 110
Kniazev, Vsevolod, 107, 234n55
Kohut, Heinz, 123
Komissarzhevskaia, Vera, 36, 128
Konevskoi, Ivan, 227n18
Korin, Pavel Dmitrievich, 250n50
Koz'min, Mstislav, 24
"Krasavitsa" (Nabokov), 257n42
Kuniaev, Stanislav, 23–24, 158–59, 221n2
Kustodiev, Boris, 145–46
Kuzmin, Mikhail, 34, 77, 103, 131, 244n25; Akhmatova's criticism of, 88–89, 97, 236n65; on Akhmatova's poetry, 234n58; criticisms of, 50, 111–12; homosexuality and, 97, 110–11, 117, 236n65; influence on Nabokov, 110, 112–15, 120–23, 125–26; *The Trout Breaking through the Ice* by, 50, 88, 125–26, 173–74, 227n20; *Wings* by, 73–74, 115–16, 118
Kuz'mina-Karavaeva, Elizaveta ("Mother Maria"), 50, 81, 83

"The Lady with the Lapdog" (Chekhov), 146–47
language, pre- *vs.* postrevolutionary, 132–34, 247n15
"The Last Romans" (Kuz'mina-Karavaeva), 81
Lekmanov, Oleg, 201
Lenin, V. I., 49
Lermontov, Mikhail, 172
Levenson, Andrei, 61
Levidov, Mikhail, 154–55
life-creation project of symbolists, 89, 112
The Life of Klim Samgin (Gorky), 132–33
L'Immoraliste (Gide), 125
"Lips to Lips" (Nabokov), 112–13
literary canon: institutionalization of, 49–50
literary museums, 75–76, 202–3
literature, Russian, 9, 229n32; apocalyptic narratives in, 255n18; appropriations from and references to, 149–50; book of Revelation in, 182, 191, 255n18; disillusionment with, 51–52, 181, 257n49; effects of October Revolution in, 39–40; evolution of, 38, 60–61, 204; goals of, 49, 111–12; prerevolutionary, 31, 229n35, 230n43, 230n53, 247n15, 257n49; preservation of, 62–63, 205; of Silver Age, 4–6, 46, 48. *See also* poetry; writers, Russian
Literature and Revolution (Trotskii), 38, 258n50
Literaturnoe nasledstvo, 28, 33
The Little Land (Brezhnev), 193

Lozovskii, Lev, 43
Luknitskaia, Vera, 100–101, 202
Luknitskii, Pavel, 69, 94, 100–102, 241n111
Lunacharskii, Anatolii, 40–41, 47

Maiakovskii, Vladimir, 40, 135; Akhmatova and, 85–87, 97; Blok and, 34, 43–44
Makarov, A. N., 166
Makovskii, Sergei, 4–5, 157, 164
Maksimov, Dmitrii Evgen'evich, 30–33, 224n50, 239n94
"Malady Sublime" (Pasternak), 127
Malevich, Kazimir, 162
Malmstad, John, 88
Mandel'shtam, Yurii, 61–62
Mandelstam, Nadezhda, 12–14, 16–17, 69, 196; Akhmatova and, 99–100, 159–60, 240n102; living conditions of, 77–78; memoirs of, 76–77, 219n29
Mandelstam, Osip, 12–13, 16, 237n78; Akhmatova and, 82, 87, 100, 104–5; as "homeless," 79–80; in other people's memoirs, 77, 172; remembering as theme for, 17–18; reviews of, 165–66; silences of, 102, 231n10
man of the 1930s theme, 57–59
"A Man of the Thirties" (Terapiano), 55
Marev, Gleb, 5
Markov, Vladimir, 111–12
Marxists, Russian, 47–48, 52
Mary (Nabokov), 110, 123, 257n44
Master and Margarita (Bortko film), 259n7
Master and Margarita (Bulgakov), 242n127
Matich, Olga, 232n17, 256n30
The Meaning of Love (Solov'ev), 190
Medvedev, Pavel, 94
Meetings with Akhmatova (Luknitskii), 101
memoirs: Akhmatova in other people's, 13–14, 76, 79–80, 164, 170–72, 240n107; Akhmatova's, 159; association with democracy and freedom, 174; Blok in Bely's, 8, 95, 134–35, 137, 224n132; Blok's death in, 34–36; censorship of, 77; Gerstein's, 219n30; Kuniaev's, 158–59, 221n2; L. D. Blok's, 73–76; Nadezhda Mandelstam's, 219n29; of 1960s generation, 206–7; as sources of history, 76–77
Memoirs (Gerstein), 13–14, 219n30
Menshikov, Oleg, 6
Merezhkovskii, Dmitrii, 60, 181, 183; *Eternal Companions* by, 74, 131–32; *The Romance of Leonardo da Vinci* by, 147–49, 192
Metropolis (literary miscellany), 183
Meyerhold, Vsevold, 9

266 — INDEX

Mints, Zara Grigor'evna, 31–32, 225n58
Mirskii, Sviatopolk, 94
Mochul'skii, Konstantin, 62–63, 257n44
modernism, Russian: failure of, 42, 227n18, 228n28; Silver Age and, 3–4, 25; Western vs., 3, 48
modernists, 46–49, 88
moralizing, traditional, 59
Moscow: restoration work in, 204

Nabokov, Vladimir, 14, 108, 115, 174, 245n50, 257n42, 257n44; characters of, 110, 123–24; criticisms of, 50, 111, 243n15; criticisms of other writers by, 109, 129; emigration and, 109, 122–23, 174; Erofeev and, 181, 194, 257n45; influences on, 109–10, 125, 149–50; Kuzmin's influence on, 110, 112–14, 120–23, 125–26; sexuality and, 123–24, 243n16; Silver Age as legacy for, 18, 194–95. *See also The Eye*
Naiman, Anatolii, 206–7
Napel'baum, Ida, 229n35
narcissism, 120–24, 245n50
nationalism, 11
Necropolis (Khodasevich), 8, 58–62
"The Neighbor from Pity Might Go Two Blocks" (Akhmatova), 70–71
Nekrasov, Nikolai, 240n107
No Ordinary Summer (Fedin), 132
Nora, Pierre, 62, 230n51
Nordau, Max, 46–47
Notebooks (Akhmatova), 157–58, 164, 172–73
Notebooks (Blok), 204–5
Notes on Anna Akhmatova (Chukovskaia), 78, 91–93, 159, 169
"A Note to a Commentary" (Brodsky), 18
Novopolin, Grigorii, 46–47

October Revolution. *See* Bolshevik Revolution
Odoevtseva, Irina, 103, 109, 157
"Ogarki" (Skitalets), 227n25
On the Border of Two Centuries (Bely), 134, 136, 224n32
"On the Death of Grandfather" (Blok), 142–43
"On the Reasons for the Decline and New Trends in Contemporary Russian Literature" (Merezhkovskii), 181
Orlov, Vladimir Nikolaevich, 31, 96, 165–67, 204, 222n9, 253n29
Otsup, Nikolai, 56–57, 112

Pale Fire (Nabokov), 125–26
Palisandria (Sokolov), 179–80
Panaeva, Avdot'ia, 240n107

Panfilov, Gleb, 259n7
Paperno, Irina, 4–5, 120
Paramonov, Boris, 10–11
Parnok, Sofia, 235n59
"Party Organization and Party Literature" (Lenin), 49
past: Akhmatova and, 17, 161–62; appropriations from, 60, 136, 144; giving up on, 39, 59, 62; link to present/future, 14, 23–24; Pasternak's relationship to, 129–30, 136, 144; writers' on predecessors and, 16–22, 19
Pasternak, Boris, 9, 13, 127, 161, 193, 248n34, 250n53, 257n40; Akhmatova and, 97, 154–55, 239n95; Akhmatova's relationship with, 87, 97–98, 104–5, 154; balanced between pre- and postrevolutionary cultures, 129, 135, 248n31; Blok and, 29, 130, 136–45; cultural mediators and, 135, 150, 154–55; death of, 154; goals in writing, 131, 141, 248n31, 248n35; influences on, 128–30, 133, 136–50, 152; innovation and, 128–29, 131, 144; poetry of, 141, 145, 248n31, 250n55; prose writing, 130, 145; silences of, 102, 231n10; sources of inspiration for, 249n41, 249n42; translations by, 130–31, 144–45; Zhivago's poetry by, 152–53. *See also Doctor Zhivago*
Pasternak, Leonid Osipovich, 129–30
Pasternak, Zinaida Nikolaevna, 68, 98, 239n95
Pavlovich, Nadezhda Aleksandrovna, 34, 35
peasants, 51, 140–41, 248n31
Pelevin, Viktor, 19
People of the Moonlight (Rozanov), 187–88
Peredreev, Anatolii, 158–59
perestroika, 9
Pertsov, Petr, 5, 217n9
Petersburg (Bely), 52, 174–75, 208
Petersburg Winters (Ivanov), 111, 164–65
Peter the Great, 135
Petrovskaia, Nina, 228n26, 229n32, 249n36
Petty Demon (Sologub), 219n23
Phaedrus (Plato), 117–21
Philosophy of the Common Task (Fedorov), 191
Picasso, Pablo, 52
Plantain (Akhmatova), 237n81
Platinum Age, 6
Plato, 117–21, 245n39
Pnin (Nabokov), 125, 174
Poem Without a Hero (Akhmatova), 82, 106, 238n86; Akhmatova's anxiety about, 20, 162; analyses of, 173–74; Dante's influence on, 106–7; past in, 17, 173; reactions of, 156, 163; writing of, 78, 105, 164, 236n74
poetry, Russian, 63; Mandelstam's legacy in, 12–13; modern, 37; prose vs., 38; public

INDEX —267

demand for repetition in, 234n58; recited, not published, 37; state of, 5, 50, 56. *See also* poets, Russian; writers, Russian; specific poets and titles

poets, Russian, 106, 253n29; appropriating from others, 19, 82, 93, 166; attacks on, 94–95, 225n53, 258n50; competition among, 103–5; feelings about past and predecessors, 16, 18–22, 82, 87–88; influences on, 24, 88, 97–98, 102–3; periodic silences of, 102, 231n10; personal lives of, 81, 167; pre- vs. postrevolutionary, 43, 154–55; publication of, 37, 166–67; relations among, 36, 89–91, 97–98, 103, 135; sources of inspiration for, 102, 241n115, 242n127; status of, 50, 70, 155, 157, 165; wives and companions of, 68, 97; writing process of, 15; Yurii Zhivago as, 150–53. *See also* artists; writers, Russian

Poets' Guild, 81

The Poet's House (Chukovskaia), 13–14

politics, 37, 48; effects of events in, 9, 25–26; stagnation in, 54, 81; upheavals in and end of Silver Age, 5, 63–64

Porter, Robert, 182

proletariat: as future of poetry, 37

propaganda: Blok used in, 28–30

prose: Blok's, 37, 145; goals of, 205; Pasternak's, 127, 145; poetry vs., 38, 173

Proust, Marcel, 253n35

Provoking Fire (Kuniaev), 158–59

psychoanalysis, 92

Punin, Nikolai Nikolaevich, 25, 241n111; Akhmatova's marriage to, 161, 164; Akhmatova's relationship with, 66–68, 70, 83–84, 90, 101–2, 234n45; Akhmatova's separation from, 78, 83, 91; Akhmatova's writing and, 164, 252n28; arrest and imprisonment of, 67–68; communal apartment of, 67–71, 93

Punina, Anna Yevgenievna, 69

Punina, Irina Nikolaevna, 234n45

Pushkin, Aleksandr, 12, 26, 88, 231n10; Akhmatova and, 19, 97, 102; Akhmatova's analysis of, 71, 101–2, 161, 241n109; Akhmatova's devotion to, 87, 97, 169–70; as cultural icon, 29, 42–43, 59; death of, 172; influence of, 4, 102, 194; literary studies of, 27, 195; Silver Age traced from, 59, 194–95

Pushkina, Natalia Nikolaevna, 68, 96–97, 102, 169–70

Pushkin House (Bitov), 175–78

Pushkinii Dom (St. Petersburg), 203, 205

"Pushkin's Children" (Tolstaya), 3

"Pushkin's *The Stone Guest*" (Akhmatova), 169–70

Putin, Vladimir, 259n7

Radio Liberty, 10–11

Ranevskaia, Faina, 239n93

Rank, Otto, 160–61, 236n74

realism, 53; Blok moving toward, 26–27, 224n50, 225n58, 249n41; symbolism and, 60–61

The Real Life of Sebastian King (Nabokov), 125

Recollections of Blok (Bely), 134

"The Reevaluation of All Values: Decadence and Marxism" (Vengerov), 48

Reifman, Pavel, 31–32

Reisner, Larisa, 103

religion, 11, 51, 186–87, 258n50; sexuality and, 187–88, 199

remembering: as theme, 17–18

renaissance, Russian, 52, 180–81, 195

Requiem (Akhmatova), 78–79, 83, 170, 196–97

Retribution (Blok), 249n41

The Return of Chorb (Nabokov), 110

Revelation, book of: in *Russian Beauty*, 185, 187–88, 198; in Russian literature, 182, 187, 191, 255n18

Revival (Brezhnev), 193, 257n41

revolutions, 41, 48, 55, 81, 225n54. *See also* Bolshevik Revolution; Russian Revolution

Riazanov, El'dar, 202

Ricoeur, Paul, 6

Road to Calvary (A. Tolstoi), 132

The Romance of Leonardo da Vinci (Merezhkovskii), 147–49, 192

romanticism, Blok's, 225n58

Ronen, Omry, 4–6, 63, 217n7

A Room of One's Own (Woolf), 72

Rosary (Akhmatova), 217n9

Rosenthal, Bernice Glatzer, 48

Roskina, Natalia, 103, 156–57, 252n18

Rozanov, Vasilii: apocalyptic symbolism of, 183, 187, 254n4; disillusionment with Russian literature, 52, 181, 257n49; *People of the Moonlight* by, 187–88

Rudakov, Sergei, 77

Russian Beauty (Erofeev), 20, 205, 223n24, 257n40, 257n42, 258n52; Apocalypse in, 182–90, 197–99; references to other writers in, 190–95; sexuality in, 182, 184–86, 190–92, 195–96

Russian Revolution, 20–21, 38–39

"Russia's *Fleur du Mal*" (Erofeev), 181

"Russia's Great Poet" (Koz'min), 24

Sabashnikova, Margarita, 228n26
Safe Conduct (Pasternak), 128
Sandler, Stephanie, 12, 241n109
Sanin (Artsybashev), 227n25
Sartre, Jean-Paul, 168
Schafer, Roy, 92
The School for Scandal (television broadcast), 11, 108, 226n1
schools: as cultural institution, 51
Schwartz, Barry, 63
Second Birth (Pasternak), 98
Selected Poems (Mandelstam), 165–66
Selected Poems (Tsvetaeva), 166–67
Self-exploration (Berdiaev), 158
Selivanovskii, Aleksei, 43
Sementkovskii, R. I., 46–47
"Seventh Elegy" (Akhmatova), 162
sexuality, 227n25; in L. D. Blok's memoirs, 73–74, 76; of Nabokov characters, 123–24; decadence and, 179–80; religion and, 187–88, 199; in *Russian Beauty*, 182, 184–86, 190–92, 195–96; in Silver Age, 199, 206. *See also* homosexuality
Shakhmatovo (Blok's estate), 51
Shalamov, Varlaam, 145
Shentalinskii, Vitalii, 45–46, 226n1
shestidesiatniki, 19
Shestov, Lev, 183, 255n18
Shields, Carol, 71–72
Shileiko, Vladimir, 68, 100, 161, 233n36
Shmakov, Gennadii, 112
Signposts, 48–49
Silver Age: all-preservationist approach to, 8–9; anxiety and, 6, 12; appropriateness questioned, 4–6, 217n7; appropriations from, 62, 147–48, 205; Bolshevik Revolution and, 8, 51, 63; conflicting attitudes toward, 11–12, 20; connotations of, 5, 9, 16, 59, 60, 63, 174–75, 198, 206; critical approach to, 61–62; cultural legacy of, 11–12, 18, 179, 194–95; declining interest in, 201–2, 206; definitions of, 3–4, 63, 174; end of, 7–8, 42, 45–46, 63–64, 218n15, 259n6; Erofeev on, 180, 193–94; independent culture compared to, 175; integrated into Russian culture, 19, 62, 201–2; "man of," 57, 59, 175–78; Nabokov and, 108–9, 194–95; popularity of, 11, 178; rediscovery of, 7, 9–10, 19, 129, 206; as renaissance, 195, 226n1; Russian modernism and, 4, 25; sexuality and religion in, 199, 205; Soviets and, 10, 51, 59, 163, 184; traced from Pushkin, 194–95; use of term, 1–5; writers of, 46, 48, 50, 66, 156, 174
Silver Age Museum (Moscow), 202

Silver Age restaurant, 1–2, 202
Siniavskii, Andrei (Abram Terts), 42–43
Sirin. *See* Nabokov, Vladimir
The Sisters (A. Tolstoi), 53–54
Petrov, Stepan (Skitalets), 227n25
Skonechnaia, Olga, 112
Smirnova, Dunia, 226n1
Smith, Kathleen, 9
Samoilov, David, 87–88
social improvement: literature's role in, 49
socialist realism, 3, 10, 25, 140–41, 174, 198
social life: intelligentsia in, 48
social order: changes in, 48, 53
social upheavals: and end of Silver Age, 63–64
Socrates, 117–18
Sokolov, Sasha, 19, 179–80
Solzhenitsyn, Aleksandr, 207–8
Sologub, Fedor, 46–47, 219n23
Solov'ev, Vladimir Sergeevich, 183, 190–91, 256n30, 259n12
The Song of Fate (Blok), 93
Sontag, Susan, 18
Soviet age: Blok and, 28–30, 42; Silver Age's relation to, 163
Soviet Blokovedenie, 31–32
Sparks, Patricia Meyer, 92
Speak, Memory (Nabokov), 109
Spektorsky (Pasternak), 141
Stalinism, 10, 49
Stalinist terror, 6, 12–13, 158, 163; Akhmatova and, 83, 92, 162, 168–70
Stepun, Fedor, 56
The Stone Guest (Pushkin), 169–70
"The Stranger" (Blok), 191
Stravinskii, Igor, 9
Stray Dog cabaret, 174
Strong Opinions (Nabokov), 14
Struve, Gleb, 155, 172–73
Struve, Nikita, 231n10
Sudeikina, Olga. *See* Glebova-Sudeikina, Olga
symbolism, Russian, 28, 31, 50, 181, 221n48; acmeists vs., 15–16; Blok and, 37, 58–59; failure of, 37, 60, 111, 112; life-creation project of, 116–17; realism and, 60–61

Taking Berlin (Ivanov), 150–51
Tartu Blokovskie sborniki, 8
Taylor, Gary, 12
Terapiano, Yurii, 55–56, 112
Tikhonov, Nikolai, 102, 165–67
Timenchik, Roman, 173–74
Time to Give Birth (Erofeev), 180
Tiutchev, Fedor, 189, 231n10
Tolstaia, Sofia Andreevna, 239n93

INDEX —269

Tolstaya, Tatiana, 3, 226n1
Tolstoi, Aleksei, 47, 53, 87, 131–32, 135, 225n53
Tolstoi, Lev, 36, 53–55, 99, 227n24, 230n43; *What Is Art?* by, 47, 228n28
Toporov, Adrian, 140–41
Toporov, Vladimir, 252n23
The Total Art of Stalinism (Groys), 10
Travelers by Land and Sea (Kuzmin), 113–14
The Trial (Kafka), 165
Trotskii, Leon, 38–40, 258n50
The Trout Breaking through the Ice (Kuzmin), 125–26; analyses of, 173–74; criticisms of, 50, 88, 227n20
Trubetskoi, Sergei, 259n12
truth, 6, 9, 55, 77
truthfulness: praise for, 56, 58
Tsivian, Tatiana, 173–74
Tsvetaeva, Marina, 18, 50, 104, 231n10; Akhmatova and, 97, 105, 239n94; *Selected Poems* by, 166–67
Tukh, Boris, 202
Tvardovskii, Aleksandr, 29, 165–66
"The Twelve" (Blok), 38–40, 50, 225n54
Tynianov, Yurii, 8–9, 15, 38

Vasilieva, Larisa, 241n115
"Vasilii Rozanov through the Eyes of an Eccentric" (Erofeev), 175
Vatagin, Mark Grigor'evich, 152
Vecheslova, Tatiana, 233n36
Vengerov, Semen, 48
Vengerova, Zinaida, 46
The Village Stepanchikovo and Its Residents (Dostoevskii), 15
Virgin Soil (Brezhnev), 193
Volokhova, Natalia, 93
Voloshin, Maximilian, 228n26
Volynskii, Akim, 46–47
Voznesenskii, Andrei, 88, 166
Vrangel', Nikolai, 223n30
Vrubel', Mikhail, 36

The Way of All Earth (Akhmatova), 78
Weidle, Vladimir, 36
What Is Art? (L. Tolstoi), 47, 228n28
What Is to Be Done? (Chernyshevskii), 111
"When in Suicidal Melancholy" (Akhmatova), 237n81

Where Are We Going? (1910 collection), 47–48
"The Wind" (Pasternak), 29
Wings (Kuzmin), 73–74, 115; homosexuality in, 110–11, 114, 117–19; influence on Nabokov, 110, 125; narcissism in, 120–23
"Without a Deity, Without Inspiration" (Blok), 220n42
Woolf, Virginia, 72, 242n127
The Words (Sartre), 168
World of Art Movement, 131, 174
World War I, 53, 55, 81
World War II, 25
writers, Russian: Akhmatova's attacks on wives and companions of, 97–99, 239n93; of alternative prose, 179–80, 205; appropriations among, 106, 131–32, 145–50; attachment to past, 16; Bely justifying contemporaries, 134–35; as characters, 106, 189–91, 194; criticisms of, 38–39, 49–50, 109, 131–32, 157–58; cultural traditions and, 21, 131, 156; emigre, 109, 157; Erofeev and, 180–81, 182, 194, 257n45; goals of prose, 205; as "homeless," 79–80; influences on, 17, 125–26, 227n24, 242n127; mid-career silences of, 71–72, 84; Nabokov as, 109–10; prerevolutionary, 48–49; private lives of, 72–73, 86–87, 105–6, 167; relations to predecessors, 19, 128, 149–50, 182, 199, 205, 257n45; relations with public, 37; remembering as theme for, 17–18; role of companions to, 100–102; of Silver Age, 50, 199; Soviet repression of, 183–84; status of, 27, 109. *See also* poets, Russian; specific authors
Writers' Union, 70, 183

Yevtushenko, Yevgenii, 166
"You Came to Russia out of Nowhere" (Akhmatova), 82

Zabolotskii, Nikolai, 166
Zamiatin, Evgenii, 34, 87
Zdanov, Andrei, 234n54
Zhirmunskii. Viktor, 165–67
Zholkovsky, Alexander, 158
Zil'bershtein, Il'ia Samoilovich, 33
Zoshchenko, Mikhail, 225n53, 247n15